NETHERWORLD

NETHERWORLD

REFLECTIONS ON WORKING FOR THE US GOVERNMENT

NATHAN D. GJOVIK

TATE PUBLISHING
AND ENTERPRISES, LLC

Published by Tate Publishing & Enterprises, LLC
127 E. Trade Center Terrace | Mustang, Oklahoma 73064 USA
1.888.361.9473 | www.tatepublishing.com

Tate Publishing is committed to excellence in the publishing industry. The company reflects the philosophy established by the founders, based on Psalm 68:11,
"The Lord gave the word and great was the company of those who published it."

Published in the United States of America

ISBN: 978-1-62295-809-2
Political Science / American Government
12.11.06

DEDICATION AND ACKNOWLEDGMENTS

This book is dedicated to my beloved wife Susette who paid a huge price for sticking with me but without whose love and support I could not have endured my employment experiences with the US Government—I love you.

Acknowledgement is also made of our now deceased rescue cats Norman and Jesus who were always there with their affection to let us know that, even as it seemed the rest of the world was bearing down on us, they always loved us. We miss them.

I would also like to acknowledge my sister Polly who took her own life while I was writing this book. I wish I could have been there for you—I miss you.

I would also like to acknowledge and thank the following individuals for their assistance in reviewing and editing this book[1]:

Ms. Molly Davis

Dr. Allan Larson

Ms. Kay Larson

Man, when perfected, is the best of animals, but when separated from law and justice, he is the worst of all.

Aristotle: *Politics*, ~330 BC.

...and you will know the truth, and the truth will set you free.

Jesus of Nazareth: *Holy Bible, John 8:32*, ~32.

To no man will we sell, or deny, or delay, right or justice.

Barons of King John of England: *Magna Carta*, 1215.

No freeman shall ever be debarred the use of arms.

Thomas Jefferson: *Draft Virginia Constitution*, 1776.

Well, Doctor [Franklin], what have we got—a Republic or a Monarchy? —Unknown Woman
A Republic, if you can keep it.

Benjamin Franklin: *Constitutional Convention*, 1787.

...the world is in greater peril from those who tolerate or encourage evil than from those who actually commit it.

Albert Einstein: *Tribute to Pablo Casals*, 1953.

I look to a day when people will not be judged by the color of their skin, but by the content of their character.

Martin Luther King, Jr.: *I Have A Dream*, 1963.

The Constitution is not neutral. It was designed to take the government off the backs of people.

William O. Douglas: *The Court Years, 1939-1975*, 1980.

In this present crisis, government is not the solution to our problem; government is the problem.

Ronald Reagan: *First Inaugural Address*, 1981.

TABLE OF CONTENTS

TABLE OF FIGURES

PROLOGUE

I wrote this book for several reasons. One was to provide a form of therapy after being brutalized by a Federal agency for nearly five years. Another was to test the adage that the pen is mightier than the sword. Another, less selfish, reason is to advise those unfamiliar with the way in which the US Government conducts its affairs of the total apathy, gross incompetence, and shear racism involved in many of its actions.

If an American company were operated in the same manner in which the US Government operates, the company would be bankrupted via a myriad of civil and criminal litigation and the responsible leaders/managers would probably face prison time. However, for some reason most Americans simply accept this and many hold the US Government up as a model.

As I see our country move toward a larger Federal presence in our lives, I am very concerned of the implications for this given my experiences, many of which I will be sharing with you through the pages of this book. I hope you enjoy the book but, more importantly, I hope you find it educational. I believe it is long past time for our once great country to revert back to its founding principles including that of equality of man and a small national government.

LIFE BEFORE GOVERNMENT SERVICE

BIRTH OF A REBEL

My name is Nathan Gjovik. I grew up primarily in northern Minnesota. I was born into abject poverty as the son of a 17-year-old boy named Merle (Mic), whose family reportedly farmed him out because they could not afford to feed him, and a 16-year-old farmer's daughter named Carol. We lived in a shack behind someone's home in Strathcona, Minnesota for some time following my birth. My crib was an old dresser drawer and our furniture was comprised of boxes and crates which otherwise would have been hauled away with the trash.

As our family grew to include a son/brother, Jason, and a daughter/sister, Polly, my father hauled us around the state of Minnesota like gypsies seeking ways of improving his/our lot. At one point it appeared that he was on track to become a wealthy and distinguished man through a company called Woodland Construction (Woodland) that he helped to found, develop, grow, and served as the President. The company specialized in prefabricated home building. I recall a local newspaper article written about the company which was in awe at how Woodland was able to get a home framed within one day.

Everything looked good until the latter half of the Carter administration when inflation caused Government policy to effect interest rates of 20+% in order to curb inflation. I guess the idea was to rein in inflation by stopping spending. Well, it worked.

The major employer in our little town of Thief River Falls, Minnesota was Arctic Cat Enterprises (Arctic). Arctic was unable to sell snowmobiles (we call them snow cats) in such an economy and bankrupted. With a large fraction of the community now unemployed the market for new homes evaporated and the cost of capital to keep things going was too high. Woodland followed suit with Arctic and bankrupted and 65 people were unemployed. My father was never the same after that. He became a bitter man with a hatred for the Government (which I would not become aware of or appreciate until years later).

WEST POINT

THE INEVITABLE OPPORTUNITY

I had participated in sports and worked very hard while I was in high school. I got good grades and applied for admission to several universities, including the United States Military Academy at West Point, New York (West Point). I followed through with the processing of my application to West Point and got all the ticket punches, including a nomination from Congressman Arlan Stangeland.

My plan was to evaluate any and all offers prior to making any available selection for post-secondary education. However, an appointment was extended to me to attend West Point. The offer arrived one sunny spring afternoon in 1981. My mother took the liberty of opening the appointment letter and sharing the news with our relatives and my proud father. My father took the liberty of telling his friends and acquaintances, including those in attendance at the school board meeting where he was vying for a position. No consideration was really given to me not taking this opportunity. It seemed that my attendance at West Point was inevitable.

R-DAY[2]

"Ladies and gentlemen, welcome to West Point," began the speech by the army officer. That was the beginning of R-Day (Reception Day). It is a highly emotional span of time when all the new cadets are brought into the academy and processed. It marks for them the end of their free civilian culture and the beginning of both a mental and physical struggle to adapt to the mechanized military way of life. It is also known as the first day of cadet basic training, aka beast barracks (beast).

After the speech I left my family with my emotions in chaos and boarded a bus with all the other new cadets (we would be referred to as "new cadets" until after we successfully completed beast) into the heart of the academy. Here we were escorted into one of the towering gray stone buildings resembling the gloomy castles of medieval Europe. We were herded through lines and issued clothing and equipment. Then we waited our turn to be introduced to the "cadet in the red sash" like convicts at the executioner's block. When instructed to "toe his line" I walked forward and stood directly in front of him staring him in the face with my fear stricken eyes. He instructed me to drop my bags. I set my typewriter case down as gently as I could and he instructed to pick it back up and drop it as instructed. I did same (and my typewriter never worked properly after that) and he commenced screaming at me until I knew exactly my place around there. After he lost interest in me I was sent on my way to various other stops where we were instructed on marching maneuvers and how to conduct our new military lives and finally to the barber shop. I then found my barracks and climbed five flights of stairs with all my gear and arrived at my room which reminded me of the cold, dreary prison cells I had seen on Alcatraz Island, except for the window which offered a bird's eye view of a back alley separating two formidable gray stone buildings.

That afternoon under a threatening sky we lined up in formation on "the plain," where all the parades took place, for the R-Day ceremonies. Here before a crowd of spectators consisting largely of families and friends of the new cadets a speaker guided us through the formal Cadet Oath upon which we all swore. As I unconsciously repeated his words my eyes searched relentlessly through the mass of people for the familiar faces of my family. All that day I had been screamed at, spit on, poked, and prodded in order for me to learn the new ways of thinking, talking, walking, eating, and dressing and I desperately needed to see their friendly, reassuring smiles, but they weren't to be seen. The speaker had mentioned that in the entire 179-year history of West Point, it had never rained on R-Day. However, after the speech as we began to march away from the field the sky rewrote the record books and drenched all, adding fuel to the fire of my misery. While we marched in procession through the downpour toward the encroaching gray stone buildings, I heard familiar voices calling my name, but I was unable to look around. Out of the corner of my eye I caught a glimpse of my father, mother, and sister huddled under a windbreaker hollering and waving at me, and my brother walking along side my platoon telling me how good I looked. I thought it would make me feel me feel better, but seeing them put a knot in my stomach and lump in my throat. How I wished I could just go home with them after the ceremony.

After the parade we marched back to our barracks where we placed our clothes and equipment in the proper places before lights out. As I laid in the darkness I started thinking about not seeing my family for six months. It had already seemed like a lifetime since I was with them but it was only that morning. Then I thought about the girl I left behind back home and how hard it was to say good-bye knowing that would be the end. I tried to visualize the last time I saw her but something clouded my eye. My mind drifted to that morning and the events throughout the day and I turned to my roommate and asked if he was asleep yet. He replied in a scared southern accent voice with a "no" and I thought I heard him roll over and start to cry. I didn't say anything because I knew how he felt. I began to get tired and closed my eyes as I heard "Taps" echo through the all-encompassing gray stone buildings.

Figure 1. West Point Class of 1985 4th Company,
2nd Platoon, 2nd Squad (1981)

Standing (l-r): Cadet Wilmer, John Aveningo, Rob
Gilmartin, Matt Corulli (Maddog), Lenny Esposito, Dave
Campbell (Soup), Mike Fleming, Ray Cruz, & Nathan
Gjovik; Kneeling (l-r): Chuck Morgan, Geoffry Clark
(Curious George), Gene Bouchard, & Molly Hagan.

CHOW GAMES

I have heard stories from others who experienced regular basic
training that chow was one of their favorite events. However, at
West Point in the summer of 1981 this was not the case. It was
simply another opportunity for hazing by the upperclassmen.
We were most assuredly presented with a great deal of great
food and desserts which made your mouth water simply being
within proximity of them. However, we were allowed to eat very

little and I was never able to enjoy the desserts the cooks worked so hard on.

The problem was the table protocols being promulgated by the upperclassman Table Commandants at their assigned tables. Depending on your seat at the table new cadets were assigned certain duties. One of them was to cut the dessert into the appropriate number of pieces. The assigned new cadet would ask permission of the Table Commandant to ask the table about dessert. Once permission was granted an announcement would be made as to what the dessert was and then a query made as to how many would like that particular dessert (not that it made any difference, because we all knew that we would not get any). Those interested would extend a fist into the middle of the table at which time they would be counted and it would then be up to the assigned new cadet to determine how to cut the appropriate number of pieces all of the exact same size (they were measured).

Upon learning of the perfectly equal size requirement most of us began carrying protractors to chow inside our cover so we had the ability of cutting the pieces to the exact size. This was done by placing a piece of bread on top of the dessert (usually pies), centering the 360° protractor on the dessert, dividing 360 by the number of those desiring dessert, and then calculating the appropriate angular measures from 0°. This was easier to calculate for certain numbers (e.g., 5, 6, 8, 10, 12) so the new cadet responsible for the dessert would typically either include or exclude him/herself depending on how many others wanted dessert so he/she could get a good number for calculating protractor angles (after all, it didn't matter anyway since we weren't going to get any). The Table Commandants got savvy to this very quickly and started to demand a commitment by the dessert cutter before deciding whether or not they wanted a piece. Typically their decision was dependent on whether or not a difficult divisor for 360 could be achieved.

Once the announcements were made over the intercom, we were properly seated (at attention with back a fist distance from the back of the chair), drinks poured, and desserts cut we could begin eating. Eating was a very formal process with each bite requiring two prongs of the fork showing at all times (e.g., if eating peas two could be skewered at a time), placement of the fork at its proper position on the plate, returning to a position of attention, and then chewing no more than three times before swallowing. We were allowed between 20-30 minutes for each meal. It probably goes without saying that there was not much food eaten at these meals, despite the huge amount being prepared. I remember being so hungry that I would develop severe stomach pains and cramping.

I lost 20 pounds in the first 12 days of my attendance at the academy (just prior to entering the academy I had completed swimming and track seasons and was in very good physical condition). When I was finally able to speak with my father and mother I told them about how hungry I was. Apparently my father called and spoke with one of the regular Army officers stationed at West Point, admonishing him that he had never sent me to bed hungry. I was subsequently called in to speak to this officer who made it very clear that he was not happy with my disclosure to my parents.

LAUGHTER AND TEARS

I recall only a few light-hearted moments during that summer.[3] One was when a squad member named Geoff Clark was stopped in the hallway by an upperclassman. Clark and I were returning to our barracks from physical monitoring for strength (primarily pull-ups) and weight in another area of the building. There was a thin line a few inches from the edge of each wall within which new cadets were expected to stay. There was only room for one person within the line and Clark was ahead of me when he got stopped. Therefore, I also got stopped. The upperclassman asked

Clark how much he weighed. Clark responded, "Sir, I weigh 90 pounds." The upperclassman fired back, "Clark, did you know that the minimum weight to get into West Point is 91 pounds?" Clark responded, "Sir, I had to go on a special weight gaining diet to get admitted." The upperclassmen warned him about falling any further below the minimum West Point standard. In my state of mind I found this exchange to be amusing. It should be noted that Clark was small in stature but he was a tough hombre and the king of the pull-ups station where it seemed he could do them all day long.

During one sunny summer afternoon while standing at attention in formation, Lenny Esposito from our squad asked permission from our squad leader, who was an upperclassman, to ask a question. It should be noted that when one asked a question of an upperclassman there had better be a good reason to ask the question, or else. After the squad leader granted permission for the question Esposito asked, "Sir, what is the air speed velocity of an unladen swallow?" This was a play on Monty Python's movie *Search for the Holy Grail*. To say the rest of us were uncomfortable would be a gross understatement. Fortunately for Esposito, and the rest of the squad, our squad leader had seen the movie and appreciated the humor and responded appropriately with "African or European?" before quietly advising Esposito in no uncertain terms that he could do Area time (punishment tour marching in the courtyard between the barracks) for such behavior.

Another light-hearted moment involved the type of headwear (cover) we were issued. As new cadets we were only allowed to wear the gray cover until such time as we completed beast and were accepted into the Corps of Cadets. Therefore, anytime one saw a white cover it was worn by an upperclassman. One afternoon Rob Gilmartin from our squad stuck his head out the window overlooking the Area while wearing his issued white cover (we were issued them but were forbidden to wear them) and hollered out "New cadets, halt!" in a deep booming voice. Dozens of new cadets remained frozen in their tracks and at attention for several minutes until they began quietly and quickly scurrying away to someplace safe.

During chow one day our Table Commandant apparently had a wild hair and began harassing one of my fellow new cadets. Hojanacki (sp?) was recruited for swimming. Apparently he was an All-American stud in the pool and was obviously of European descent. However, the Table Commandant asked him if he was Mexican. Hojanacki popped off, "No, Sir!" The Table Commandant responded, "Hojanacki, you look like a Mexican. I want you to tell me how much you love being a Mexican." Hojanacki responded, "Sir, I love being a Mexican!" The Table Commandant was not satisfied and shouted back, "Hojanacki, tell me in your Mexican voice how much you love being a Mexican!" Hojanacki obliged in a high pitched nasally "Mexican" voice much to the delight of the Table Commandant.

The light-hearted moments were few and far between and I spent most of my time wondering what I was doing there. One evening a squad member named John Aveningo came to our room in tears. He had just come back from what was known as the "Magical Mystery Tour" of the rooms of various company officers. It was very shocking to me to listen to John tell my roommate David Campbell and I about his experience and how at least one of the upperclassmen company officers tried to goad him into a fight. John was as STRAC (standing tall right around the clock) as they come. He had attended a military prep school to specifically gain entrance into the academy. He wanted to be there badly and he was viewed by at least me as one of the best, if not the best, we as a class had to offer. To hear him now talk about being unsure if he wanted to continue rocked whatever foundation I had.

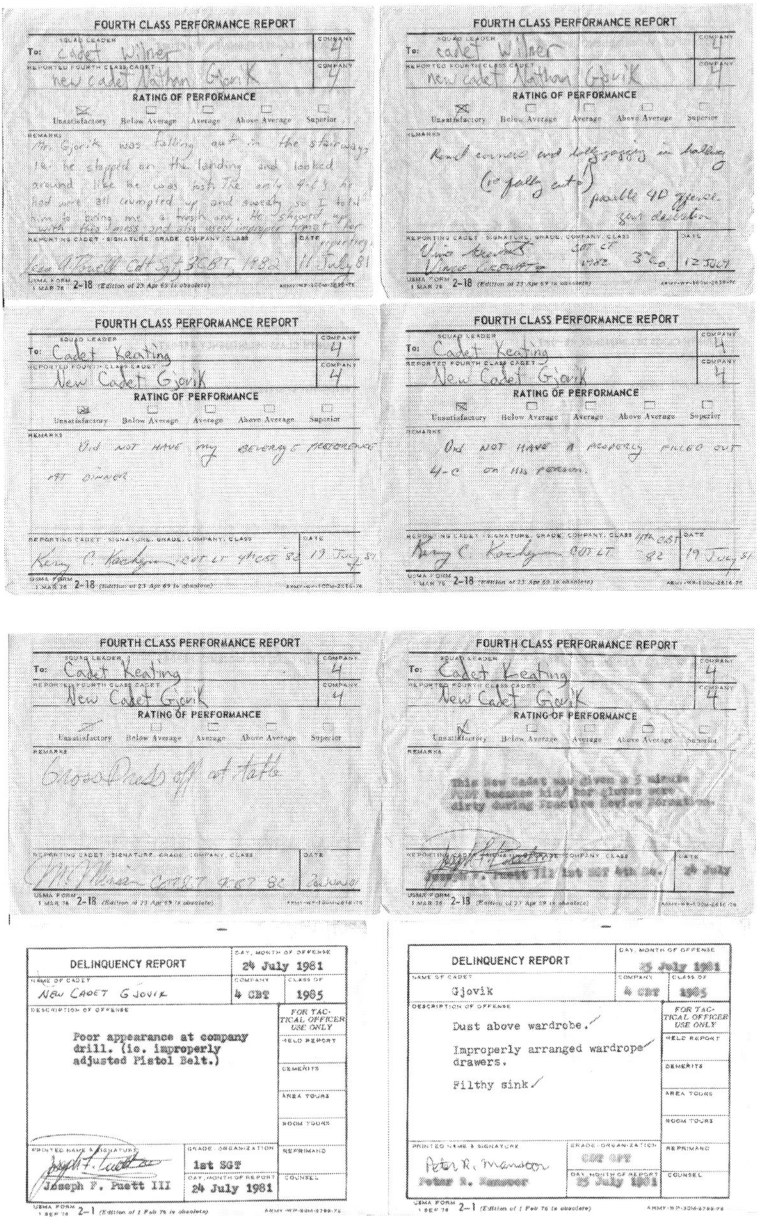

FOURTH CLASS PERFORMANCE REPORT
To: Cadet Wilner — Company 4
Reported Fourth Class Cadet: New Cadet Nathan Gjovik — Company 4
RATING OF PERFORMANCE: Unsatisfactory
Remarks: Mr. Gjovik was falling out in the stairway. He he stopped on the landing and looked around like he was lost. The only 4-C's he had were all crumpled up and sweaty so I told him to bring me a fresh one. He showed up with this mess and also used improper format for reporting.
Reporting Cadet: [illegible] Cdt Sgt 3CBT 1982 — Date: 11 July 81

FOURTH CLASS PERFORMANCE REPORT
To: Cadet Wilner — Company 4
Reported Fourth Class Cadet: New Cadet Nathan Gjovik — Company 4
RATING OF PERFORMANCE: Unsatisfactory
Remarks: [illegible]
Reporting Cadet: Vince [illegible] CDT LT 1982 3rd Co. — Date: 12 July

FOURTH CLASS PERFORMANCE REPORT
To: Cadet Keating — Company 4
Reported Fourth Class Cadet: New Cadet Gjovik — Company 4
RATING OF PERFORMANCE: Unsatisfactory
Remarks: Did not have my beverage preference at dinner.
Reporting Cadet: Kerry C. [illegible] CDT LT 4th CBT 82 — Date: 19 July 81

FOURTH CLASS PERFORMANCE REPORT
To: Cadet Keating — Company 4
Reported Fourth Class Cadet: New Cadet Gjovik — Company 4
RATING OF PERFORMANCE: Unsatisfactory
Remarks: Did not have a properly filled out 4-C on his person.
Reporting Cadet: Kerry C. [illegible] CDT LT 4th CBT '82 — Date: 19 July 81

FOURTH CLASS PERFORMANCE REPORT
To: Cadet Keating — Company 4
Reported Fourth Class Cadet: New Cadet Gjovik — Company 4
RATING OF PERFORMANCE: Unsatisfactory
Remarks: [illegible] off at table
Reporting Cadet: [illegible] CBT [illegible] 82

FOURTH CLASS PERFORMANCE REPORT
To: Cadet Keating — Company 4
Reported Fourth Class Cadet: New Cadet Gjovik — Company 4
RATING OF PERFORMANCE: Unsatisfactory
Remarks: This New Cadet was given a 5 minute [illegible] because his/her gloves were dirty during Practice Review Formation.
Reporting Cadet: Joseph F. Puett III 1st SGT 4th Co. — Date: 24 July

DELINQUENCY REPORT
Day, Month of Offense: 24 July 1981
Name of Cadet: New Cadet Gjovik — Company: 4 CBT — Class of: 1985
Description of Offense: Poor appearance at company drill. (ie. improperly adjusted Pistol Belt.)
Printed Name & Signature: Joseph F. Puett III — Grade, Organization: 1st SGT — Day, Month of Report: 24 July 1981

DELINQUENCY REPORT
Day, Month of Offense: 25 July 1981
Name of Cadet: Gjovik — Company: 4 CBT — Class of: 1985
Description of Offense: Dust above wardrobe. Improperly arranged wardrope drawers. Filthy sink.
Printed Name & Signature: Peter R. Mansoor — Grade, Organization: CBT CPT — Day, Month of Report: 25 July 1981

Figure 2a-b. Fourth Class Performance and Delinquency Reports (1981)

DOUBLE STANDARDS AND DISILLUSIONMENT

The first class of female cadets had graduated the previous year and it was clear that many of the male upperclassmen did not care for the presence of female cadets on the campus. Over the course of the summer during beast it became more and more evident that there existed a very obvious double standard between males and females. Females were not required to have a military haircut or perform the same physical training. They also were not subjected to the level of hazing administered by the male cadets (one upperclassman, who served as our company commander, actually seemed to be at least infatuated with one or more of the women in my squad) nor were they held to the same standards during military exercises.

I recall one training exercise in particular on how to provide cover fire, low crawl, and assault an enemy position. We were presented with a cleared field within a forested area which was setup with a staggered log formation which led to an enemy pillbox location at the far end where the enemy was supposed to be firing at us. The training mission was for groups of two to assault the enemy position by having one provide cover fire for the other as he/she moved via low crawling (i.e., face in the dirt and mud) to the next closest log to the enemy position. When the first person arrived at the log they would then in turn provide cover fire for the second person as they moved via low crawling to a forward position. This process would repeat until the team was at the log closest to the pillbox where one team member would low crawl below enemy fire and throw a grenade into the pillbox firing hole where the enemy was located. Two women performed this exercise just before me and I was able to watch them. They did not low crawl during the exercise as each simply stood up and ran up to next log before flopping down on the ground. When they got to the log closest to the pillbox one of them stood up and approached the pillbox, looked into the firing hole through which the enemy was supposed to be shooting at her, pulled a dummy grenade from her belt, and tried to get it into the hole only to have it bounce off the hardened concrete exterior surface and blow up between them. Pretty funny stuff until you realize that one of them may be your partner someday.

The kid glove treatment was not reserved to the women. Several individuals had been recruited for sports, including Lenny Esposito (lacrosse) and Rob Gilmartin (hockey) from my squad. Toward the end of beast the rest of the upperclassmen started arriving back on campus and meeting with their new cadet teammates. Often this resulted in "recognition" of these new cadets/plebes by their upperclassmen teammates (i.e., they would actually be recognized as a human being with a name). This often brought with it certain protections from hazing by certain other upperclassmen. I guess this was my first lesson on how the "good ol' boy" system works.

During one of our bivouacs I was given the "honor" of carrying the radio for the company commander. The radio appeared to be an old technology and weighed in around 95 pounds with nice thin straps (I wore the reminder of that honor in the form of strap marks in my shoulders for a couple of days after that experience). However, it did offer the opportunity to get to know the company commander and listen to some of the conversations he was having with others in the field. One of those conversations had to do with the theft of some copies of *Bugle Notes*, otherwise known as the plebe's Bible. I found this very disturbing as the Cadet Honor Code is "a cadet will not lie, cheat, steal, or tolerate those who do." I was led to believe by the reputation of the academy and the upperclassmen who were harassing us every day that we were special. However, what I was seeing was a group of young people who seemed no different than many or most of those with whom I had grown up, with all of our collective human frailties.

It was clear that I had been disillusioned about West Point and as I learned more it meant less to me.

R-DAY 2

I became convinced that West Point was not for me and I simply wanted to leave and placed another R-Day (resignation day) on the calendar in our room. There were a number of rumors of other new cadets doing interesting things to leave, temporarily or permanently. One involved new cadets taking bayonets to themselves in order to be placed within the safe confines, albeit temporary, of the hospital or to be sent home. Another involved a new cadet who lived somewhere close to the campus who escaped at night. Academy officials apparently starting getting concerned over the number of new cadets leaving and began counseling those of us who were considering resigning.

I was provided counseling one night with an upperclassman who must have been training to be a counselor. He ordered me to stand with my head outside his window and holler out something he thought would help me vent my frustrations and thus, resolve my situation. However, my situation did not revolve around frustration. It was associated with the will to be there. What little I had before going was now gone.

I also had to speak with one of the regular Army staff members before being allowed to resign. I remember his frustration with me as I explained to him that I wanted to return to northern Minnesota in time to attend classes at the University of North Dakota that fall. I guess that was the end of his patience with me as the pencil he was tapping on his desk took a little flight across the room and he began decompressing by advising me of how fortunate I should feel to be there and that I had taken a slot that somebody else could have had.

Despite the "encouragement" to stay I was steadfast in my desire to leave. I began returning my issued gear. However, my resignation path was not official until I turned in my epaulettes. I did same and ran back to my barracks. I don't recall ever feeling as free as I did at that moment. It was like I had just escaped from East Berlin and was on my way to a better life in the West.

Several upperclassmen shouted for me to stop as I ran up the stairs of my barracks, right down the middle and jumping up two or more steps at a time, but I ignored them and pressed on. I stopped in my barracks to collect my personal effects and say goodbye to my squad mates and wish them well. A couple of the upperclassmen in my platoon had conversations with me about leaving (I guess it was their last ditch effort to try to keep me there) before I reported to the outprocessing barracks.

The outprocessing barracks was more like a quarantine station as we were kept apart from the rest of the cadets (wouldn't want to contaminate the rest of the herd). There were guards posted to make sure we didn't wander. During a conversation with one of them he shared that he was envious of me because I was going home. His father had gone to West Point and, by God, he was going there as well. He also wanted to leave but could not because of his father's expectations. I felt sorry for him. I knew there would be many who would be disappointed in me for leaving. However, I also knew it was my life and I didn't belong there.

When I deplaned in my hometown of Thief River Falls, Minnesota, my mother commented on how emaciated I looked. I got a positive greeting but it was clear that my parents were very disappointed in me. They did not want me back at what I had previously called home. However, they did set me up as a caretaker of some apartments my father's company had built and were leasing in Grand Forks, North Dakota (home of the University of North Dakota).

UNIVERSITY OF NORTH DAKOTA-TAKE 1

FREEDOM TO FAIL

By the time I got to the University of North Dakota (UND) the fall semester was beginning and there was not much available in terms of classes. I had no idea what I wanted to do anyway so I enrolled in coursework that sounded interesting and might be helpful down the road. My memory of that time is that staff at the UND were not helpful in my decision making processes and I very much felt like I was on my own in a hostile environment. This was especially true when it came to parking. Parking was a premium on the campus and the parking office ran their operation like German SS troops terrorizing the student population. There was no forgiveness and certain cars, like mine (I had a jacked-up Camaro), were targets. I recall being parked for 30 to 60 seconds outside Merrifield Hall as I ran at full speed from my car to my instructor's office to grab a graded final paper and then return at full speed to my car to find a freshly issued parking ticket.[4]

I was working as a caretaker of my father's apartments, for which I got free rent. I furnished my apartment with the typical suite of junk furniture (my parents gave me the desk and dresser I used at their home before leaving for the academy) including a couch which I had dug out of the trash and reupholstered myself with some clearance fabric from a local supply house. I also got a job at the iconic Bronze Boot steak house as a busboy on the north end of Grand Forks.

During that first semester at the UND I simply was not ready for school, after my regimented existence in high school followed by my academy experience. I was in class only a fraction of the time and got my first and only "C" in any class (ironically it was American Government I). Despite this I was still able to pull off a 3.22 GPA. However, I did not return to the UND the next semester, or the next several semesters.

This period of my life was essentially one in which I was lost and at risk for making poor choices. I fell in with a group of people connected to another busboy at the Bronze Boot who used drugs and alcohol and began to participate in same, if for no other reason than to simply have some "friends" since I knew nobody else in Grand Forks. We did many stupid things during some of those alcohol fueled parties and I'm surprised that nobody in our group got seriously hurt, or worse. I'm not proud of this period of my life.

COMMUNITY NATIONAL BANK

LIFE AS A TELLER

I am not clear as to how it is that I ended up working at Community National Bank (CNB) in Grand Forks. However, I recall one conversation with a counselor at the Job Service North Dakota office. He looked at my resume and advised me that I didn't give him much to work with. I was unimpressed with this State employee and wondered what kind of credentials he had when he was 18. Be that as it may I applied for a part-time position as a teller at CNB and was offered same. Little did I know at the time the impact this would have on my life.

When I first started working as a teller there were several things which were different for me. I found it very odd to have access to all of that money within my drawer, especially when I had so little myself. Also, most of the other tellers were women which, for a young single guy, was a pretty good deal. However, these women knew how to take advantage of me on the job.

In one situation one of the female tellers vouched for a customer who had presented to me to cash a check. Based on this I cashed the check and, of course, it bounced. The Chief Operating Officer (COO) was not happy with my decision to cash the check and asked me to personally collect the associated funds. I found out from the teller that vouched for the young woman who cashed the check that they were simply acquaintances from a local bar (nice). I ended up having several telephone conversations with the young woman for whom I had cashed the check. During those conversations I learned all about her various crises—she had no money and was pregnant and the father didn't want to have anything to do with her and …

I provided a significant amount of cash to another customer on another day. At the end of the day I was $30.00 off while "proving" my drawer. I suspected that I had inadvertently given out a $50 dollar bill as a $20 bill to one of my customers. I called the one that had received the large amount of cash and they confirmed that they had received an extra $30, but they had no intention of returning it because it was my mistake (nice). I had to go talk to the bank auditor, a tough guy named Dean Hruska. This was a scary proposition and I was worried that I might lose my job. Ironically, Dean would later become a fixture in the lives of me and my wife (funny how life's pathways cross sometimes).

ADVANCING TO CUSTODIAN

I did pretty well working as a teller, but it was part-time and I needed additional money in order to make ends meet. The bank had decided that they were going to consolidate several part-time cleaning, maintenance, and other functions into one full-time position. The job paid $12,000 per year and I needed it badly. I recall speaking to the supervisor of the new position and, essentially, begging for the job. I got it and I worked like a dog. In addition to the various duties they had originally envisioned I went through all of their storage spaces and cleaned and organized them. This turned a fairly significant amount of unused space into very usable space. I was spending 60-80 hours a week working this new job. I guess they were happy because I got a 50% pay increase after only a couple of months. This made me happy and I became a proud member of the CNB team. As I worked in my custodial position I spent a great deal of time moving around the bank. Through this I saw many facets of the bank operations and learned a great deal about effective management and strong leadership from simply watching.

DISTANCE LEARNING

CNB was founded the same year I was born so it was relatively young when compared to its competitors. Also, the population within the state of North Dakota was shrinking. Therefore, the business climate in which CNB was competing was highly competitive. However, we were making money. The reason for this became clearer to me years later as I was completing a master of business administration degree—management at CNB knew how to manage.

Probably the key motivator was their willingness to fire people. Management had very high expectations of their employees and those who didn't meet those expectations were escorted to the door. I recall one teller who had been an employee for approximately 10 years. She borrowed money from her cash drawer to buy a snack during her break. The COO, a big believer in management by walking around, happened to audit her drawer upon her return from break and discovered the shortage. Taking money from one's drawer was not allowed and everyone knew it. However, this teller apparently thought that reimbursement of her drawer at the end of the day was acceptable. It was not and she was escorted to the door.

CNB management also understood the importance of having the right people in the right places. In late 1987 the bank President who was one of the founding members of the bank died of cancer. The remaining founding member was then named CEO and President. Approximately one year following the death of the President the other founding partner and CEO/President decided to retire. CNB management was structured like most banks in that they had several vice-presidents (VPs). Each of the VPs was vying for becoming anointed into at least the position of President. However, the board of directors understood the importance of selecting the correct individual. They conducted a search and hired someone from outside the bank (and the local area). I believe this upset many of the VPs. However, over time the wisdom of the selection crystallized as the bank became wildly successful. They made a gutsy move but it paid off in big dividends, literally.

I learned a great deal from my experience at CNB even though I was observing it at a distance due to my role as a custodian and a computer main frame operator (see below).

GENERAL LEDGER

Sometime in 1987 I added additional duties to my CNB employment. At that time we had a main frame computer and check sorting machine which required its own approximately 15-foot by 20-foot room (about the size of a good-sized professional office). The main frame computer was used primarily to maintain and update the bank's general ledger. Typically this would be updated each evening to reflect the day's work by part-time staff.

The previous part-time computer operator, shall we say, had some issues—like relationship and drug and … Therefore, one-half of the part-time position was offered to me. Several months later the other half was offered to an attractive young woman named Susette. I had to train her in and she thought I was a nice guy (fooled her). A year later we would be engaged and two years later, married.

L.G.

During the time when Susette and I were working at night on the computer, Dean Hruska, Auditor, woke up one morning with a splitting headache. He went to the hospital to get checked out and ended up in emergency surgery for a brain aneurism. His life changed that morning. The brain surgery affected his memory, among other things, and subsequently he lost his wife, his home, and his job. However, the bank stood by him. They allowed Dean to rehabilitate by helping Susette and I update the general ledger in the evenings.

During those late nights working with Dean we got to know him very well. I watched while he struggled with the realities of his new life. Usually this involved him simply getting very quiet, walking away, and hiding in another room until his eyes dried. Susette and I understood his pain as our lives were extremely difficult as well. Therefore, we felt a natural bond to Dean and began to hang out with him as time permitted.

One of the events that Dean invited us to was bingo at a local hall. It was finals week at the UND and I was very, very tired. However, the opportunity to be with both Susette and Dean was something I couldn't pass up. We were each playing two bingo cards. I had a prime seat behind a support column so I couldn't see the full board. Somebody won the regular bingo round, then the shape on the card, and finally blackout. I was disappointed because I had only one space left on a card for blackout. When Dean looked over at my card he hollered out that they had called that number a long time ago. I had apparently missed the call on the number and I could not see that part of the board to check my card. I was crushed. The prize for the win was $150.00. On the drive home all I could think about was all of the things I could have purchased with the $150.00 (like a new winter coat which I really needed). I haven't played bingo since that night.

Susette and I kept encouraging Dean to try to find himself female companionship as another step in putting his life back together. However, despite his seeming outgoing personality he's shy with women and we both knew he would never make the first move in engaging a woman for anything more than giving her a hard time (in a good way—he is a jokester). Therefore, I wrote a quasi-joke letter for him to post in the local classifieds. The letter extolled the virtues of Dean's manhood and was signed Dean "the love gun" Hruska. From that point on he became known to me as L.G. Over the years we have maintained contact with Dean and, as he got older and his dentures began to be nonconforming, the L.G. changed meaning to "love gums."

It so happened that when Dean lost his home he moved into an apartment in the same building where I would also later live. I recall his numerous visits to my apartment when he knew Susette was visiting (he'd probably see her orange Mazda out front). We always knew it was Dean from his distinctive knock. On at least one occasion we were home and did not answer the door because we wanted to be alone. Both Susette and I feel guilty about that now and have often talked about how much we miss having Dean knock on the door. Too bad we don't sometimes understand that those little opportunities we often take for granted and assume will be available indefinitely eventually end and we're left with only treasured memories (if we're lucky).

Dean now lives in a nursing home in Grand Forks and is unable to leave without nursing assistance. We visit him as often as we can and when we do he speaks of dying. I programmed our cell phone numbers into his cell phone so we, once again, occasionally get that, now welcomed, interruption from Dean. I try to keep the conversations positive and give him a hard time like I have over the past many years, but the visits are not the same and we both know it. I miss him already.

UNIVERSITY OF NORTH DAKOTA-TAKE 2

TAKE NO PRISONERS

I had to speak to a counselor before being readmitted to the UND. At that time I was considering pre-dentistry. The counselor asked me why I chose pre-dentistry and I explained in a very matter-of-fact way that I wanted to make sure when I got done I would be able to make some money. He seemed surprised by my response and indicated he wished more students shared my focus on being employable when they graduated from college. However, pre-dentistry was rather short lived once I discovered the additional college (seems ironic now in retrospect) and subsequent training which would be involved before becoming a dentist. I understood I was very good at math and science and turned toward engineering. I later declared civil engineering because I wanted to be able to be outside as part of my job (again, ironic in retrospect).

I'm not sure if there is anything more motivational to improve one's skill sets than spending some quality time each work day cleaning toilets. When I went back to school at the UND I was highly motivated to do well. I wasn't very popular with some of the other students, especially in math and science classes, because I got consistently high scores on the exams and most professors graded on a curve so the bar was raised—good! I worked hard on my studies while I was working 60+ hours at the bank. I've noticed empirically through my life that there seems to be an inverse relationship between having time available and effective use of available time. I had little time for studies and yet I was almost always better prepared than others who had nothing but school to keep their time occupied.

CRUSHING CALCULATION

Working the kind of hours I was and trying to complete a difficult field of study like engineering was almost impossible. I wondered from day to day if I was actually going to be physically capable of continuing the program (I had to keep my job in order to pay the bills). Yes, I was motivated, but I was getting taxed to the maximum both mentally through school and physically through my job. The only way I could get all of my homework and studies done was to do much of it at night. There were many nights when the lights did not go out at my apartment (or at the bank where they let me use their computers). I knew I was pushing it too hard when I would start to get nauseous.

I recall one morning as I was making my rounds cleaning the bathrooms. I was carrying my blue plastic cleaning tray with my cleaning supplies and running through in my mind (this was how I kept my sanity: thought about other things while cleaning) how much longer it was going to take me to complete the engineering program at the current rate (I could only take classes as they fit into my work schedule). I had already been doing it for over two years and it felt like forever. However, based on my mental calculations it was going to take another five years. That was definitely a low point. I thought I could have simply rolled up into the fetal position and let the world haul me off.

LOOKING UP

Time passed and the coursework got done. Engineering school was much more difficult than the general science classes, especially for one on a strict time budget, and I was competing against others who were also good at math and science. Despite that I was recognized in my "senior" year with a merit-based scholarship from the Associated General Contractors (AGC). It was the highest award given by the civil engineering department (John Jardine Memorial Scholarship) and I really needed and appreciated it (and still do). The only thing I didn't much appreciate was listening to Dean Fletcher's favorite opera selections during the 3½-hour drive each way to the annual North Dakota AGC conference in Minot to accept the award. I survived and was incredibly honored to receive the award (thank you, AGC!).

Around that same time I was nominated to be inducted into Tau Beta Pi, the engineering honor society. I was provided with my flat casting of the bronze Bent (society's symbol) which I was supposed to refine through filing and polishing before it was to be placed on my membership plaque. The induction ceremony seemed like something I had heard about for many of the various campus fraternities and I was about as far from being a "frat boy" as one could get. However, I tried to overlook that and was honored to be considered and included.

NORTH TO ALASKA

In early 1988 David (Dave) Apanian, the son of Dr. Ronald Apanian (then Chair of the UND Civil Engineering Department), came on a recruiting trip to the UND. Dave was a UND alumnus and was stationed in Alaska as a commissioned officer with the US Public Health Service (USPHS). Dave's pitch sounded very exciting to me and I started checking into it. I spoke with my supervisors, David Putbrese and John Ouradnik, at CNB. They had both been supportive of my educational efforts. However, this would be an extended absence from both jobs (full-time custodian and part-time main-frame computer operator) for approximately 3 months. They both thought they could make it work (thank you both!) and I tendered an application for the USPHS Commissioned Officer Student Training and Extern Program (COSTEP). On the application I noted that I would only be interested in working in Alaska. I never expected anything to come of it, but I was offered a COSTEP position in Alaska that summer.

During that time of my life nearly everything was hard simply because I had limited income and little or no time for anything. I was excited about the opportunity to work that summer in Alaska but it was hard simply getting there. Susette and I were dating and I was not looking forward to leaving her for three months. She helped me get my apartment temporarily moved into a storage garage run by a friend of mine named Mike Thompson. Of course, as usual, the move took longer than expected and I was moving out of the apartment late into the night and didn't get everything wrapped up until the early morning hours (thanks, Mike, for coming back and letting me into the storage facility that night/morning). My flight left for Anchorage early that (next) morning. Therefore, I got little or no sleep that night.

It was very hard to say goodbye to Susette that (next) morning and the extremely poor customer service from Northwest Airlines did nothing to help the situation. However, we got off the ground and the rain started falling inside the aircraft cabin. I called her from Seattle and then again from my room in Anchorage (no cell phones then so being able to talk to someone several time zones away could be a pretty big deal). I also called my summer preceptor and he directed me to get some rest and report the next morning—sounded great to me and I did same. I think I slept for around 12 straight hours.

Sleep came at a premium that summer. I found an apartment just one block from Chilkoot Charlie's bar (one of the biggest, rowdiest bars in Anchorage). Typically they had at least one band playing until the early morning hours and, whenever I was actually in Anchorage, they could be heard from within the apartment building.[5]

LIFE AS A COSTEP

The USPHS uses the COSTEP to recruit young talent from universities around the country into the service. Typically the tours ran during summer break and students would need to have completed their sophomore year in college and be studying a health related field. Engineering was included since the service also included preventative health programs (e.g., provision of safe water and sewer/solid waste collection and disposal) and medical device engineering programs.

I was assigned to what was known at the time to be the Alaska Area Native Health Service (AANHS), Office of Environmental Health and Engineering (OEHE), Division of Sanitation Facilities Construction (DSFC) program. It was the mission of the DSFC program to provide safe water, wastewater, and solid waste facilities to Native homes and communities.

That summer there were six COSTEPs assigned to the AANHS. We came from different states and walks of life. Prior to my departure from North Dakota I had joked that I'd probably end up with a roommate who is a surfer dude from California. That is exactly what happened.

Since I was one of the first COSTEPs to arrive in Anchorage the lease was in my name. This gave me dibs on the only bed in our apartment. When my roommate arrived it just so happened that someone in our apartment complex upgraded their mattress. Their old mattress was retrieved by my roommate from the dumpster, cleaned up a little bit, placed on the floor in the living room, and he was in business.

One night I was awakened by the sound of a window sliding open in the living room of our garden level apartment (I have always been a light sleeper). I got up and noticed someone trying to sneak in through the window. I got my little .22 caliber pistol and had it ready for a not so friendly greeting for the intruder when my roommate moved (he was sleeping on the floor under the window). This startled the would-be intruder and he quickly changed his mind. I doubt he ever knew how fortunate he was by not coming into our apartment that night.

Figure 5. Alaska Area Native Health Service
Engineering COSTEPs (1988)

From left to right: James Spehalski (roommate), Don
Proctor, Mark Davidson, Mark Wilgus, Nathan Gjovik,
Pat Doyle, Ben Pritchard.

During one of my many trips out of Anchorage (I volunteered
for as many as I could) my roommate was about to help himself
to a blueberry muffin from a bag of rolls I had purchased some
time ago. That was until he noticed that the blueberries appeared
to be a bit hairy and, upon further inspection, he discovered they
weren't blueberries at all! We shared a good laugh over these
moldy rolls.

Working as a COSTEP was a priceless experience, but it
was a great deal of work and Alaska, at least at that time, was
very primitive and dangerous. There was a story shared with us
of a newly-wed couple who drove their 3-wheelers around the

Anchorage mud flats at low tide until the young bride got her legs wedged into the mud trying to free her stuck machine. The frantic young groom had to watch her drown as a rescue crew tried to save her when the tide came back in, but she was held fast by the clayey mud. It was a tough place to live and work.

THE FIRST TRIP

Shortly after my arrival in Anchorage I was off with my preceptor, LT Mark Pearson, to a village called Metlakatla at the extreme southern end of the Alaskan panhandle. LT Pearson was the field engineer for a project which provided a new water supply and treatment system for the village. The project was near completion and we needed to assist in placing the new pressure filtration system into service.

The new village water supply was a mountain lake located several hundred feet above the new water treatment plant (WTP) and village. This was high enough to create very high pressure within the piping system at the WTP. Reportedly the piping used outside the WTP was rated for 300 psi and then there was a series of pressure-reducing valves (PRVs) inside the plant to bring the pressure to within a workable pressure which would not damage equipment (less than approximately 75 psi). However, nothing inside the WTP had been placed into service.

A brief discussion was held about the plan of action and I discovered that the "EP" in COSTEP may more appropriately stand for "Expendable Person." I was asked to descend into the valve vault outside the WTP. This was a confined space approximately 8 feet deep which housed the large (gate) valves which controlled the water supply feed into the WTP. Each valve weighed several hundred pounds empty (without water) and was fitted with a wheel to allow opening and closing of the valve. I was asked to begin opening the main valve feeding water to the WTP. As I did so the water from the mountain lake began flowing through the valve with a deafening scream and the whole valve and piping assembly inside the vault began to shake. I looked up through the vault access for some sort of assurance from LT Pearson as to whether or not this all seemed right and simply got a smile and a gesture indicating that I should keep opening the valve. I did and things seemed to settle down once the system had achieved pressure equilibrium across the valve.

I exited the vault and we went inside the WTP to begin opening the final supply valve to the treatment system. Just downstream of this valve was a very large PRV which looked nearly as tall as me and had to be extremely heavy. As soon as the final supply valve was opened the mountain lake water starting screaming through to the large PRV and the valve started bouncing around like it was on horseback. LT Pearson and I looked at each other with what appeared to be the same level of doubt and fear (a cartoon depiction would have included a shared bubble over our heads reading "we need to get out of here before this whole place goes") wondering if it was safe for us to be standing so close and we slowly walked away (after all we both had an image to maintain).

At the time I found the experience in Metlakatla to be very exciting. However, in retrospect, this was simply my first exposure to what I would find to be "seat-of-the-pants" project management within the agency.

TENAKEE SPRINGS

While in Metlakatla I had a discussion with LT Pearson about visiting the daughter of Kay Larson, a woman who was like my second mother back in North Dakota. Debbie Lockhart is the daughter's name and she and her family lived in the southeastern Alaska village of Tenakee Springs (Tenakee). LT Pearson decided to take the ferry back from Metlakatla to the hub community from where we had caught the bush flight to Metlakatla. It just so happened that one of the stops made by this ferry was in Tenakee. LT Pearson authorized leave, I made contact with

Debbie, and spent the next couple of days in Tenakee visiting her family.

The village is located on the east side of Chichagof Island, on the north shore of Tenakee Inlet and is known for its mineral spring public bath house. The bath house was at that time a dark cave-like structure with a naturally heated pool of water in the middle of a sunken floor. Since it was rather primitive (i.e., had no dressing rooms) it had separate hours for men and women. I bathed there two nights while breathing in the moist sulfide-laden air and holding conversations with a one-armed Native drifter named Dick Blue Sky who spent his time "looking for a nice place to live."

Down on the beach there was an outhouse which emptied onto the beach (rumor had it that the area was known for its brown trout). The community was great. It was like a picture postcard at every turn and incredibly peaceful. The people were all very nice including Debbie and her family. Two of her three children were home on summer break and another child was off fishing with her husband Glen. Glen and Debbie were working on their home at the time and it appeared they were finishing things as money and available equipment and materials allowed. However, given the setting it was beautiful and comfortable and I am very grateful to Debbie and her family for their hospitality and to LT Pearson for the opportunity to visit (thank you all!).

Figure 6. Tenakee Springs Community Center
with Primitive Outhouse (1988)

Figure 7. Tenakee Springs Post Office (1988)

Figure 8. Tenakee Springs Garden (1988)

BACK COUNTRY ADVENTURES

One of the projects I was given was to develop record drawings (as-builts) and establish local monuments (steel cards screwed into permanent fixtures) for locating recently installed water and wastewater utility appurtenances (e.g., manholes, valves, etc.) within the village of Holy Cross (monuments were needed because the actual appurtenances would be covered by snow in the winter time). Holy Cross was established as a Catholic outpost along the Yukon River. There was still a Catholic presence there which was staffed by nuns. I got to know the nuns pretty well because they had one of the few telephones available to a non-resident (use of the phone usually involved my having to first get my butt kicked by one of the nuns in cribbage).

Prior to leaving North Dakota I had seen a young comedian special on television in which one of the comedians commented about staying in a town so small when he dialed "9" to get an outside line he reached someone's home. Holy Cross was a similar experience. I had an assistant helping me get around in Holy Cross. I asked him how I could reach him and he said his number was 15 (could have been a different two digit number). I smiled after he said it and then he explained that the prefix and first two numbers were the same for everyone in the community. As it turned out this assistant was the brother of a guy who had recently murdered the store owner (and their father owned the bunkhouse where I was staying—nice).

I ended up staying and working over the weekend in Holy Cross. I met Jim and Betty Johnson during my travels through the community. She was Native and he was a big Scandinavian and they were both incredibly friendly. They invited me to join them for salmon fishing one night and I took them up on it. We fished the Yukon River that night until around 12:30 am (and the sky was just getting pink from the setting sun). They rewarded my efforts with a 40-lb king salmon—thank you!

Future trips took me to Akhiok, Hydaburg, King Cove, Kodiak, Ouzinkie, and Port Graham. It seemed that each trip had its own story and many of the stories included something associated with the flight to or from the destination village.

During our trip to King Cove the pilot attempted to land on the airstrip only to have our plane, while on approach, bounce around like a yo-yo from the winds created by the surrounding volcanic peaks. He brought it around again, gained elevation, brought it down at a radical angle (hot), and we bounced off the airstrip as he brought the aircraft to a stop on the ground.

We conducted our business in King Cove and returned to the aircraft. LT Pearson always offered me the opportunity to sit in the copilot's seat on the bush flights. I always accepted as I found this to be very interesting. As we left the King Cove airstrip I noticed the pilot jamming on a lever between us. I asked him what was wrong and he explained that he could not get the landing gear up. I thought about this and then asked if this was a problem. The pilot responded that having the gear down would create more drag which would not allow us to get all the way back with the remaining fuel on board. Therefore, the pilot decided to land on a little sand spit called Nelson Lagoon. I was curious as to how he was planning on resolving the issue and got out with him and watched as he kicked the landing gear struts. We re-boarded the aircraft and he pulled the lever and the landing gear came up (then I was concerned about them coming back down).

During our trip to Akhiok the clouds were socked in on the southern portion of Kodiak Island. It made for beautiful scenery as we flew above the clouds with rugged mountain peaks extending up through the clouds like volcanic islands in an ocean of white cotton. It was beautiful until I started wondering how the pilot was going to get below the cloud cover knowing there were mountain peaks everywhere. Later I found out. The pilot had identified a small hole in the cloud cover and proceeded to take a radical angle to descend through the hole. We got through and he followed a river to the coast which led us to Akhiok. However, the return trip wasn't quite so relaxing. Our aircraft for the return flight from Akhiok to Kodiak was a Widgeon (Grumman G-44) which has overhead wings and wing-mounted engines. Shortly after takeoff I heard what must have been an engine backfire followed by thick black smoke which billowed through the cabin from front to rear. I thought we were goners but the pilot was cool as a cucumber and neither said nor did anything in response. I later found out this was simply the manner in which his aircraft performed as the same thing happened several more times during the remainder of the trip.

During another return trip to Anchorage we were flying over the Cook Inlet and I was again sitting in the copilot's seat. Passengers had exhausted their various discussions and we were left listening to the constant drone of the engines. I started getting the "head bobs" and was about to take a nap when I turned and looked at the pilot who was fast asleep. I quickly started talking which startled him awake. I decided it was in our best interests to talk to him about anything. So he started telling me about how he had just kicked his cocaine habit as I looked down at the deep, dark water of the Cook Inlet—nice!

MOUNT SUSITNA AND DIAMOND TOOTH GERTIES

It was difficult for Susette and me to be separated for what seemed to be so long. So she bought airline tickets to come and visit me in Anchorage. As she was buying tickets I was buying a ring and on July 10, 1988, I proposed to her while we watched the sun set behind Mount Susitna (aka The Sleeping Lady) from an Anchorage city park (she said "yes").

Figure 9. Sunset Behind Mount Susitna from Anchorage (1988)

This was an exciting time as I got some time off from work and we decided to make the best of it. We travelled down to the Kenai Peninsula (south of Anchorage). While in Seward I asked a local if they knew of a place we could park our vehicle overnight. We didn't have much money and were planning on sleeping in the bed of the 1983 yellow/rust Datsun pickup which I was renting from one of the engineers in the office. They asked if we had an RV. My mind flashed a picture of our Mexican made (i.e., it didn't have the necessary features to be normally registered in many of the states in the lower 48) rusty pickup with a topper and I smiled as I responded in the affirmative. We were directed to Camp Mary at Lowell Point. This was our first night on the road of what would become our own odyssey.

Figure 10. The Rented "RV" (1988)

We next travelled north to Fairbanks and enjoyed a carnival ride before they shut it down and began correcting some problems which must have become evident while we were riding—nice. I guess risking our lives gave us healthy appetites as we feasted on king salmon (from Holy Cross) baked over a campfire. We remember this meal to this day.

Our next stop brought us into the Canadian Yukon Territory. I normally kept a pistol with me, but I could not take it across the border so I checked it at a shop in Tetlin Junction. At the border crossing the agent asked if I had any animals in the vehicle and

I replied, "Just her," as I pointed to Susette. He didn't appreciate my humor (probably heard it before), but we were allowed to pass and our entry into Canada was eerie as we traversed the mountain pass with the passing clouds.

We arrived in Dawson City late in the day and began looking for a place to spend the night. It was cold and wet and, after spending several nights in the back of the truck, we really wanted a roof over our heads. However, the hotels in town were very expensive—too expensive for us. I recall looking up the stairs leading to the rooms within one of the hotels we had to leave and I promised myself that someday we would return when we could afford to stay in one of those beautiful old historic buildings. We ended up staying at Mary's Rooms for approximately $20 (American). This was not what we had in mind, but the price was right. Following a meal of sandwiches and water we caught the cancan show at Diamond Tooth Gerties. Despite our lack of funds we enjoyed the show and it seemed to make the trip worthwhile.

Figure 11. Mary's Rooms in Dawson City,
Yukon Territory, Canada (1988)

Fuel was very expensive in Dawson City and I didn't want to have to buy more there than I needed. I had used approximately ½ a tank from Tetlin Junction so I added enough to have approximately ⅔ of a tank on board before leaving Dawson City. As we left town it started raining again and the truck wheels churned through the muddy road. Several hours later the fuel gauge read empty and I noticed our road wrapping around another mountain on the horizon. I started trying to conserve every drop of fuel by coasting down all declines in elevation. We would be travelling very fast by the time we would reach the bottom of a hill and I would coast up the other side as long as I could before applying the accelerator. While coasting down one of those hills I drove over a large rock which tore the exhaust system off the truck (it's probably still rusting away along that rocky road). This further dampened our spirits as we now had to endure the unbaffled noise of that little Datsun (chainsaw) engine.

Susette began to look concerned and shouted an inquiry as to why I was driving like I was and I reluctantly had to shout a response that we were almost out of gas as I tried to keep a calm exterior. Out of the corner of my eye I kept noticing the dense forest leading up to the edge of the road and could only think of how much I wished I had my pistol with me—at least I would have some means of protection if we ended up stranded. I guess the big guy upstairs was looking out for us as we reached Tetlin Junction on what must have been the last remaining fuel vapors in the truck. I picked up my pistol at the shop which was still open (also very lucky), fueled the truck (full this time), and we proceeded to return to Anchorage. We had had enough of our Alaskan travel adventure (the lack of an exhaust system probably cinched it) and I drove straight through to Anchorage, stopping only for fuel and restroom breaks. A nice hot shower, safe place to sleep, and rest felt really, really good.

Susette returned to North Dakota two days later and we both returned to the realities of our separate worlds—her to explain that she was going to marry the custodian at the bank and me to face some new challenges in my Alaskan adventure.

FIRST COSTEP IN UNIFORM

C. Everett Koop was the Surgeon General (SG) of the USPHS in 1988. SG Koop was intent on establishing esprit de corps within the USPHS. At the time many or most USPHS commissioned officers wore uniforms only occasionally (usually on a designated uniform day). SG Koop rightly believed that the USPHS commissioned corps should look and act like other uniformed services and was strongly promoting, via his limited power over the USPHS commissioned corps, all commissioned officers to be in uniform. SG Koop went so far as to send free shoulder boards to all COSTEPs that summer along with a letter of instruction on how to apply for a uniform allowance.

All of the COSTEPs in the office inquired individually as to the uniform allowance. However, they were all rebuffed by CAPT Jim Crum, OEHE Executive Officer, except me. CAPT Crum made personal visits to each COSTEPs cubical and "convinced" them that they should not apply for the uniform allowance (I think he thought it would come from his budget). However, I was convinced that this should be part of the COSTEP experience and, since the SG was promoting it, it certainly could not be wrong. I applied for my uniform allowance, even after receiving my intimidation visit from CAPT Crum, and on August 8, 1988, I became the first COSTEP in AANHS history to report to work in uniform. I was an ensign (O-1).

Figure 12. Ensign Nathan Gjovik in Anchorage (1988)

BARROW

I was waiting to board a flight from Kodiak back to Anchorage late one Friday afternoon in August when the gate agent announced that the flight had been overbooked and they were looking for volunteers to give up their seat in return for a free round trip ticket anywhere Mark Air flew. I discussed it with my travel partner from the office and he didn't think there would be any issues so I volunteered. To my knowledge Mark Air only flew within Alaska and I wasn't aware of any more trips planned for me since my COSTEP tour was almost over. I had heard a great deal about Barrow and I had not been in the northern part of the state. Therefore, I made reservations to fly up to Barrow the next day (Saturday).

The flight from Anchorage to Barrow occurred in two steps: Anchorage to Fairbanks and Fairbanks to Barrow. There were several people on the flight from Anchorage to Fairbanks.

However, nearly everyone deplaned in Fairbanks. I stayed on board and watched as the Fairbanks ground crew unloaded baggage and shipping items from our plane's cargo bay before beginning to load endless cases of beer. This got me a little concerned and I started looking around to see who was actually going to Barrow. There were only a handful of us and the others looked like characters out of a Jack London book. I asked one of them if he was from Barrow. He asked if I had ever been to Barrow. I responded in the negative and noticed a little smile develop within the mess of unkempt hair under his nose followed by silence.

Upon my arrival in Barrow I changed my return flight to Anchorage to the next available flight. However, that flight would not occur until the next morning. I called the hotels in town and discovered, once again, that their rates were very high (too high for me at least). I asked airline staff if I could sleep in the terminal and was told in no uncertain terms that this was not possible. So, I thought I would walk around and see what happened. This was an odd feeling for me to not have some sort of plan for a place to stay. However, the whole summer was about new experiences for me and I was trying to maximize them.

I ate a very expensive modest lunch and then found my way to the USPHS hospital in town. Upon my arrival I introduced myself as a student extern (COSTEP) from Anchorage and became an instant celebrity (I think they were simply happy to see a new face). One of the doctors invited me to stay at his place that night. I took him up on it and ended up meeting several staff from the hospital at his place. One of the nurses gave me a tour of the town by 3-wheeler and we ended the night by watching a video which had been shot the previous weekend on the beach in Barrow. It seems that the ice flow had just broken up enough on the Arctic Ocean surrounding Barrow to allow necessary supplies to finally arrive by barge. Therefore, several in the community had a party the previous weekend at the beach. The video showed some guys drinking beer and throwing the Frisbee as their dog watched on. Invariably the Frisbee flew off into the nearby Arctic Ocean and the guys coerced the dog into retrieving it for them. The Frisbee fun continued on the beach until it, once again, went flying off into the Arctic Ocean. The dog wanted nothing to do with it this time as he was still trying to get warm. Therefore, one of the guys emptied a nearby trash barrel and gathered up a couple of sticks and began to float his way out to the Frisbee. This worked just fine until his sticks were no longer long enough to reach the bottom and keep him upright and in he went. He quickly climbed up on a nearby floating piece of ice and then began trying to jump from one piece of ice to another to get to the Frisbee. Eventually he got it and got himself wet again as he came ashore. However, this sparked an impromptu Polar-Bear-Club event as several on the beach tore off their clothes and jumped into the ice-laden water.

I had a great visit to Barrow thanks to the hospitality of the staff at the USPHS hospital and I am very grateful for same—thank you!

HOMECOMING AND UND WRAP-UP

I returned home (Grand Forks, North Dakota) in late August to a new apartment which Susette had found for me. It was in a great location (Library Lane) and happened to be in the same building as our friend Dean (L.G.). I got things settled fairly quickly since classes at the UND were starting back for me almost right away. After such an exciting summer I had mixed feelings about returning to my custodial/IT work at CNB. Regardless, it was good to be home with my new fiancé and all of the familiar faces.

My last year at the UND was another grind. Working 60+ hours a week and going to engineering school is not easy. However, the time passed and it was very exciting interviewing for engineering positions and I took advantage of every opportunity to do so. Graduation was an exciting time, especially when I found out that I would be graduating with honors (magna cum laude). My parents even attended the event and life seemed good, but there remained difficult decisions to be made.

POTATOES OR PIG ROASTS

It was the fall of 1989 in Grand Forks. Susette, my future bride, and I were trying decide where we would be making our first mark in the world—Idaho or Oklahoma. I had graduated from the civil engineering program at the UND the previous spring. Engineering was hot and I had several interviews and offers. We had narrowed them down to two.

The positions (I had my choice of two) in Idaho were with Westinghouse which was involved as a contractor to the Idaho National Engineering Laboratory (INEL) near Idaho Falls and Pocatello. One was performing cleanup of hazardous waste from various scattered locations across the INEL property. The other was designing facilities to treat and store nuclear waste. I was interested in the latter primarily because it sounded very exciting. However, the site was very isolated and secure.

The isolation was of concern for two reasons. The first was daily transport to the site and back since the INEL is located in a remote area. However, even if it was closer to a population center the security issues may have precluded me from discussing work issues with Susette (we share everything). The high level of security also required a security clearance which took time to process, especially in the days before E-mail and web-based databases. This was also a problem as I was already pushing the envelope by still working my custodial job at CNB where both Susette and I were employed. I could make at least 100% more money as a civil engineer (as opposed to a "maintenance engineer"). However, I would have to leave Susette behind since she was still trying to complete her bachelor's degree in public relations. Also, CNB had a good profit sharing plan in which I would be fully vested if I stuck it out through the end of the year.

Therefore, it made sense for me to continue working at CNB through the end of the year, but no longer than that. So that was our plan—I would continue to work as a custodian and IT person at CNB through the end of the year, we would get married in January (also allowed us to avoid the "marriage penalty" Federal income taxes in place at the time), and we would start new employment shortly thereafter.

The other position was with the Cherokee Nation located in a quaint little town in northeastern Oklahoma called Tahlequah. I had interviewed with the Cherokees due to a recommendation from the USPHS Indian Health Service (IHS) Area Office (IHS regional offices are called "Area" offices) in Oklahoma City. Apparently the new District Engineer in Muskogee, LCDR Michael R. Weaver, had done some research at the USPHS headquarters, where he had been stationed prior to accepting the assignment in Oklahoma, and found my name in a list of COSTEPs and forwarded it on to Oklahoma City who then forwarded it on to the Cherokees.

The Cherokees provided a fly-out to interview with them. It was an interesting trip which was made even more interesting when I missed my turn to Tahlequah while driving through Wagoner in the wee hours of the morning prior to my interview with George Bearpaw. I got only a couple of hours of sleep that night. However, I guess it was enough to get an offer.

The offer actually came through the Oklahoma City Area Office from CAPT Wayne T. Craney, Director, DSFC. CAPT Craney was trying to recruit me to the position as a USPHS commissioned officer to be detailed to the Cherokee Nation. I vividly recall the nature of my phone discussions with CAPT Craney. He has a very interesting and memorable personality and his use of cartoon character voices (Popeye, Brer Rabbit, etc.) was very different than the calls from other recruiters and made a lasting impression.

CAPT Craney advised me of the pay and benefit package and indicated that he thought he could arrange for approximately two years of credit toward pay due to my COSTEP experience (and continued student status following same). Also, since I would be a commissioned officer I would have the ability to retire at 20 years of service. These considerations made the offer very competitive, especially for a young person who did not have much and was very future oriented.

So there we were, Susette and me, on a cold, dreary weekend afternoon in my apartment on Library Lane in Grand Forks trying to figure out where we would begin our lives together—potato country (Idaho) or rural Oklahoma where pig roasts are major events. During our discussion the television was on in the background. We started noticing the repeated presentation of a commercial for Idaho potatoes. The commercial extolled the virtues of Idaho-grown potatoes while featuring beautiful scenery from the state. We thought that perhaps this was an omen of some kind and maybe this was the path we should take (in hindsight this appears to have been accurate). However, we opted for the position with the USPHS in Oklahoma, probably because it represented a more stable and secure path (and would not involve me having to wear a radiation monitor). I accepted the offer, executed my oath of office via my supervisor at the bank and began the paperwork to return to uniformed service on February 4, 1990.

LIFE DURING GOVERNMENT SERVICE

USPHS AND THE COMMISSIONED CORPS[6]

The origins of the US Public Health Service rest in a Federal act passed in 1798 that provided for the care and relief of sick and injured merchant seamen. The act established a number of marine hospitals to care for merchant seamen along the East Coast. Marine hospitals were later established in additional port cities as the nation expanded south and west. Funding for the hospitals was provided by a mandatory tax of about 1% of the wages of all maritime sailors.

A reorganization in 1870 converted the loose network of locally controlled marine hospitals into a centrally controlled *Marine Hospital Service* and a Supervising Surgeon (later *Surgeon General*) was authorized to administer the Service. John Maynard Woodworth was appointed as the first Supervising Surgeon in 1871. Woodworth adopted a military model for his medical staff, put his physicians in uniform, and created a cadre of mobile, career service physicians who could be assigned as needed to the various marine hospitals. The commissioned officer corps (now known as the Commissioned Corps of the US Public Health Service) was established by legislation in 1889. At first open only to physicians the Corps has expanded to include a number of other professional disciplines including dentists, engineers, nurses, pharmacists, physician assistants, sanitarians, scientists, veterinarians, and other health professionals.

The expansion of the professional disciplines within the Corps was driven by expansion of the scope of activities of the Marine

Hospital Service. Quarantine was originally a state function rather than Federal. However, the National Quarantine Act of 1878 vested quarantine authority with the Marine Hospital Service. As immigration increased dramatically in the late nineteenth century the Marine Hospital Service was assigned the responsibility for the medical inspection of arriving immigrants at sites such as Ellis Island in New York. Commissioned officers played a major role in fulfilling the Service's commitment to prevent disease from entering the country.

Due to the expanding scope of the Marine Hospital Service its name was changed in 1902 to the Public Health and Marine Hospital Service and again in 1912 to the Public Health Service. Today USPHS commissioned officers serve their country by controlling the spread of contagious diseases such as smallpox and yellow fever, conducting biomedical research, regulating the food and drug supply, providing health care to underserved groups, supplying medical assistance in the aftermath of disasters, and in other ways.

The current mission of the Commissioned Corps is "Protecting, promoting, and advancing the health and safety of the Nation."

INDIAN HEALTH SERVICE

The IHS, an agency and operating division (OPDIV) within the Department of Health and Human Services (DHHS), is responsible for providing Federal health services to American Indians and Alaska Natives. The provision of health services to members of Federally-recognized tribes grew out of the special government-to-government relationship between the Federal government and Indian tribes. This relationship, established in 1787, is based on Article I, Section 8 of the Constitution, and has been given form and substance by numerous treaties, laws, Supreme Court decisions, and Executive Orders. The IHS is the principal Federal health care provider and health advocate for Indian people, and its goal is to raise their health status to the highest possible level. The IHS provides a comprehensive health service delivery system for approximately 1.9 million American Indians and Alaska Natives who belong to 564 Federally recognized tribes in 35 states.[7] The health service delivery system is comprised of 33 hospitals, 59 health centers, and 50 health stations. Thirty-four urban Indian health projects supplement these facilities with a variety of health and referral services.[8]

The IHS has a formal hiring (and informal promotion, and award, and …) policy called Indian preference which provides absolute preference to Native American applicants (i.e., non-Native applicants who apply will not be considered if there is a "qualified" Native candidate). It should be noted that Native American status is determined by individual tribal policies (some have no minimum Native American blood quantum requirements) and the determination as to whether a particular candidate is qualified is determined by human resource "specialists" who are predominantly Native American.

CHEROKEE NATION OF OKLAHOMA

A LEADER AMONG TRIBES

I started my career as a commissioned officer with the USPHS, assigned to the IHS, and detailed to the Cherokee Nation of Oklahoma (CNO).[9] These were the best year's of my IHS/USPHS career. The people I worked with were great, the work was interesting, and northeastern Oklahoma is beautiful.

The CNO was one of the forerunners of a concept known as "self-governance." Modern tribal self-governance efforts are based on Public Law 93-638, the Indian Self Determination and Education Assistance Act (ISDEA). The law basically allows individual tribes to determine whether or not they wish to manage the various Federal programs for Native Americans. If they do and if they can demonstrate that they are capable of implementing the program (this was usually a rubber stamp exercise) under a "638" contract (Title 1) with limited Federal oversight then they are allowed to compact (Title 3 which later became Title 5 under the reauthorization) the program and utilize the associated Federal funding pretty much as they see fit.

The CNO had recently entered into the Title 1 phase of a "638" self-governance contract for various IHS Office of Environmental Health and Engineering (OEHE) programs. I was commissioned into the US Public Health Service, assigned to the Indian Health Service, and then detailed to the CNO. Therefore, I was a commissioned officer but was technically an employee of the CNO. This place on the fence was often nice because I wasn't completely associated with either the Federal or Tribal governments. However, I felt dirty about many of the activities in which I was involved.

GAMESMANSHIP

The legendary Wilma Mankiller was the Chief of the CNO at the time. Her husband, Charlie Soap, had just been removed from his position as the Director of the Community Development Department due primarily to fiscal irresponsibility. Based on what I was told by others I think he was simply too kind to serve as the director. He helped each and every person who walked through the door regardless of their level of need or available program funding. As a result he ran the program into a deep fiscal hole. A new director was brought in who had a strong accounting background by the name of George Bearpaw.

George is a former Green Beret who served in Viet Nam. I'm sure his management style was radically different from that of Charlie Soap. I think he was the right man for the job. However, probably just as he had to in Viet Nam, I think he was involved in covert activities at the CNO. In this case it was a fiscal shell game to hide the fact that the Tribal program had been mismanaged, lest they jeopardize the opportunity to advance their "638" contract into a compact. Ultimately, the CNO was granted a "638" compact for various IHS programs and there is now little or no oversight of the Federal funding utilized for same.

One of the functions of the CNO's Community Development Department was to provide water, sewer, and solid waste facilities to homes and communities where Tribal members lived. I'm sure the noble idea and image planted in the minds of lawmakers when they passed the law was to help poor, medically indigent Native Americans by providing them with safe water and sewer/solid waste collection and disposal. However, like probably every Government program, it evolved into a mechanism for people to manipulate the system.

Because the CNO had no minimum blood quantum requirements to achieve Tribal enrollment (they were trying to increase their numbers and, therefore, political muscle) we were routinely providing services to people who were a very small fraction Cherokee (e.g., 1/2048th Cherokee which meant that they may have had a great-great-great-great-great-great-great-great-great-grandparent who was ½ Cherokee).

We were also serving many homes which were far from being needy. I vividly remember driving up to a new multi-story home which we had just provided with a free well and septic tank and drainfield sewer disposal system. There were a couple of new vehicles parked outside and several power toys (motor cycles, four wheelers, etc.). As a matter of fact, I recall preparing for a visit from an IHS headquarters delegation and having difficulty finding an appropriate site (i.e., a place without modern amenities like a satellite dish occupied by people who appeared to be truly in need of our services) to match the lawmaker's and upper level IHS management's perception of a truly needy Native American home which benefited from our program.

There was also slight-of-hand involved in classifying many older homes as "like new" in order to qualify them to be served with "housing" funds which were more ample than the "regular" funds used to serve existing homes.

As noted above the CNO is/was very sophisticated. They were one of the five "civilized" tribes relocated to Indian Territory in the 19th century.[10] This level of sophistication is a good thing, to a point. When applying for grants it was better for a Tribe to appear to be less sophisticated since this provided a political advantage (better to be viewed as poor and unsophisticated when applying for free money). The Tribe was in need of a new or upgraded sewer collection and treatment system to serve the Tribal complex. A grant proposal was developed for same. It was well written and very polished, too polished. Therefore, it was decided to "dumb it down" a little in order to improve the chances for it to be funded. The strategy worked and the project got funded with a significant Federal grant.

I am not proud to have been associated with the above activities. My only defense is to suggest that I was young and did not know any better at the time.

COSTEPS

I had two engineering COSTEPS during my tenure at the CNO. They were very different from each other which served to provide me with excellent experience in managing diverse professional staff.

TED SCHLEUTER

Ted Schleuter is an exceptionally bright individual from the University of Arkansas who was a great deal of help to me as a COSTEP engineer over the course of my first summer with the CNO. I assigned him a major project, a hydraulic analysis of a small community water system in an area called Redlands, and he did it well. Along with our professional relationship we became friends and kept in contact with each other over the next several years. Ted went on to work for a private consultant as well as the state of Arkansas. However, as his career progressed he began looking for better pay and benefits which the state could not match.

Several years ago he called me about coming back to the USPHS to work for the IHS in Oklahoma. I warned him against this advising him of my highly discriminatory experiences. However, as is the case with most people, the promise of the pay and benefits provides a smokescreen for the bad things, like discrimination.

JON FOGARTY

Jon Fogarty is another highly intelligent COSTEP I had during my tenure with the CNO. He came from North Dakota State University and also did a good job on the projects assigned to him. However, Jon has a strong "type A" personality which created some issues with me. In one instance I recall him not performing a construction staking job as I had instructed him to do. When I asked him about it he made no bones about telling me how I was wrong. I thought this was pretty bold for a student and subordinate, but I gave him the benefit of the doubt and provided him with a very positive review for the summer.

Jon is fractionally Native American and most people would not recognize his Tribal heritage simply by his appearance. However, Jon knows how to use his fractional Native American racial makeup to his advantage within the IHS. I recall my supervisor at the time warning me that I would probably be working for Jon at some point in time in the future. This turned out to be very prophetic.

LEADERSHIP

My CNO chain of command included Wilma Mankiller, Tribal Chief, George Bearpaw, Director of Community Development, Richard Acorn, Director of Construction Programs, and Bill Reid, Senior Tribal Environmental Engineer.[11] Bill is a retired USPHS commissioned officer who had done a great deal of work with the CNO while on active duty. He had retired as an O-6 officer despite his southern rebel demeanor (he's from Arkansas). However, he was active duty at a time when the IHS was young and in dire need of professional staff who were able to get things done. Therefore, his southern rebel demeanor was not a hindrance to him. Bill became a strong mentor for me and, for better or worse, his demeanor served to reinforce my own beliefs. The USPHS leadership had changed significantly in the 30 years since Bill had been commissioned and they no longer tolerated rebels.[12] This had a significant impact on my career.

My USPHS chain of command included CAPT Wayne T. Craney, CAPT H. Ward Conaway, and LCDR Michael R. Weaver. As described above CAPT Craney is a rather eccentric individual. However, it is this eccentricity which is appealing to many, including me, and he became a mentor for me during the relatively short time I worked under him. CAPT Craney was commissioned about the same time as Bill Reid and, like Bill, was from the generation of leaders who got things done (as opposed to sitting around and considering all of the various political nuances associated with each potential action). However, as noted above, the service and agency winds were changing. The new leadership did not care much for the likes of CAPT Craney and they let him know it during an unscheduled review of the Oklahoma City Area just prior to his retirement. CAPT Craney left with some resentment which I thought was highly inappropriate for the newer generation of leaders, who owed their comfortable existence to leaders like CAPT Craney, many or most of whom had very little actual experience in the field. CAPT Conaway was what I would describe as a transitional leader between the old guard (those like CAPT Craney and Bill Reid who had built the IHS) and the young guns (the new generation of politicos). One of this new generation was LCDR Michael R. Weaver.

LCDR Weaver came from a family of USPHS commissioned officers. His father had retired from the service and his older brother was a ranking member of the management team in the Anchorage Area. Therefore, the road to success for LCDR Weaver had already been cleared and paved. This knowledge apparently brought with it a certain arrogance which was not appreciated by the CNO. They are a powerful Tribe and took issue with the arrogance exhibited by LCDR Weaver in his dictates to the Tribe. CNO leadership had contacted the Choctaws, another powerful Tribe in Oklahoma which LCDR Weaver served. The two tribes were planning a strategy meeting on how best to remove LCDR Weaver from his post. At the time I believed LCDR Weaver to be not only a supervisor but a friend as he and his family had shared time and meals with my wife and me during several seasonal events (none of us were originally from Oklahoma and LCDR Weaver's wife was from North Dakota so we had something in common with her). Because of this and my natural sense of loyalty to my leadership I called LCDR Weaver one night from our home to advise him of the pending meeting between the tribes. I was told later by his wife that he spent the rest of that night in a nervous pose as he must have been strategizing on how to keep his job. Whatever he did it must have worked because he stayed at his post in Muskogee another few years until he accepted a position with the Portland Area IHS where I would later work for him again.[13]

Figure 13. LTJG Gjovik and RADM Bill Pearson, Chief Engineer,
at USPHS Engineer Career Development Seminar (1991)

Figure 14. Oklahoma City Area IHS OEHE Surveying Class (1991)

OKLAHOMA CITY AREA INDIAN HEALTH SERVICE

UNIVERSITY OF OKLAHOMA

One of the reasons I had sought out the opportunity for a permanent change of station (PCS) to Oklahoma City was the educational opportunities for both my wife and me at the University of Oklahoma (OU). This was actually surprising to me since my bachelor's program was so difficult (because I was simultaneously working 60+ hours a week) and I had promised myself that I would never go back. I guess education is like childbirth—you develop amnesia regarding the associated pain and do it again. At any rate, I had already completed three graduate engineering classes from the University of Arkansas via distance learning (which was by video tape at the time) and been admitted to the OU Graduate School for engineering. Likewise, my wife had applied and been admitted to the OU Graduate School for public relations and mass communication.

We ended up renting an apartment in Norman, OK (home of OU). This made for quite a daily commute for me, but made it more comfortable for my wife and provided us with the opportunity to experience life in a big college town. The apartment we rented was noisy due to our upstairs neighbors' habit of partying until the early morning hours. One night we had enough and called the complex's security service. The neighbors responded in kind and called security one early evening when I had our stereo on while I was studying. The stereo was not loud, but apparently it was loud enough for them to hear it from upstairs. We received a notice on our door the next day from management that if our irresponsibility persisted we would be evicted.

I went in to talk to the apartment complex manager about the note and explained what had happened. He was very aloof and arrogant as he responded that I needed to be responsible. I advised him that he should treat me better because he and I might have to do business together in the future. He responded with, "I don't think that's gonna happen." My statement turned out to be very prophetic.

As a result of the experience in the apartment we began looking at buying a home and found a nice little brick house just a couple of miles away. At the time of our checkout I provided our forwarding address and discovered our new house was in the same subdivision as the manager's home. Later, as we were in attendance at one of our new homeowner's association meetings, he nominated himself to be the new President, which would benefit him significantly since he was an employee of the subdivision developer. Those in attendance were asked if anyone had any objection to him being elected President. I fixed my eyes on him and he glanced up at me as he sheepishly fidgeted with his feet. I'm sure my statement was echoing through his mind, as it was mine. Despite my inclination I said nothing and everything seemed better between us after that.

My wife and I worked very hard over the next 2-3 years on our respective graduate programs and completed same in December 1993. We rewarded ourselves with a trip to the winter Olympic games in Lillehammer. We were able to visit my Norwegian relatives (they had visited us several years prior in the US) and see the US hockey team play in my namesake city of Gjovik, Norway.

We took the next two semesters off before we were back in the Sooner Schooner riding toward another set of degrees. My wife had tasted the limited benefits of having a master of arts degree and decided to pursue her dream of becoming a dietitian. She got into the program and I got into a dual master's degree program—master of business administration and master of public health. I thought having more education would help me with employment within the USPHS as well as outside should

I decide to leave. I was wrong on both counts. I didn't realize that most managers are insecure and do not want to hire those with superior credentials to their own. If I had to do it again, I wouldn't. We completed our programs in December 1996 and May 1997.

LEADERSHIP

My USPHS chain of command included essentially the same individuals mentioned above with one exception. That was RADM Robert Harry, Jr., Oklahoma City Area IHS Director, whom we always referred to as Dr. Harry (he is/was a dentist). My expectations for a flag rank officer are very high. Dr. Harry is/was a nice guy but he did not meet my expectations for a flag rank officer. However, he is partially Native American so he met that primary agency prerequisite.

ELEVATOR INCIDENT

One morning while working in my cubicle in the Oklahoma City Area office I was approached by an out-of-breath LTJG Darren Buchanan. Darren provided information technology (IT) support for our office and he and I had commuted into Oklahoma City together from Norman for several weeks when I first started working there so we knew each other well. In between deep breaths he explained that Lisa Young, a young attractive IHS employee who worked down the hall from us, was trapped in the elevator on the first floor and asked if I had something which could be used to pry the doors open. Of course this piqued my curiosity so I grabbed the longest screwdriver I could find in our toolbox and headed down to the lobby.

Upon my arrival in the lobby I saw Dr. Harry with his fingers jammed into the elevator door gap trying to pry them open while he was ringed by a bevy of onlookers. I am the sort of person who takes action when I believe it is called for and this certainly seemed like that sort of situation. After all, our Area Director was personally involved in this effort so it must have been important. I simply could not understand why others were not assisting as well. So I stuck my fingers in the door gap above where Dr. Harry was working and noticed him giving me an odd sort of threatening look which I did not understand at the time.

We were able to pry the doors open enough to see a very healthy and very embarrassed Lisa Young standing beside a television cart which was tilted off to one side. We were able to speak to her. From what I gathered she had entered the elevator on the second floor and did not realize the power cord on the cart was dragging on the floor behind her as she entered the elevator. The elevator door closed and trapped the cord plug on the second floor as she was on her way to the first floor. Apparently the elevator had a safety feature which locked it in place once it sensed resistance to motion and the doors won't open unless you are aligned with the landing floor or you have an elevator door key. It seemed clear to me that the solution was to try and send the elevator car back to the second floor. However, I guess Dr. Harry saw it differently as he barked out to onlookers to "call 911!"

A few minutes later firefighters, police, and an ambulance crew showed up in the lobby of our building. The ambulance crew brought in their cot so they would be ready to resuscitate Ms. Young from her life threatening condition of extreme blushing once the firefighters rescued her. Dr. Harry and I joined the bevy of onlookers and watched as the firefighters began hooking up the hydraulics to their jaws of life extrication tool. I asked them if this was going to damage the elevator doors and was told by one of the firefighters, in the presence of Dr. Harry, "Oh yes, this will damage the doors significantly." Meanwhile the building custodian had found his way to the scene of all the action in the lobby and was trying to get the attention of the testosterone fueled emergency crews who were preparing to "significantly damage" his building. Fortunately the custodian did not spend much time in the lobby since nobody seemed to care that he was trying to tell them he had the key to the elevator control room. As the firefighters were queuing up the jaws of life into the door gap, the custodian apparently found his way to the correct reset switch and sent the elevator back to the second floor. To the best of my knowledge, not even the ambulance crew, saw hide nor hair of Lisa Young that afternoon. Fortunately, she was able to extricate herself and recover all on her own once the elevator car reached the second floor. It was a miracle!

I later found out the emergency crews were not the only people present at the elevator incident who were fueled by testosterone. I was told by others in the office when I described the highly inappropriate manner in which Dr. Harry had managed this incident, and the funny look he gave me when I tried to assist him, that he was pursuing Lisa Young. It appeared that Dr. Harry was attracted to Ms. Young more so than his own wife who was also an IHS employee in the same building. Apparently this ultimately resulted in a claim of sexual harassment and, in typical agency fashion, Dr. Harry was promoted to the headquarters office where his skills were heralded and he became an example to all.

The USPHS commissioned corps is splintered into various racial special interest groups. One of them is the American Indian/ Alaska Native Commissioned Officers Advisory Committee (AI/ANCOAC). Apparently they were quite impressed with RADM Harry, who is fractionally Native American, and his accomplishments as presented in the Commissioned Corps Bulletin (see Appendix 2).

RADM Harry retired in February 2006.

BLOWN OFF BY THE SURGEON GENERAL

Early in my 5-year tenure at the Oklahoma City Area IHS tour of duty we had a visit from then SG Antonia C. Novello. SG Novello was on official business in Tulsa which is only about a 90-minute drive down the Turner Turnpike from Oklahoma City. The Oklahoma City branch of the USPHS Commissioned Officer Association coordinated with SG Novello to visit Oklahoma City. We had rented a limo to pick her up and drive her to the IHS Area office. The preparation for the visit was almost comical. The Area office was packed full of USPHS commissioned officers, many of whom held rank of CDR (O-5) or CAPT (O-6). However, many or most of these officers had no clue as to how or when to render military courtesy. You see many of these officers had no military experience (as a matter of fact many of our global leadership at the time had joined the USPHS commissioned corps to avoid military service during the Viet Nam war) and the USPHS had no officer training or even a basic training requirement. So there they were bouncing around trying to form a receiving line as I agreed to man the elevator.

Figure 15. SG Antonia Novello (1990-1993)

I was joined in the elevator by LTJG Donna Frank. She was a female Native American officer. We were both in uniform and located on either side of the elevator car as SG Novello and her aide walked in. Both Donna and I greeted her and her aide as she entered and I hit the button to take us all to the third floor. SG Novello was standing beside me and her aide beside Donna. The SG gave me a quick head-to-toe once-over and then leaned across the elevator car to shake hands with Donna and exchanged some small talk with her. When the elevator reached the third floor she again looked at me and then reached across and shook Donna's hand warmly and expressed "it was so nice to meet you," as she left to provide her speech to the awaiting excited group. It was obvious that SG Novello wanted nothing to do with me. I was a young officer and felt terribly slighted by SG Novello, our service's highest ranking officer.

Donna and I followed SG Novello and her aide out of the elevator and I immediately advised CAPT Conaway, my supervisor, of the SG's grossly dichotomous treatment of Donna and me. CAPT Conaway did not respond which implied that I should simply ignore it. This was my introduction to the recurring agency theme of simply ignoring obvious double standards by minority persons and the need for me to simply "suck it up."

SG Novello's behavior sensitized me to her agenda. Prior to her retirement on June 30, 1993, she authored a farewell address which was published in the Commissioned Corps Bulletin. In the address she utilizes a female pronoun numerous times and a male pronoun 0 times to describe her various accomplishments. In the same address she cites the vaccination of all of the children of Puerto Rico (she is of Puerto Rican descent) as her crowning achievement. Keep in mind that this came on the heels of the 1991 rejection by the people of Puerto Rico to be considered for statehood in the United States. However, she met the Clinton administration's primary qualification: she is a female (and a minority—bonus). Therefore, the political machine was able to lay claim to nominating the first female Surgeon General.

It bears noting that former SG Novello was indicted in New York State in 2009 on one count of defrauding the government, three counts of filing a false instrument and sixteen counts of theft of government services. She apparently worked out a plea bargain and pled guilty to one felony count of filing a false instrument in exchange for a lighter sentence. The former SG had also reportedly abused her authority over New York Health Department staff by "turn[ing] her staff at the Health Department into her personal chauffeurs, porters and shopping assistants during her seven-year tenure"[14]—just makes me swell up with pride.

SHINING EXAMPLE OF A GOVERNMENT WORKER

As noted above the IHS has a policy known as Indian preference which has its roots in 25 U.S.C. 472. The policy apparently took a major shift in 1979 as a result of litigation involving an IHS employee who happened to be a Native American from Oklahoma named Don Tyndall (I do not have a cite for this case, but it is likely called Tyndall v. U.S.). The current policy is to grant absolute preference to Native Americans in virtually every aspect of employment actions within the agency—hiring, promotions, etc. Native American is defined as anyone who is affiliated with a Federally recognized tribe. As noted earlier some tribes manipulate this system by not having any minimum Native American blood quantum threshold.

As it so happened Mr. Tyndall was still employed by the IHS and had an office in our building which was just outside the Area Director's office. He was a typical Native American from Oklahoma (had some small fraction of Native American ancestry or "blood" as they call it) who had a unique look, at least for Oklahoma at the time. He was portly with long braids on either side of his head which would fall below his hat. I also remember that he drove a yellow Mercedes Benz sedan.

I knew virtually all of the agency staff in the building and what they did. However, I did not know what Mr. Tyndall did since I did not see him much and his office door was normally closed. However, one morning he walked into my office holding what appeared to be a ream of paper in one arm. He peeled a sheet off the top and proceeded to hand it to me. I paused my phone conversation, accepted the paper from him, and examined same. It was an informational sheet on different types of sailing ships. I looked quizzically back at Mr. Tyndall seeking an explanation and he responded with "I just thought you would be interested in this" and proceeded on to the next office down the line. Apparently Mr. Tyndall found something to occupy his time that day—make hundreds of copies of something he personally found to be interesting and disseminate them to staff throughout the building.

This person is/was the apparent standard bearer for the Federal Indian preference policy—you just can't make this stuff up.

REAL EXAMPLES OF (REVERSE) DISCRIMINATION

RECRUITING ENGINEERS AT THE UNIVERSITY OF OKLAHOMA

While completing my master-of-science degree in civil engineering at the University of Oklahoma, I became friends with a female graduate student. She graduated the summer before I did and at a time when civil/environmental engineers were not in big demand. She was young and, to my knowledge, had no professional engineering experience other than that which was related to her research project. However, she was able to find employment immediately in the community of her choice performing work of a highly esoteric nature while her male peers, who in some cases possessed superior academic records and experience (at least one of whom was also professionally registered), struggled for interviews.

WEST VIRGINIA UNIVERSITY AND THE NATIONAL SMALL FLOWS CLEARINGHOUSE

I had become very disenchanted with the IHS and began looking for employment elsewhere in 1994. I applied for many positions including two with the National Small Flows Clearinghouse, a Federal government contractor focused on providing primarily educational and research resources to small water and wastewater systems throughout the United States. The program enjoyed the sponsorship of the late Senator Robert Byrd from West Virginia and is, therefore, located on the campus of the West Virginia University.

I was called to arrange a fly-out interview one afternoon and made the mistake of mentioning during conversation with a secretary named Ms. Hanson, who was going to call me back the next day with a proposed itinerary, that, like her husband from whom she got her last name, I was also of Norwegian descent. Weeks passed and I heard nothing back from the contractor. I began reflecting on my conversation with Ms. Hanson and was convinced that the only possible reason for the lack of response was my naive comment about being of Norwegian descent (I suspect that due to the unique spelling of my last name and the fact that I work for the IHS led them to believe that I was Native American).

I went to the Federal Equal Employment Opportunity Commission (EEOC) office in Oklahoma City to seek assistance. As I was waiting in the lobby for a case counselor, I noticed that there was not one Caucasian male to be seen anywhere in the office and I was made to feel very uncomfortable by the lack of conversation and glaring looks from office workers passing by. During the interview the case counselor told me that there was nothing the EEOC could do for me as I had no definitive proof that I had been harmed. I asked if they could call the organization to see if one or both of the positions had been filled and was told that they could not.

Soon after I called the contractor and was told by a human resources secretary they had filled one of the positions. I called the EEOC to provide the case counselor with this information. I left a message to please have my call returned as the individual was unable to speak to me. However, I was never called back.

Approximately 10 days after visiting the EEOC office I received a call from the contractor in West Virginia to arrange the fly-out interview after all. Over breakfast during the interview process I was told by one of the selecting officials that the reason it had taken so long to schedule my fly-out was that their EEO/AA office "was not happy with the candidate pool" implying that there were not any minority or female applicants and that they had to readvertise the position in venues with predominantly minority audiences.

I have never heard anything back from the contractor following my interview other than to receive my travel reimbursement. However, I have learned via their newsletter, to which I was a subscriber, that the positions were filled by a graduate student from the Middle East and a Canadian citizen. I guess it may be possible that the student working on his master's degree with no professional credentials was somehow better qualified than myself who had (have since greatly expanded credential base) a master's degree from a highly reputable, accredited school (University of Oklahoma), registration as a professional engineer, and several years of professional experience.

CONGRESSIONAL AND ACLU APPEALS

I was becoming more and more disenchanted with the IHS and frustrated with the lack of opportunities available to me within and outside the agency, despite my having achieved the usual pinnacle engineering career ticket punches (a master's degree and professional registration). It was my strong belief that the primary reason for my lack of opportunity was due to the policies being promulgated by the Clinton administration. I was a Caucasian male in a Caucasian male dominated profession. It didn't seem to matter how well I had done in school or what my credentials were. This was all secondary as every application form I completed was prefaced by an affirmative action form which required disclosure of the primary credentials hiring officials were now looking for (race and gender). I had even gone so far as to place an ad in a nationally published professional newsletter to which I received one reply for a position on a remote island off the coast of British Columbia.

As my frustration grew I started reaching out to my elected representatives for assistance. On October 13, 1995, I wrote letters to Congressman J.C. Watts (R) and Senators Jim Inhofe (R) and Don Nickles (D) from Oklahoma. I received a cursory but sympathetic response from Senator Inhofe—that was it.

On December 18, 1996, I wrote a letter to the American Civil Liberties Union (ACLU) of Oklahoma asking for assistance in stopping affirmative action so people of European descent would have the ability to compete fairly for employment. I received no response.

On October 11, 1999, I wrote a similar letter to the ACLU of Washington State, after we had a PCS to Washington. I received a hand written note in response from Kathleen Taylor, Director, that they did not have the resources to pursue such a matter. This struck me as highly duplicitous since they always seem to have adequate resources to make sure so called "disadvantaged" people get a fair shake. I guess the fact that I am Caucasian automatically means that I have lived a life of advantage—I wish this were true.

SECURITY NATIONAL BANK

While I was stationed in Oklahoma City my wife worked in the human resources department of a small town bank. Her bank was targeted by President Clinton's Department of Labor (DOL) for a labor audit (euphemism for assurance that quotas are being met). They determined that her bank was not doing enough to hire so called "disadvantaged" people. The DOL threatened fines of $500,000 if it was not corrected immediately. Coincidently, the next several hires were African Americans. Some of these individuals did turn out to be good hires. Others did not, but they had to be hired or the small town bank would have been levied the fine (less costly to hire the individuals and deal with possible inefficiencies or employment problems associated with not hiring the best candidate than to face the litigation and fines).

One of the positions available at the time was that of mail handler. The selectee would be responsible for sorting and distributing incoming mail and affixing postage to outgoing mail and ensuring proper delivery of same to the post office. This was a position for which the bank's human resources department had received visits from a retired elderly gentlemen who had virtually begged for this job (probably because it was relatively low stress and it was something he could do to keep himself active). However, the DOL's threat precluded award of the position to a man, especially a white man. Therefore, the bank hired an African American female into the position. Unfortunately, she was fired sometime later for stealing postage.

I guess this form of discrimination against predominantly Caucasian people is not considered discrimination since President Clinton had called for an end to racial discrimination and it was his DOL which was making the threats against small town businesses who did not hire what they deemed to be an adequate number of minorities (i.e., forcing them not to hire Caucasian males).

I recently heard former President Clinton make a statement that he does not know where this rise of racial identity came from—I just about choked. It was his Secretary of Labor who was promulgating these policies by forcing people to disclose their gender and racial/ethnic makeup so they could determine whether or not the proper candidates would be hired. Therefore, he was directly responsible for the very thing he now claims to have only been an innocent bystander.

Figure 16. Ken McKenzie in DOE Journal (2005)

COUSIN KEN

Following the retirement of CAPT Craney there were few people for me to relate to within the Oklahoma City Area IHS office. Most of the employees were Native American and they had no problem with the current state of events because they were beneficiaries—they had Indian preference inside the agency and affirmative action outside the agency—the sky was the limit. My supervisor, CAPT Conaway, certainly had no empathy as he had little or no experience applying for job after job and not being considered due to his race. I believe in his mind when I would mention my frustrations I was simply a whiner who needed to suck it up. Therefore, the only person who really understood was another (Caucasian) engineer within the office by the name of Ken McKenzie.

(Cousin) Ken was from Alabama and was four days older than me. I gave him grief that I was born just about the time his mother was probably trying to stuff him inside a dumpster in Birmingham. He had a great sense of humor and responded in kind by mocking my erect posture and flat affect in a little comedy routine he liked to perform for office staff. (Cousin) Ken understood my frustrations as he was experiencing the same situation I was, except it was occurring out in the open within the office. Despite his significantly greater level of experience and his stellar reputation within the agency he was not considered for promotion to Director of his division due to his race. This was a source of significant frustration for him over many years. We called and spoke to each other a couple of times a year after I left Oklahoma City.

As the story goes on July 6, 2009, (Cousin) Ken left work to have lunch with his girlfriend in Oklahoma City. Apparently something happened either physiologically or psychologically or both. He was reportedly driving his car extremely recklessly and ultimately drove it off the road and into a water reservoir outlet dam. He died instantly.

(Cousin) Ken was one of my few friends. I miss him.

BOMBING OF THE ALFRED P. MURRAH FEDERAL BUILDING

The morning of Wednesday April 19, 1995, seemed like the start of just another beautiful spring day in Oklahoma. At 9:02 am I was sitting at my work station on the second floor of Five Corporate Plaza just off the Northwest Expressway when the floor felt as if it were lifted up and set back down. For some reason I thought a large truck must have hit our building so I ran downstairs to check. As I exited the building I noticed what appeared to be a mushroom cloud rising above downtown. I went back into the building and advised Rogers Barton, Acting Director, OEHE, of what I saw and we began to scramble to get a television setup so we could follow news reports.

The following several minutes/hours are fuzzy. I remember my wife and father calling to check on me. My father's voice seemed shaky as he said my name, like he wasn't really sure it was me who answered the phone. Apparently he had been trying to reach me for some time and all of the lines were jammed. They lived in another state and had been called by my mother's sister who had heard news reports that something terrible had occurred at a Federal building in Oklahoma City.

The initial news reports were all over the map. The thought of a terrorist attack was not even on the radar until sometime later. Nobody knew what had happened. We only knew that it was bad. I asked Rogers if we should be doing something. There we were, a building chock full of uniformed service members, most of whom being medical providers, only a few miles away from the incident. However, Rogers had to wait for instruction from his supervisor, Dr. Harry.

Dr. Harry did exactly as the rulebook stated—you sit on your hands and wait for the state to request an emergency declaration and then begin to mobilize resources through proper channels to provide assistance in the recovery phase. I guess he didn't understand that this was an emergency event which required true leadership and an immediate and thoughtful response. One person who did realize this was Jim Cousins, IHS Service Unit Director, in Shawnee, Oklahoma which is approximately 30 miles east of Oklahoma City.

Mr. Cousins is/was a military combat veteran who understood the need to immediately provide critical resources to the scene. He coordinated the mobilization of two teams of individuals. One team was a medical provider team to assist with triage at the scene. The other team was an OEHE team comprised of an engineer, sanitarian, two equipment operators, and several pieces of equipment including radios, two tractors with backhoe/loader, and a bulldozer. This equipment was used to provide ingress/egress routes for emergency crews to/from the Alfred P. Murrah (Murrah) Federal building.

Figure 17. Bombing of Alfred P. Murrah Federal Building (1995)

Meanwhile those of us stationed at the Area office in Oklahoma City were sent home early with instructions to monitor the news and be available by phone in case we were needed.

I was called by CAPT Greg Haase, Acting Director, DSFC, the division I worked for, at approximately 4:15 am Thursday April 20, 1995, to report to the Murrah Federal building bomb site in relief of CDR Don Reynolds, Shawnee Engineer Consultant. I reported to the site in uniform at approximately

5:30 am. I provided my name, rank, organization, and USPHS identification card to guards posted around the site perimeter and explained that we had equipment on-site and was allowed into the "ground zero" area surrounding the north face of the Federal building which had a temporary chain-link fence perimeter.

Upon arrival at the scene, I entered the on-site command center (garage/storage area located at the northwest corner of the Murrah Federal building) and inquired on the status of the bulldozer and two backhoes which CDR Reynolds had left at the site. One of the backhoes was being used to clear debris from 5th Street which fronts the north face of the building. The remaining backhoe and bulldozer were parked near the northwest corner of 5th and Robinson (Robinson runs along the east face of the building). There was a sense of urgency and chaos as I briefly spoke with several individuals including Commander Doyle (name assumed from information CDR Reynolds had provided CAPT Haase as I was never introduced), Oklahoma City Fire Department, who was in charge of on-site operations; Jay Coon with FEMA; Ben Kates, Construction Supervisor, Midwest Wrecking; Major Gary Bouteller, Army National Guard riot control unit; and several FBI and other law enforcement officials concerning the situation and how the USPHS could assist. I was told that I should notify logistics which was located at the main command center on the corner of 8th and Harvey (three blocks north of the northwest security gate) of my presence and what the USPHS had to offer. A decision was made by Commander Doyle to temporarily suspend heavy equipment operation in order to accommodate the efforts of a rescue team which had arrived with sensitive listening equipment. I left the Murrah Federal building area to speak to the logistics command.

While walking up to the command center I called CAPT Haase on my cellular phone and gave him an update on the situation and explained that we may need jackhammers with extended hoses (if available) and air compressors. It appeared that there may be a need for such items for removal of concrete in order to gain access to pockets within the debris.

Upon arrival at the main command center, I asked several individuals where logistics could be found and was given blank looks. I found my way to a table where site entrance permits were being issued by the Oklahoma City Police Department. I received a permit and inquired about the location of logistics. Nobody knew what I was talking about, however, an FBI agent overheard my discussion and brought me to a central area within the command center (commandeered parking lot serving as a personnel staging area). I spoke with a ranking official of the Oklahoma City Fire Department and explained who I was and that I was with the USPHS and that we had equipment on the scene. He requested a list of the equipment we had and could provide. While preparing the list I overheard one of his subordinates discuss a concern over what I would call assistance overload (i.e., that they did not know how to handle the flood of assistance arriving in support of the rescue efforts). I explained that our equipment was already at the building and was being used in the rescue effort and left him a list of the requested data (two backhoes and a bulldozer on-site, also provided makes and model numbers, and the possibility of jackhammers and air compressors, if needed) along with my name, rank, organization, and cellular phone number and departed to return to the Murrah Federal building area.

While walking back to the Federal building area, I reflected on my short visits to the Murrah Federal building and "logistics center" (if that's what it was) and was struck by the seeming lack of organization and coordination. However, I understood that time was of the essence in saving lives and that was where the efforts were focused.

When I arrived at the northwest security gate for the second time, security had been increased considerably and I was not allowed back in as a decision had been made to limit the number of personnel on-site in order to mitigate losses should the remaining structure collapse. While surveilling the situation from outside the fence, an individual identifying himself as a member of a FEMA team asked me how he could get two pallets of equipment inside the fencing to the rescue teams. I asked him what type of equipment he had. He replied that he had portable generators, saws, and jackhammers. I got the attention of the security guards and explained that two pallets of equipment had arrived which needed to be delivered inside the fencing. The security guards coordinated the delivery with the FEMA member and I called CAPT Haase to let him know that we would not be needing jackhammers or compressors.

While surveilling the situation I noticed there was one critical column located along the north face of the Murrah Federal building at ground level near the edge of the blast area which appeared to be supporting a significant portion of the northwest quadrant of the remaining structure. I also noticed a truck with scaffolding loaded on a trailer parked near the intersection of 6th and Harvey just down the block from the north face of the Murrah Federal building which I assumed had been brought over in support of the rescue efforts. I proceeded to the security gate and explained to the guard there was a trailer full of scaffolding nearby which could be used for access to the northwest quadrant of the structure and that I was an engineer and may be able to assist inside. The security guards had me sign my name on a legal pad which they were using to track how many personnel were within the fenced perimeter and allowed me back inside.

Once inside, I worked my way through the crowd around Commander Doyle (along with several others) in order to explain there was a trailer full of scaffolding that may be used to provide better access to the northwest face of the building. He was preoccupied with other things at the time, so I left to take a look at the critical column that I had noticed earlier from outside the fence. On the way, I stopped to talk to a group of individuals gathered in front of the Federal building. They were discussing erection of a temporary man lift elevator along the northwest face of the structure where I had thought the scaffolding could be placed (Flintco Inc. was to build the man lift). Among the group were Don Cook, FEMA team member from Phoenix, and Jack Stevens, President and CEO of JLS Group, Inc. from Carrollton, Texas who are both engineers. Mr. Stevens stated that he was involved in the original design of the building in the early 1970's. I introduced myself as an engineer and they invited me to accompany them in an examination of the remaining structure via boom basket along the north face.

We examined the critical column along with support columns above it and the support columns of the northwest corner before examining the interior blast area. We were glad to see rebar in the upper depth of the concrete roof slab which was cantilevered over the collapsed region of the building. However, we became concerned about cracks and spalling in the concrete and the appearance of bending in the critical column near the building's northwest corner.

Once down on the ground we formulated a plan to brace the interior of the critical column with a 12-inch, schedule 80 steel pipe followed by wrapping the column with steel cable in order to reduce its buckling potential. Boldt Construction was to provide the materials, fabrication, and installation. Don Cook left to get some rest as he had been working at the site for nearly 12 hours following his arrival late the previous evening and was exhausted.

Jack Stevens and I decided to examine the structure from the inside and proceeded to the on-site command center to get permission to gain access to the building. Commander Doyle assigned two firemen to accompany us and we proceeded to the building's south side stairwells. Starting with the second floor, we worked our way through the accessible portions of the remaining structure floor by floor all the way up to the rooftop checking the extent of structural damage. Jack suggested that the elevators could be made operational as at least five of the six elevator shafts were relatively unscathed (i.e. rails appeared to be straight and cabling was under tension suggesting that the cars were still operational). While in the mechanical room, I recorded the information off the elevator motor housings in case it would be needed later. Upon our exit from the building we approached Commander Doyle about the possibility of making the elevators operational which we thought would assist tremendously in the rescue efforts through increased transport speed and access. He agreed to call in the elevator company representatives to consider the possibility, but he was not very keen on the idea of providing power to the building.

While in the building I had experienced vibrations from choppers flying overhead. Once outside, I advised Commander Doyle and several FBI agents of the need to implement a chopper no-fly policy in the vicinity of the building as there was much loose debris hanging precariously over the rescuers working in the collapsed area below the broken floor slab edges. This was subsequently implemented.

Jack Stevens and I were still concerned about the stability of the critical column near the building's northwest corner. We had not yet seen the back side of the column. We asked for and were granted permission to climb the ladder to the second floor from the north face in order to gain access to the back side of the exposed column. However, much of the column was hidden by debris. What we could see of the upper portion had relatively substantial cracking which extended into the nonvisible area. Upon our descent, we asked Commander Doyle for a crew to clear the debris from the second floor area immediately behind the critical column and a crew was dispatched to perform same.

As it was now close to noon and my cellular phone battery had expired and I had not spoken with CAPT Haase in several hours and had not seen CDR Reynolds who had called at around 10:30

am to tell me he was on his way back to the site, I departed for my vehicle to plug in the phone and make some calls. I tried calling several individuals including CAPT Haase and CDR Reynolds before CDR Reynolds called me on his cellular phone from the northwest security gate near the Federal building. I departed my vehicle to meet him.

CDR Reynolds met me at the security gate and he and I entered the secured area together. I introduced CDR Reynolds to Jack Stevens and briefed him as far as the general situation and the activities that Jack and I had been involved in. We began formulating a proposed plan to remove the large concrete slabs which had pancaked on top of each other in the collapsed region by bringing in a large boom (100-200 ton) to peel back the upper slab (i.e. roof slab) and gain access to the lower regions. I believe CDR Reynolds left to check on getting a larger boom truck to the site.

By this time, the fire crew had completed cleaning the debris from behind the critical column and Jack and I climbed to the second floor and examined the inside face to assess damage. The concrete cracking and spalling on the inside face was fairly significant and appeared to be worse than the outer face. There was also visible flexural cracking of the second floor support beam which tied into the midpoint of the critical column. We descended the building to check on the status of the pipe brace fabrication effort.

Don Cook reappeared at the site after getting some rest and approached me about the size of the cracks on the critical column. It was his opinion after being gone for several hours that the cracks had grown longer and wider since his departure. He and I went over to look at them together. I was unsure as to whether or not they had gotten bigger due to my constant presence. However, I agreed that nonessential personnel should be evacuated from the scene and Don and I approached Commander Doyle to discuss the issue with him. Meanwhile Jack Stevens commandeered a bucket truck and started measuring and marking the cracks on the critical column in order to get a sense as to whether or not they were, in fact, getting worse, and if so, to what extent.

Commander Doyle came out to check the cracks for himself. CDR Reynolds and Jim Allen, Dolese Brothers, Inc. engineer, approached and Commander Doyle explained that this was still very much a rescue mission and that he could not pull personnel out of the building unless collapse was imminent. He instructed the engineers present to get together and provide him a best estimate of the chance of structural failure. We decided that in order to provide an estimate we needed data, so we decided to split into two groups. CDR Reynolds and Jim Allen would monitor a shoring effort on the south side of the building and Jack Stevens and I would monitor the critical column on the north face. Don Cook continued his efforts with the FEMA rescue team from Phoenix inside the building.

Jack and I had heard that the elevator company had been consulted about making the building elevators operational and that Commander Doyle had nixed the plan. We proceeded to the on-site command center to speak to him about the situation and were able to convince him that it was worth the effort to attempt to make them operational and that the effort would not interfere with rescue efforts as the mechanical room was near the roof. The elevator company was called back to the building.

Jack and I returned to the critical column to check the cracks again. We noticed that a vertical hairline crack had grown approximately two inches beyond the mark left only one-half hour earlier. I began to get a bit anxious as we continued to check the remaining cracks. However, it appeared that none had grown longer or wider and there was no slippage along the cracks. Jack felt that if the column were to fail, it would not be in shear and that it would probably be manifested via a buckling failure which would hopefully provide ample warning to evacuate the site. We decided to continue to monitor the cracks while the bracing efforts continued.

Over the next couple of hours the cracks did not worsen and the bracing was successfully installed on the inside edge of the critical column. CDR Reynolds and Jim Allen obtained a transit from Dolese Brothers, Inc. At CDR Reynold's suggestion, Jim and Jack placed witness marks along the line of support columns above and including the critical column on the north face in order to detect any changes in alignment.

During down time between checking the cracks, Jack Stevens, CDR Reynolds, Jim Allen, me, and a FEMA engineer formulated a layout plan for the large boom truck which had arrived on the scene. The plan involved placement of the large boom as near as possible to the bomb crater in order to facilitate removal of the largest concrete pieces. The large boom was to be flanked by two smaller booms working the periphery regions where the debris was smaller. There would also be a clear strip immediately north of the booms where the removed debris could be placed for subsequent off-site removal by payloaders and dump trucks.

The plan was presented to Commander Doyle by Jack Stevens, CDR Reynolds, Jim Allen, and the FEMA engineer. I understand that a series of two or three meetings with all of the engineers followed in the on-site command center. It appeared that several other engineers had arrived on the scene by that time and were probably involved in the meetings. I continued to coordinate removal of debris for equipment placement along the north face.

Figure 18. Boom Trucks Being Rigged at
Murrah Federal Building (1995)

CDR Reynolds and Jack Stevens approached me around 7:30 pm
after a meeting in the on-site command center. They were angry
and dejected. They explained there was a turf battle ensuing
inside between the FEMA coordinator, Mark Ghillarducci, and
the Oklahoma City Fire Department which had manifested an
outburst of displeasure by Mr. Ghillarducci at the efforts of the
non-FEMA engineers and the plan which we had developed.
Jack explained to me he had been involved in other emergency
rescue efforts (e.g., Mexico City earthquake and one or two
hurricanes) and was simply in Oklahoma City volunteering his
time as a way of repaying society for the comfortable life he had
been provided and that he was going to leave since his presence
was not desired. I asked CDR Reynolds where the two backhoes
and dozer were and he responded his crew had picked them up
earlier that afternoon so we no longer had a need to be at the
site. Jack, CDR Reynolds, and I watched in relative silence for
several minutes as the large boom was being setup before us.

CDR Reynolds and I said goodbye to the people we had been working with at the site and left at approximately 8:00 pm. As CDR Reynolds and I left the site we were approached by several media reporters. I wanted desperately to speak my mind about what was happening on the site since I was convinced it was not right. However, thank God, I didn't, nor did CDR Reynolds as this would have fueled a media frenzy.

I called CAPT Haase upon my return home and briefed him on the day's events. I was only at the site for approximately 14½ hours. However, I was completely spent due to the emotional, mental, and physical intensity associated with the work at the scene. I called my parents to let them know I was alright. I remember my father asking me if I had seen anything real bad. I explained the victims who were reachable had already been transported to other locations by the time I had arrived at the scene. However, I remember seeing a stuffed animal (purple monster) on the floor along with other debris (children's records, books, etc.) in the daycare as we walked through. That bothered me. My wife then graced me with a back and foot rub as I dozed off to sleep.

I later learned that the rescue plan developed by the non-FEMA engineers, including myself, was ultimately nixed by the FEMA coordinator in lieu of a bucket brigade (rather than removing large concrete floor/roof slabs via boom truck they would be broken up into small pieces which would be manageable by hand). This sealed the fate of any survivors still trapped in the building. I struggled with this for a long time and it was exacerbated a year later when I attended a briefing by the state epidemiologist who had various statistics associated with the bombing some of which were gathered from autopsies performed on the victim's bodies. Apparently some were, in fact, alive for unknown periods of time as evidenced by the presence of dust in their lungs.

One of those who died in the incident was the child of a neighbor in Norman. A monument was erected in his memory which overlooks the neighborhood pond. The surviving family members moved away shortly thereafter. We would also move about a year later.

LESSONS LEARNED

BOMBING RESPONSE

During a major emergency event the local resources will, more than likely, be stretched thin or be inadequate. Therefore, it is incumbent upon those managing supplemental resources to be proactive in offering assistance. I think the extremely negative publicity following Hurricanes Katrina and Rita has changed the political paradigm for emergency response.

The Federal government seems to have a natural propensity to expand its power in spite of limitations placed upon it. In the case of the Oklahoma City bombing response, the FEMA's function was supposed to be support of local command (as in any other Federal response). However, the FEMA coordinator apparently did not do this as he changed the existing rescue plan utilizing boom trucks to debris removal by hand via jackhammers and bucket brigades which would take significantly longer. As a result the fate was sealed for any living victims who were inside the building waiting for us to find them. The lesson, therefore, is that the Government needs to be kept in check. See the next lesson learned for an idea on how this can be done.

CONTRACTING CUTBACKS

In the mid-1990s, as part of the Clinton-Gore reinvention of government initiative, there was an emphasis placed on moving limited Federal resources as close to the customer base as possible (i.e., reduce the overhead associated with the provision of services). This resulted in the IHS offering buy-outs and early-outs to civil service employees working in administrative offices.

On the surface this seems like a good idea. However, the net result is the loss of those who are most able to gain employment elsewhere, leaving those who may be the least experienced and employable (outside government) to carry the weight. Many of those who may be most employable include contracting staff.

Approximately 75% of the contracting staff in the Oklahoma City IHS Area office accepted the buy-outs and early-outs. At the time I was managing the Area-wide construction contracts being utilized in support of our field operations. I, and those above me in the chain of command, was very concerned as to how we were going to be able to continue to function given this extreme loss of support staff. It was downright eerie. On the Friday afternoon before the effective date of the buy-outs and early-outs the contracting office was filled with staff. The following Monday morning the office looked empty and you could almost hear crickets chirping in the background. I thought we were doomed to failure. However, something unexpected happened. The Director of the Division of Acquisition Management (DAM—appropriate acronym) was forced to begin evaluating how he could do things better. Rather than simply asking for more staff whenever somebody complained about being overworked he actually scrutinized productivity and the involved processes to seek higher efficiencies. The net result was that existing contracting services were not only maintained, but they improved.

This was an important lesson for me—the key to government efficiency is to force lean operations through limitations on funds and staffing.

GOVERNMENT HUMAN RESOURCE MANAGEMENT

There was a secretary working within my division in the Area office. It was obvious to me that she contributed little to the success of the division. However, she was Native American so addressing her poor work habits was apparently not high on the priority list for division management. I asked for and was given the responsibility of supervising her. I began documenting her work habits and her inability to perform the simplest of tasks I was asking her to perform. Her typical work day involved arriving late for work, signing in, and then leaving the building to pick up breakfast somewhere nearby. She would then buy a newspaper on the way back into the building and read it while she ate her breakfast. After breakfast she would begin communicating with her friends throughout the building via phone and E-mail.

I started assigning her very specific tasks to perform each day and then reviewing her progress (this was a significant burden on me to supervise this individual). During one of these productivity reviews it was clear that she had literally done nothing the previous day. I had given her a markup with less than ten revisions on a hardcopy which needed to be done as a first priority. It was not done the following day and she had no qualms about telling me she did not get it done. Her demeanor was almost one of daring me to do something about it. So I did. I made arrangements to discuss her performance with Woodrow Kinney, Director, Human Resources Management.

It was clear from the start of my discussion with Mr. Kinney, who is Native American, that he was not supportive of me as a supervisor with a problem employee. As a matter of fact, he became hostile toward me and began raising his voice. I asked him why he was behaving that way and asked him to be supportive. His response was that he was put out when he started talking to me and I glanced off to the side as if I didn't care what he was saying. I calmly noted I did not recall that, but I did recall making a recent glance outside when it had begun to rain. The secretary stayed and was only removed from her position at the end of her temporary appointment by allowing it to lapse.

There were two lessons I learned from this experience. The first was that race trumps all else when it comes to human resource issues with the government. The second is that it is to management's advantage to keep as many employees working under temporary appointments. In this day of extreme political correctness the end of a temporary appointment may be the only real method available for a government manager to remove a problem employee who happens to have some kind of minority status.

Figure 19. Oklahoma City Area IHS OEHE Volleyball Team (1996)

Faces superimposed on 1996 US Olympic volleyball team player bodies (from left to right): Nathan Gjovik, Angela Primeaux, Jack Christy (cartoon face), Harold Cully, Bobbie Gonzalez, Al Frejo, Mitch Baroff, Bob Springer, Mary Barnett, Ken McKenzie, & Diane Harjo.

PORTLAND AREA INDIAN HEALTH SERVICE

LEADERSHIP

Now *CDR* Michael R. Weaver hired me for a Senior Field Engineer position in Toppenish, Washington. Apparently he was impressed enough with me from our Oklahoma experiences to hire me again. However, neither of us had changed and our differences in personalities and ethics would become an issue down the road. CDR Weaver was the District Engineer for the Portland Area IHS DSFC program located in Seattle. CDR Weaver's supervisor was initially CAPT Michael Peterson and then CAPT Kelly Titensor. CAPT Peterson seemed to have the qualities one would expect from a ranking officer—including intelligence and the ability to think for himself. However, he was passed over for the Director position for which he should have been the obvious selection. I guess his ability to think for himself was not appreciated by his supervisor CAPT Richard Truitt, Associate Director, Portland Area IHS.

CAPT Truitt took micro management to a whole new level. He once authorized the purchase of two new desktop computers for our office in Toppenish (an office he never visited during my 4-year tenure) for which I was very appreciative. However, he personally specified on which desk the computers were to be placed. I was the office manager, but I was not asked and I was simply supposed to do as I was told. I began calling his management style "nano-management." I am unsure as to why he would involve himself in such relatively insignificant issues since he spent most of his time ingratiating himself with the power players at IHS headquarters in Rockville, Maryland. I guess it paid off for him as he kept getting his commission extended beyond the mandatory 30-year retirement. CAPT Truitt had over 40 years of commissioned service before he retired and then was hired back as a civil servant into the same position. I guess he is/was viewed as an irreplaceable asset to the agency. It should be noted that CDR Weaver shared with me that CAPT Truitt had told him the primary reason he continued on active duty for so long was to dilute the percentage of his retirement he would have to pay his ex-wife (i.e., since they divorced while he was on active duty she was entitled to a pro-rata share of his retirement based on the proportion of years they had been married to those he was on active duty). I wonder if the power players who kept extending his commission were aware of this—probably not.

CAPT Truitt's "right-hand man" was Wes Bell, Director, Facilities Management. I met Mr. Bell during my first visit to the Portland Area Office. He started right in on me about a water service line I was apparently responsible for getting installed for a new warehouse facility behind the Yakama Health Center. I explained that I had only been in Toppenish for a few weeks and was unaware of the need to install a water service line for his program. He proceeded to make me feel like an idiot due to my lack of awareness. When I returned to Toppenish I immediately arranged to have the water service line installed to the warehouse building. We were almost complete when I received a call from the Project Manager (PM) in Seattle.[15] The PM explained that the building was not yet ready for water service and asked if I could have the contractor stand down. I described to him the grief I had taken from Mr. Bell during my trip to Portland and politely clarified that there was no way I was not going to finish the job. I asked the contractor to install an extra gate valve so we could duly isolate the building. I finished the job but Mr. Bell still had issues with me.[16]

CAPT Kelly Titensor had similar "nano-management" tendencies to CAPT Truitt. I once spent weeks working up a design to perform a water main replacement on the Burns (Oregon) Paiute Reservation via a trenchless method. This was not a new technology and I was a registered professional engineer and I had the design reviewed by another registered professional engineer. However, this was not good enough for CAPT Titensor. He was not comfortable with the technology so I had to spend another couple of weeks changing the design package to a conventional trenching style of construction. The project cost using conventional trenching was higher and the timeline longer, but CAPT Titensor was satisfied so I guess it was all right.

As you have probably guessed I was less than impressed with the IHS Portland Area chain of command. However, I was impressed with several members of the Yakama Nation Tribal leadership, primarily a department manager by the name of Marlene White. Marlene was the manager of the Tribal Maintenance and Water and Sewer programs. She is/was tough and intelligent and wise (from years of having to face adversity). I was able to get to know her pretty well through our work together on numerous projects, some of which involved our having to spend some significant windshield time to and from project sites. She is/was a Yakama Nation Tribal member and, during one of our several trips together, she explained to me that the primary problem on the Yakama Nation reservation was the irresponsibility of their men. I had never looked at things that way, but I started taking note and, over time, came to believe she was right. The general exception to this was those men who had been in the military and returned to the reservation. It seemed that those individuals with military experience typically had discipline, some type of skill training, and some level of leadership experience. Because of this and the seeming ubiquitous tribal admiration of the warrior culture (i.e., this was not limited to the Yakama Nation) many men became Tribal leaders because of their military experience. However, those individuals were the exception rather than the rule.

CLOUDVILLE

I received a call one day from one of the Yakama Nation Tribal managers concerning a suspected case of meningitis in the village of Cloudville. She asked me if I could check out their water system to see if the problem could be associated with their water supply (people always seem to think their water is the culprit for various malaise). I agreed to do so.

Cloudville is located on the northern bluffs overlooking the Columbia River. It is a beautiful location. However, the family group that lived there apparently did not believe in cleaning up, picking up, or maintenance. From the road it looked more like an illegal dump site than a cluster of homes. I brought another person from the office with me to pull a water sample from the suspect home.

We found our way to the home through all of the piled up junk surrounding it. The door was wide open and I could see the kitchen and dining room from the threshold. Within the kitchen there were domestic and farm animals passing through and a barefoot toddler on the kitchen floor which contained various scattered feces. I could also see the kitchen sink which was surrounded by piles of dirty dishes some of which looked and smelled like they had not been washed in weeks. I knocked several times with no success and asked the toddler several times if he/she could get their mommy or daddy. No adult ever came to the door. However, we had just driven approximately 90 minutes to get there and we could see the kitchen sink, our target, from the doorway. I announced our presence and walked into the kitchen over to the sink. I peeked around the corner and saw two adult males sitting on the couch in the living room with their heads tilted back. They were breathing so it appeared they were "gorked out" on something. We collected a water sample from the kitchen sink, said goodbye, and promptly left. I doubt any of the adult members of the family had any idea we were ever there (certainly helped to confirm that Marlene was right).

I reported the household environment to the Tribal program manager and later provided her the results from the water sample which, remarkably, was negative for bacterial contamination.

GEORGEVILLE

Georgeville is another family enclave which is located north of the Columbia River and within the vicinity of Cloudville. Georgeville was compromised of approximately 20 Department of Housing and Urban Development (DHUD) homes occupied primarily by members of the George family. The community had been provided with its own, very expensive, water and wastewater systems for which each household was responsible for paying $10 per month to the Tribal Water and Sewer program for maintenance of same (my wife and I were paying approximately $100 per month for the same services in the city of Yakima). Only a few actually paid with the rest claiming that they did not have available funds to pay for their water and sewer services. However, driving through the community one could see a satellite dish on nearly every home. Also, during one trip to Georgeville one of the Tribal Water and Sewer operators collected several large trash bags full of empty beer cans which were left on the ground at the local party spot near the water tower. He was able to bring them to a recycler and make a couple of month's worth of water and sewer payments in that one trip.

I'm sure there are many who would make excuses for the residents of Georgeville (enablers). However, it was clear to those of us familiar with the situation that the people of Georgeville had plenty of time and money for entertainment (at least satellite television and alcohol), but did not have same when it came to paying their utility bills or cleaning up their neighborhood.

OFFICE MANAGEMENT ISSUES

Working in an IHS field office was difficult. There were numerous pressures from a host of stakeholders—contractors, employees, and Tribal and other customers. CDR Weaver did not seem to understand this because he worked behind a secured door in an ivory tower, literally, in downtown Seattle. Despite the fact that I had the heaviest workload in the Area and was getting a great deal accomplished he was constantly applying a great deal of pressure on me to produce more. As he was doing this he was providing very little in terms of support for my situation which also included significant challenges associated with Native American staff (who essentially could not be fired, and they knew it). In particular there was one secretary who had been in the office for awhile and seemed to have a hatred for white men (in addition to me she also hated her previous supervisor who is/was also a white devil in her mind).

The secretary was militant about certain issues, including her inability to answer the phone while 15 feet away from her desk in the room where the copier was. When I had the audacity to suggest that whenever she was in the office and not on break she should be the person answering the phone and routing phone calls she got quite upset with me. When I explained that this was in her, and only her, job description she seemed to grow to hate me even more. Her demeanor began to affect that of a young, male engineering technician, who is also Native American, and things got worse.

CDR Weaver, in all his infinite wisdom, decided that it was time for him to make a visit to our office and set things right. He had a meeting with staff while I was gone to a meeting off site and decided I was the problem—nice. Based on this I wrote a memo to his supervisor, CAPT Titensor in Portland, OR (see Appendix 3).

I view the concepts included within this memo (the need for local management to be vested with the responsibility and authority to deal with local management issues and for the chain of command to support local management) to be a combination of common sense and entry level management skills. However, the memo was not received well by any of the Portland Area chain of command members. CAPT Titensor responded with an offer to help me transfer to Portland to work directly under him. I did not take him up on it.

Apparently, once again, the expectation was for me to overlook poor performance and conduct issues by Native American employees, simply because they are Native American.

THE TRANSFORMATION OF YAKIMA

During my tour in Toppenish my wife and I lived in nearby Yakima, Washington. In the early 1990s Yakima had been designated an all-American city. It was still relatively clean, safe, and prosperous. However, it was a community in transition. What used to be migrant farm workers had become "resident farm workers" (i.e., illegal aliens from Mexico) and Yakima was rapidly becoming the crime capital of the state. Unemployment was near 20% and it was commonplace not to hear a word of English spoken while shopping in local stores. Many Caucasian Americans were having difficulty finding employment in the area because many employment criteria required candidates to be bilingual (English and Spanish)[17]. The Immigration and Naturalization Service, which was managed locally by a Hispanic male, had a "crackdown" on local fruit packing plants. Local plants were investigated and required to fire any illegal aliens in their employ. Thousands were fired, but none were deported. The local Latino and Chicano organization immediately cried foul and began to try and extort money from local businesses in the name of humanitarian relief for the fired illegal aliens. If they did not receive the money ($500 per business) then they would boycott the offending businesses. However, this was never presented on the television news. It was left to the local news radio programs to present.

We had a nice home in Yakima and the area is beautiful and has great weather (~300 days of sunshine per year) since it is on the dry side of the Cascades. However, it was clear that Yakima was a community in decline due to poor immigration policy and policing and we were glad to leave.

LESSONS LEARNED

There are many people in positions of power who enable the bad behaviors of others (e.g., poor performance and/or conduct at work, unwillingness to pay bills, laziness, etc.) simply because of some kind of perceived disadvantage which was foisted upon their ancestors. Many of us (and our ancestors) have histories of adversity and disadvantage in the current day, but because we don't fit the stereotypical racial features of skin, hair, and/or eye color we are expected to "suck it up."

PHOENIX AREA INDIAN HEALTH SERVICE

LEADERSHIP

The person who hired me to join his team in the Eastern Arizona District Office (EADO) as the Engineer Consultant for the DSFC was CDR Mitchell Constant. I would like to believe CDR Constant and I share many similar attributes, including physical. To some we look like we could be brothers. CDR Constant is very devout in his Christian faith so I joked privately that I must be his evil twin. I have a deep respect for CDR Constant and together with an outstanding cadre of field engineers we got a great deal of work accomplished on behalf of the Hopi and San Carlos and White Mountain (formerly Fort Apache) Apache Tribes in eastern Arizona. However, the chain of command above CDR Constant was made up of ranking officers with strong appetites for easy living. I had seen this before and called it the pre-retirement cruise—ranking members of IHS management, many of whom were USPHS officers, essentially abdicating their responsibilities as they quietly floated their way to their retirement date while punishing those brash young boat rockers, like me, who dared to make any kind of a ripple in their pond.

RETIREMENT PLANS

Before I accepted the position in the Phoenix Area I had requested of CAPT Chadwick a fly-out so I could scope out the area for housing and employment opportunities for Susette. He refused to provide a fly-out until I accepted the position.[18] I accepted and then flew out, with Susette (which we paid for), to check out the area.

The duty station was located in Pinetop which is beautiful. However, homes are generally very expensive and can be difficult to resell (some of the homes we were looking at had been on the market for over four years). Good jobs were also difficult to come by. Susette was experiencing a very successful career path as a dietitian in Yakima. She had been selected for a highly coveted position at a new oncology center in Yakima, was the President of the local chapter of the American Dietetic Association, and was recently named the young dietitian of the year within the state of Washington. With this portfolio of strong credentials in hand she applied for a position at the local IHS hospital in Whiteriver (~20 miles south of Pinetop).

Apparently she was able to overcome whatever reservations CAPT Ann Farrar, Supervisory Dietitian, had about her and she was offered a position as an entry-level GS-7 civil service position. Typically, a new professional staff member is given credit for their previous experience. However, CAPT Farrar was unwilling to support crediting Susette's four years of previous professional experience. As time went on Susette started to understand what was going on. CAPT Farrar was just another in a long list of IHS management disappointments.

This was Susette's first exposure to employment within any governmental organization. However, she was routinely deprived of virtually all training as CAPT Farrar burned up the training budget on herself, just before retiring. We also noticed her more than once carrying supplies from the hospital to her home, which was behind ours, to care for her ailing father (who did not appear to be Native American). CAPT Farrar also allowed the continued harassment of Susette by some female Apache food service workers who seemed to delight in making the life of my beautiful young wife a living hell via their hostile demeanor and, according to rumor, their use of hexes which they seemed to be continually placing on her.

In addition to the hostile work environment and poor management the Phoenix Area human resource department had placed her into the civil service retirement system (CSRS) which had been closed to participation for 14 years (since 1987). Therefore, she had been contributing to a retirement system from which she could never receive any benefit—and she was the only person to take note of this (i.e., nobody within the Phoenix Area had noticed the error over a period of several months). She started asking questions which only fell on deaf ears (i.e., nobody cared or knew enough to correct the situation). The situation culminated in the involvement of several Congressional offices and the regional DHHS office in San Francisco. The final letter from Susette, dated March 31, 2003, got their attention (see Appendix 4).

I think the letter does a good job of documenting the gross incompetency of at least the Phoenix Area IHS. However, it probably goes without saying that it probably did not help my career much—but it felt good for us to send it. The issue was eventually resolved by a technician in the DHHS Regional Office in San Francisco—I guess the IHS was devoid of human resource staff competent enough to figure out how to correct or explain such a situation.

2001: A (HOUSING) SPACE ODYSSEY

We left a beautiful 2200-square-foot home in Yakima to enter an unknown housing situation in Arizona. Since Susette had accepted a professional position with the Whiteriver IHS Hospital we had the opportunity to live in a manufactured home behind the hospital available for our use as a rental. After searching unsuccessfully for suitable housing we decided this was the best option. However, we soon discovered that even this was poorly managed. There were several people who were renting government homes behind the hospital who were not eligible, but they were allowed to live there simply for political reasons (i.e., they were Native American). At least one of these families was heavily involved in distributing drugs and we personally witnessed highly suspicious interactions on more than one occasion. We reported them. However, nothing ever seemed to be done.

Eventually Susette reached her frustration threshold with Government service and she decided that it was better to simply leave. However, if she left her Government employment our housing would no longer be available (which was not necessarily a bad thing). We developed a decision matrix for housing options. The matrix included portable housing (e.g., a camper or motor home). We worked our way through the matrix and ended up with this option. We contacted a former colleague of mine whom I had known in Toppenish, Washington who was also currently stationed in Arizona. He and his wife had been living full-time in their motor home for a number of years. He informed me of an advertisement for what appeared to be a very nice motor home in the Arizona Republic. We had already been looking at them and decided to check this one out since we were going to be in the Phoenix area. We setup an appointment and ended up taking the financial plunge to purchase the 2001 Monaco Dynasty during the visit. It seemed very impetuous at the time. However, it turned out to be a good move as we ended up living in it for 5½ years.

MY FIRST ELK

I was returning one fall night to Pinetop in a Government-owned vehicle (GOV) from a meeting and work with our Polacca, Arizona field office on the Hopi Indian Reservation. I crested a hill in a rural area between Snowflake and Show Low while traveling south on Arizona state highway 77. The sun had completely set and there was little, if any, moonlight. I was using my vehicle's low beams as oncoming traffic was fairly heavy. The lights from an oncoming vehicle partially obscured my vision as it approached. As the car passed I discovered an adult elk standing broadside to my direction of travel in the middle of my lane and facing west (i.e., the outside of the lane/road). I attempted to brake and swerve my vehicle. However, with the little reaction time I had available, I was only able to strike a heavy blow to the rear quarters of the elk with the right front corner of my GOV. The elk apparently swung around the vehicle and struck the right rear of the vehicle smashing the right rear window.

After the impact I immediately pulled the vehicle off the right side of the road. As I looked in the rear-view mirror to check on the elk I noticed there were no other vehicles in the area at the time of the incident (other than that which had just passed and disappeared over the hill) and could not see anything behind me. I called 911 and was told a highway patrol officer would be dispatched to my location. I then surveyed the vehicle and discovered that in addition to the obvious body damage the radiator was also damaged and the right front quarter panel had been collapsed into the wheel. I then called the Government Services Agency (GSA) to report the accident and arrange for a tow.

A few minutes after the collision a southbound car parked behind my GOV and the driver approached my GOV and asked if I needed assistance. I said that I was fine and thanked him for checking. He then turned and went back to his vehicle and drove off northbound.

As I waited for the highway patrol I was unable to check on the status of the elk as it was too dark to distinguish anything without a flashlight. A southbound truck driver stopped to check if I needed assistance approximately 15 minutes after the collision and left just after the highway patrol arrived.

The highway patrol officer asked if I was alright and if I needed a tow and then explained that accident reports for that area were normally generated by the Snowflake Police Department. He then called same and asked for an officer to be dispatched to the area. While we waited for the Snowflake police we searched the roadside for the elk. Approximately 10 minutes after the call was placed the Snowflake police arrived with two vehicles.

I provided some details of the incident to Officer Mortenson from the Snowflake Police Department and then he and the other officer from Snowflake assisted the highway patrol officer and me in searching for the elk. We found the elk approximately 200 feet north of where I had parked my GOV. We surveyed the elk and determined it to be dead. It appeared that the elk was killed instantly as there was no sign in the surrounding grass and brush of it struggling. The highway patrol officer then explained that he could issue me a Big Game Salvage Permit which would allow the elk to be legally butchered. I was wearing my service dress blues so I indicated to him that I didn't really feel as if I was prepared to field dress the elk. However, I accepted after Officer Mortenson explained that I could donate the animal and that he knew of a needy family in Snowflake that could use the meat. I asked Officer Mortenson to make contact with the family. He did same and I provided the permit to Officer Mortenson to give to the family. The family's husband/father arrived approximately 10 minutes after the call and began field dressing the elk. I then provided the remaining details to Officer Mortenson for completion of the accident report along with a business card so he could fax it to me the next morning. It should be noted Officer Mortenson informed me that was the 6th or 7th accident involving an elk he had personally responded to that year at the same location.

The tow truck arrived about an hour later and I called Susette. She likes to talk and I had to listen to the details of her day before being able to tell her about the accident (still makes me smile). We got back to Show Low and CDR Constant gave me a ride back to the office where my personal vehicle was located. This wouldn't be the only accident I would be involved in with CDR Constant.

SAAB STORY

Shortly before we arrived in Arizona CDR Constant and his family were involved in a significant car accident with their SAAB sedan on a nearby mountain road. His wife was taken by air ambulance to a local hospital. Everybody fully recovered and they were just getting the pieces put back together from the impacts of the accident, including replacement of their SAAB sedan and completion of their new home construction project.

CDR Constant asked if I could assist him with the compaction of his switchback driveway leading up to his house. I agreed and we made plans for the following weekend. While he was placing rock with a skid-steer I was making compaction runs with a drum roller. Everything was going fine right up to the time when I was trying to get the rock compacted next to the concrete apron outside his garage. The garage door was open and as I stood up to check how close the drum was getting to the structure my knee caught the levered speed control and off I went—right into their brand new replacement SAAB sedan.

Having to tell my supervisor that I had just possibly destroyed his new car was one of the hardest things I have ever had to do, especially after he had just purchased it to replace the other one which was totaled in the mountain road accident. He was obviously not happy, but he handled it well. I tried to buy myself some redemption by paying his insurance deductible. However, even as I write this chapter some nearly 10 years hence I still feel awful about it. I/we were very fortunate in that nobody was hurt, especially his young daughter who was standing near the compactor at the time I was working the garage apron area. I/we were also very fortunate in that the house was not affected. Therefore, we were very lucky that this SOB only impacted that SAAB.

FLOODS

While working in the EADO we experienced several instances of significant leaks within the office due to heavy rain or snow melt. I was told that this was a common experience within the office. This seemed very odd to me since we were renting the office space from a private landlord. I thought Federal office space would have associated high standards. I know that if I was associated with the maintenance of the office and we experienced just one roof leak I would have immediately demanded repair of same. However, between the six O-6 officers in the Phoenix Area Office and the one managing our office they could not seem to muster the courage to call and make this very simple demand. What made it even more perplexing to me was that the rental contract was being managed by the GSA. Therefore, all one had to do was call the GSA and ask that they demand repair of the leaky roof. However, this was apparently too much to ask of all those O-6 officers.

During one of the significant leak events I apparently had at least two significant waterfalls which occurred in my office (occurred at night during non-duty hours). The water damaged or destroyed several of my professional books, a radio, and my treasured Glamour Shots® photo of Susette. Following this I contacted the GSA directly and was promptly rebuked for not following the chain of command. The recommendation made to me was to move my office to another which was unoccupied and had traditionally experienced fewer leaks. During the phone call with CAPT Chadwick I asked why a demand wasn't made of the GSA to get the leaks fixed. I was met with silence and made to feel as if I was some sort of radical. I moved my office (lost at least a day of productivity in the process) and continued to suffer damage from roof leaks after the move, albeit less significant.

I guess my pressure to get the roof repaired eventually worked since, after years of experiencing roof leaks, the chain of command eventually worked up the courage to call the GSA and ask them to ask the landlord to repair the roof (and the landlord did same).

FIRES

During our tenure in the White Mountains of Arizona we experienced two major wildfires, the first of which was the Rodeo-Chediski Wildfire. This wildfire caused the evacuation of the entire communities of Pinetop, Lakeside, and Show Low.

We had just completed our move into our motor home and looked like geniuses as we simply relocated our new home on wheels down the mountain to Whiteriver. Fortunately, since we were able to get ourselves easily relocated, we were able to help others secure their homes and possessions. I was also able to assist in the preparation of our office in Pinetop for potential loss from fire. This was necessary since our O-6 office manager had disappeared in the dead of the night prior to the mandatory evacuation and, apparently, did not find it important to prepare the office or let any of the remaining office staff know of his location. I personally found this to be completely irresponsible. However, I guess my expectations were simply too high for this ranking officer. This was only one of several disappointments I found with office management.

OFFICE MANAGEMENT ISSUES

After a series of poor management choices and poor work ethic being exhibited by the local office manager, an O-6 officer, I felt it necessary to author another memo on office management issues (see Appendix 5). From my perspective it was clear that he had been derelict in his duties as the office manager in regard to both the leaks in the roof as well as the evacuation effort necessitated by the wildfires.[19]

As predicted in my memo the outcome of the subsequent non-action by the Phoenix Area chain of command was that both CDR Constant and I were gone within several months.

A PARIAH IS BORN

CDR Constant transferred to a Director position with the IHS Albuquerque Area Office. After all of the above experiences I requested a meeting with CAPT Alan Croft, Associate Director, OEHE, and CAPT Kevin Chadwick, Director, DSFC, to see where I stood in terms of applying for CDR Constant's position. CAPT Croft is a sanitarian and was CAPT Chadwick's supervisor. CAPT Chadwick is an engineer and was CDR Constant's supervisor. It should be noted that the two dysfunctional employees in the EADO were both sanitarians and there is a long standing general resentment between engineers and sanitarians due to the relative ease of becoming professionally registered as a sanitarian and the fact that sanitarians generally make significantly less money than engineers on the open market. However, within the USPHS they have complete parity with engineers and often rise through the chain-of-command because their work is generally less demanding than that of the engineers which allows more time to write themselves and each other up for awards. Therefore, in the USPHS sanitarians are generally extremely well paid and receive high accolades for their labors. When an engineer like me comes along and is perceived by a poor manager as attacking a fellow sanitarian the manager may be prone to simply protect their brethren. I believe that is part of what happened to me in the Phoenix Area.

I was on leave during my trip to Phoenix to meet with CAPTs Croft and Chadwick. My wife Susette was with me. I wanted her to attend the meeting. However, CAPT Chadwick was apparently intimidated by her presence and asked her to leave. The meeting was a flop for me. CAPT Chadwick played the political line and encouraged me to apply for CDR Constant's position. However, CAPT Croft showed up late, did not provide any type of greeting, and left early without any words. The message was loud and clear, "Boat rockers need not apply."

LESSONS LEARNED

The Phoenix Area IHS was the quintessential real-world example of the ill-informed walrus (see Appendix 6). However, I suspect the primary driving force behind this behavior was apathy—management officials had already started their pre-retirement cruises.

Engineers Field Test Trial Uniform

Engineers from the Eastern Arizona District of the Phoenix Area, Office of Environmental Health, are part of an ongoing uniform field test. They are wearing the trial uniform for 30 days. LCDR Thomas Moeller reports, "We all enjoy being involved with the test, and we all like the new uniform for the field." LCDR Moeller and his fellow Indian Health Service engineers are shown in the photo below.

Bottom Left: *LTJG Kevin Chapman, LCDR Thomas Moeller, LT David Mazorra, and LCDR Christopher Brady.* Second Row Left: *LCDR Nathan Gjovik, CDR Mitchell Constant, and LCDR Michael Stover.*

Figure 20. Field Deployment Uniform Trial
by EADO Engineers (2002)

INDIAN HEALTH SERVICE DIVISION OF ENGINEERING SERVICES

LEADERSHIP

The person who selected me for the project management position with the Division of Engineering Services (DES) in Seattle, WA was CAPT Richard (Rich) Melton. CAPT Melton was a very good manager as far as IHS management goes. He has a good blend of technical and human resource skills. I respect him both personally and professionally. CAPT Melton's supervisor was CAPT Kenneth (Ken) Harper (Retired). Ken is one of those individuals who retired from active duty and then returned to the same position as a civil servant. Perhaps it is this decades of experience in a given location which develops in one a certain arrogance. Ken has it in spades and apparently believes that he had seen and done it all. I actually heard him say this to now *CAPT* Michael Weaver who had transferred to this division from the Portland Area IHS (two floors down in the same building) and was now managing the Technical Services Division (the sister division to the Project Management Division where I was employed).

I had accepted the position with the DES because I knew that I would not be working under the supervision of CAPT Weaver. Our working as colleagues seemed to improve our relationship. CAPT Weaver had recently remarried after divorcing his long-time wife, reportedly due to her drug and alcohol abuse. His new wife was one of the contract specialists in the office named Monica. She is smart and attractive and the two seemed like a good match.

Susette and I joined the Weavers for meals at their home in Redmond on several occasions (we were living in our motor home and had very little room for guests). We always brought something to the table and the meals were nice and everyone was cordial. We were even asked to assist them in watching their first child the night their second child was born and we obliged. Things seemed good and we felt comfortable sharing personal stories, including our involvement with my extremely dysfunctional family. Little did I know at the time how CAPT Weaver would later utilize this information, with some embellishment, to destroy my career. However, this would occur only after he became my supervisor again following the retirement of CAPT Melton.

IGNORED BY THE SURGEON GENERAL

Figure 21. SG Richard Carmona (2002-2006)

Early in my tenure at the IHS DES we had a visit from SG Richard Carmona. I was impressed by the SG because of his impressive resume. I thought we finally had a SG who was selected based on merit. During the meeting I provided him with a brief statement on the damage that was being perpetrated on the IHS by Indian preference and then asked him about his thoughts on the issue. He suggested that it was a difficult issue and that I should formalize my question in written form and forward it to him through his aide for a more thorough response. I did same (see Appendix 7). However, I never heard anything further from the SG regarding this important issue. I later found out that he is of Puerto Rican descent which may explain why he was allowed the wide variety of opportunity which is highlighted by his impressive resume and why I never heard anything further from the SG on the issue of discrimination (i.e., he may have personally benefitted from it).[20]

A SECOND AMENDMENT REQUEST

Susette and I had our motor home parked at a nice RV resort in Everett which is approximately 20 miles north of Seattle. I was taking the bus to downtown Seattle every work day. I had to walk to the bus stop which was only a few blocks away. However, across the street from my path to the bus stop was what appeared to be an illegal dump site and, on occasion, I would see people hanging out in the area amongst the trash. I assumed they were probably drug users (fairly common in the Seattle area—I once saw a couple of people torching up joints at the bus stop in downtown Seattle). I carried a backpack with me which contained various emergency items should I need them while traveling to and from Seattle. One morning one of the (presumed) "meth-heads" from the dump site came across the street. He appeared to be coming for me (and my nice big backpack). This was quite surprising to me since I have a fairly large stature and build, but it supported my belief that the group was probably into drugs and, therefore, not thinking logically. I pulled my walking stick from my backpack and prepared for action. He picked up a big stick from a wooded area on my side of the street and kept coming. I kept walking to the bus stop (mostly backwards as he was approaching from my rear) and, fortunately for us both, the bus arrived at the stop just as I arrived and an incident was averted. However, the lesson was not lost on me that I may need more than a walking stick to defend myself against "gorked out" zombies.

Within only a few weeks of the above near incident the London bus bombings occurred and I began evaluating the bus commuting situation in the Seattle area. I was nearly always very vigilant about my surroundings, but it seemed there were very few like me riding the buses. I wondered what I would do if a terrorist jumped up and started screaming "Allah Ahkbar!" while brandishing a weapon of some sort. Again, my walking stick was probably not going to cut it.

I had duly applied for and been granted a permit to carry a concealed weapon within Washington state. I desired to carry a weapon with me during my commutes to and from Seattle. However, I was not sure where I could keep the weapon during the time I was at work. The Government has a strict prohibition against taking weapons into any Federal space (makes no sense to me since this only places law-abiding citizens and employees at risk of being slaughtered like sheep should some nut show up with a loaded weapon and bad intentions). I was well aware of the prohibition, but I was also aware that our building was not a Federal building—it was a commercial building within which various Federal agencies were renting space. Therefore, I asked whether or not I could store a weapon within my locker in the fitness center, which, as far as I knew, was a space available to all building occupants who paid for a membership (i.e., it was not a Federal work space). The response came back that this would not be allowed since the fitness center was also considered Federal space and that was it, so I left it at that.

I thought this was a simple request. However, apparently others viewed me as some sort of right-wing extremist for simply asking. This simple request was also later utilized by Ken Harper and/or CAPT Weaver to characterize me as having tendencies for workplace violence.

DEPLOYMENT TO NEW ORLEANS FOLLOWING HURRICANES KATRINA AND RITA

Part of the dysfunctional response to the Gulf Coast region following Hurricanes Katrina and Rita revolved around the involvement of the USPHS. The USPHS is a uniformed service. However, it has no leadership academy like other services and those who rise to the top generally do so as a function of their ability not to make waves (i.e., absence of leadership). I also knew the primary emergency response coordinator, CAPT

Andy Stevermer (I worked in the same building with him in Seattle). Therefore, it came as no surprise to me that the Federal relief response following Hurricanes Katrina and Rita was dysfunctional.

I was deployed initially to Lake Charles, LA. Therefore, I rented a four wheel drive upon my arrival in Baton Rouge (the closest we could get to New Orleans at the time) and proceeded to find the State Emergency Response Team (SERT).

When I arrived the situation was chaotic with most people having had little direction from above. I was eventually assigned to the Principle Federal Official (PFO) office in New Orleans, LA (NOLA). The drive to NOLA was surreal—like being in the middle of an apocalyptic nightmare. The primary mission of the USPHS was to try to get the area's hospitals back into service. I had driven down to NOLA with a USPHS nurse officer who was reporting in relief of an administrator at one of the hospitals.[21] It sounded like she had a tough assignment ahead of her as she would be expected to temporarily work and live in very Spartan-like conditions within the hospital to which she was assigned.

As it turned out I had the opposite experience. I got to share a room at one of the very nice downtown hotels for approximately one week before FEMA floated a cruise ship in for us to stay in. We each had to share a berth with another deployed uniformed service member and it was close quarters, but I certainly was not about to complain.

I was asked one morning if I had a need to see the area from above. I responded that it would be beneficial for me to see where the various hospitals were and what type of external damage they each had, so off I went. Seeing NOLA from the air really drove home how widespread the damage was and it was very helpful for me to see the hospitals.

One of the hot issues being discussed at the PFO was the request made by local officials on behalf of their constituents to remove and dispose of debris from private properties. This was not something which was usually done as there was the assumption that individual homeowners would perform such tasks as in other Federal responses. However, the Federal response was already highly politicized and we didn't need any additional bad press by the news spinmeisters. Therefore, some sort of blanket easement was developed which allowed the Army Corps of Engineers (ACOE) official access to private property (and the bad press continued unabated). However, based on what I saw, it was clear that the bulk of the problems with the government response were due to poor state and local leadership (and perhaps graft associated with maintenance of the levee system, which an ACOE staff member told me was the responsibility of the parishes).

Figure 22. French Quarter Cafe for Emergency
Responders in New Orleans (2005)

At the French Quarter Café one night I sat across the table from a deployed national guardsman from Baton Rouge. He was disgusted by the lack of personal responsibility being exhibited by the local population and the inept local leadership. His statement, "All these people know how to do down here is party" pretty much summed it up.

Mayor Ray Nagin was concerned about the NOLA population who had fled to other cities returning to their compromised homes. He was pushing an initiative to return people to their homes immediately. While on the surface this may sound like a good idea there were a number of issues— like the lack of safe utilities in many of the areas (i.e., no water, sewer, electricity, etc.). I had significant concerns over this plan (e.g., water-borne disease, inability to fight fires with a compromised water distribution system, and the high possibility of fires given the lack of electricity for cooking and lighting) and voiced them during a PFO planning meeting with US Coast Guard (USCG) officers. The USCG had command of the PFO under ADM Thad Allen. At our next stakeholder coordination meeting the USCG Captain acting on behalf of ADM Allen made it clear that our job was to support local officials (it seemed that this was directed toward me). He was correct and I fell back into line.

Figure 23. CDR Nathan Gjovik Working the
ESF-8 Desk at the NOLA PFO (2005)

CDR Sharon White, also deployed to the PFO with me, and we spent most of our time trying to determine what assets the USPHS had on the ground in the area. In an organized relief effort this would have been accomplished with a simple phone call. However, the right hand had no idea what the left hand was doing.

Several months after my deployment I was asked, along with several other USPHS officers, to provide a briefing on my Katrina/Rita deployment experiences. I described my experiences truthfully (see Appendix 8). However, this was not received well by CAPT Stevermer who was in attendance at the briefing.

CAPT ANDY STEVERMER

CAPT Andy Stevermer was the emergency response coordinator for Region X. He had a strong reputation based on his extensive experience as an emergency responder. I respected him for that. However, he was like many type A personality types in that he believed that he had all the answers and did not require any input from lesser experienced persons like me, not realizing that we all have weaknesses and, therefore, we could all use help from others who complement our skill sets. CAPT Stevermer may very well have been a great emergency responder when it came to making responsible decisions quickly. However, he was not a good organizer and it showed in his performance at Katrina where he was the lead USPHS responder.

As noted above CAPT Stevermer was present when I provided my deployment briefing. I know he was not pleased with me but I said what he needed to hear. Our response to Katrina and Rita was poor and one of the primary reasons was his inability to get it properly organized.

CAPT Stevermer and I also did not see eye to eye on our local emergency response preparations. I saw the commissioned officers located within our building, most of whom were registered clinicians, as extremely valuable, immediately deployable assets should Seattle suffer a major event (the Seattle area is at risk for many different types of major events including earthquakes, tsunamis, volcanic eruptions, and terrorist attacks). I had recently completed an EMT-Basic course from Everett Community College. Based on this training, I had made recommendations through my chain of command as to what medical equipment and supplies I thought we should have within the building. The equipment and supplies would allow USPHS commissioned officers the ability to respond to an emergency event with victims both inside and outside the building should the normal emergency response system be unable to reach us (a distinct possibility under any of the potential major events). CAPT Stevermer apparently believed that the liability and maintenance associated with providing the equipment outweighed the potential benefit. I guess reasonable persons can argue this both ways. However, I believed that enabling USPHS commissioned officers to be able to utilize their skills when needed during a major response was in accordance with our mission as well as the expectations of our customers, American citizens. CAPT Stevermer's argument prevailed and our first aid kits were replenished with Band-Aids® and aspirin.

WHO IS YOUR CUSTOMER?

CAPT Stevermer was not the only person I encountered who seemed to lack understanding of service to customers. The DES had two primary functions, one to design and construct new facilities and the other was to manage maintenance and improvement (M&I) projects for existing facilities. An upper level management decision had been made to allow the IHS Areas to manage their own M&I projects if they so desired. Every one of the Areas being serviced by the Seattle DES office opted to manage their own M&I projects. To me this was a statement. However, the Seattle staff members each had their own rationalizations as to why the Areas pulled their work back.

I was one of very few members of the Seattle DES staff who had actually worked in the private sector for any length of time (and not been fired). To me it was clear that the office lacked proper leadership (and the vision associated with same) and, consequently, staff had no fundamental understanding of who their customers were or the expectations associated with good customer service. Therefore, response times and follow-up were poor and while providing the poor customer service they would mock their customers, some of whom I knew personally. I started asking them the very basic question, "Who is your customer?" The responses were mixed and I suggested to Mr. Harper and CAPT Weaver that we should discuss this at our next office meeting. They agreed to do same and agreed, privately, with my perspective on customer service. However, when I mentioned this during the presentation they quickly backed away from their support—wouldn't want to disagree with any of the long time staff. Instead of supporting a new healthy vision of providing high quality customer service they opted to stick with the tried and true path to failure.

The long time staff members got the message and continued with their comfortable existence which included spending significant blocks of duty time playing office games, designing their home remodel projects, etc. Once again, any similarly situated business managed in such fashion would be bankrupted by the loss of their customer base and, potentially, litigation for nonperformance, poor performance, etc.

WINNEBAGO HEALTH CARE CENTER

I was asked by the PM of the new Winnebago Health Center, which was under construction, to review the engineering specifications regarding some civil work which was to occur on the site. There was a question as to whether or not the work was included within the contract. I saw the work clearly indicated within the contract documents and made mention of same to the contractor during a teleconference later that afternoon. The contractor was claiming this as extra work and was upset by my assertion that it was included in the contract and started trying to rationalize why he should not have to do it. I responded that he would because it was included in the awarded documents. Apparently the PM was not happy with my assistance since the contractor got angry (he apparently always tried to keep the contractor happy, even if it meant paying for something twice) and I was not invited back for involvement in his projects again.

In the summer of 2004 the Federal government, in conjunction with the Winnebago Tribe in Nebraska, dedicated a new health care facility. However, rather than provide thanks for the new $60 million facility the Winnebago Tribe unveiled a time capsule with a bronze plaque cover which essentially stated that the facility was owed to them.

Figure 24. Time Capsule Cover at New
Winnebago Health Care Center (2004)

What is not said within the plaque is that the limited treaty requirements for health care expired in 1859. This was mentioned right in their treaty (see Appendix 9) which was printed inside the dedication ceremony document (which called the new facility the "Winnebago Treaty Hospital") provided to attendees (if anybody had bothered to read it like I did).

It is also worth mentioning that this new health care center was built in the middle of a Federal government tear on constructing replacement facilities for Native Americans (as this was). I was privy to the numbers and I was unaware of any health care facilities being closed in Indian Country without a concurrent replacement and significant upgrade. Many of the facilities being replaced were built at times when the same day surgeries and simple procedures using today's medical technologies were not existent and they typically required an inpatient stay. Therefore, even though the tribes receiving the new facilities were receiving far more and better services than were provided in the older facilities, most of which were hospitals, the new facilities for smaller reservations or service areas were generally health care centers (i.e., they do not have in-patient services because they are no longer required). I'm sure the Winnebago Tribe of Nebraska understood this.

SISSETON HEALTH CARE CENTER

ELECTION IRREGULARITIES

While Tom Daschle was the Senate Majority Leader from South Dakota he was the pork master. He engineered approval and funding for a number of new IHS health care facilities within the state of South Dakota. According to a conversation I had with a county commissioner in South Dakota as part of one of Senator Daschle's projects, the Senator would arrive in the area and meet with the Tribe and leave (i.e., he had no interest in meeting with his non-Tribal constituency). The Tribes apparently knew this and rewarded him with delivery of a controversial Senatorial election in 2002 for his Democratic party via sending Tim Johnson back to Washington DC. Senator Johnson won the election by 524 votes over John Thune amid reports of voting irregularities on Indian reservations. While managing the construction of the Sisseton Health Care Center two Tribal elders, who were former Tribal officials, joked about how they would sort the ballots and trash the undesirable votes (i.e., Republican). John Thune was able to overcome this criminal disadvantage in 2004 as he defeated Tom Daschle.

PROJECT STARTUP

Whenever a construction project benefiting one or more Indian tribes is funded the various aspects have to be offered to the benefiting tribe(s) for their execution of the project with the available funding. Tribes are eligible if they are able to receive an acceptable audit from the National External Audit Review (NEAR) Center which generally shows they are administratively capable to perform the work. If they meet the audit requirements and have the desire and capability to perform the project, as evidenced by an acceptable budget and schedule, award can be made to the tribe. The tribe can then request transfer of the project funding leaving the role of the associated IHS or BIA program to simply monitor the general performance of the project to ensure the work conforms with provided specifications and Federal law. At least this is what is supposed to happen.

The SWO had expressed their desire to perform the construction for the ~$20 million health center and associated 62 quarters. A contract was awarded to them in 2003 for nearly all of the work (everything except design). However, the SWO had not met the requisite audit requirements. In 2004 it was discovered that the Tribe had a NEAR alert for at least the previous audit year. The DES was advised by the Tribe that the next audit would yield the same results. The Tribe was then allowed to hire their own accounting firm to certify their administrative systems in order to satisfy part of the capability determination. This audit resulted in at least one significant finding (probably the same one causing the repeated NEAR alert). Tribal staff advised me that the finding was the absence of a Tribal procurement system. Not having a procurement system when your capability for managing $20 million in construction work is being evaluated should be a very big deal. It would be akin to a company being evaluated to be able to make timely payments on a large loan and discovering they had no bank accounts. However, even this seemed to be overlooked as it was never clear if the Tribe's administrative systems were actually certified or if the contract award was made based on a promise that a procurement system would be developed and implemented.

Another part of the determination as to whether or not the Tribe would be awarded a contract was the development of a project budget and schedule. Kathy Block, Senior Contracting Officer, CAPT Melton, and I flew out to South Dakota to meet with SWO staff and assist them in the development of their budget and schedule. The meeting was held in a quiet conference room away from the Tribe's administrative complex. The meeting started with participants introducing themselves and getting to know each other. However, this was interrupted by the sudden, unexpected, and peculiar arrival of approximately 20 Tribal members, who were all men, walking purposefully into the room and taking standing positions around the perimeter of the room. I think we were all made to feel nervous by this behavior. I began asking why they were there and found out they were apparently construction workers who were expecting us to start making some sort of employment guarantees to them for the construction work. I explained the contract administration would be a Tribal function, assuming they were awarded the contract, and we were simply there to assist in the development of the budget and schedule and their presence would not help in that process. I guess they weren't quite sure what to do at that point and so I restated it a little more directly by asking them to please leave so we could perform our work. They left and Kathy commented to me that she was impressed at how I handled the situation. When we finally got down to business it was clear that the Tribe did not know what they were doing. They simply wanted to get their hands on that $20 million check. The Tribal delegation assigned to develop the budget and schedule left the meeting early and both items were developed by Ms. Block, CAPT Melton, and me on behalf of the Tribe.

By every measure there should not have been a construction contract awarded to the Tribe for any amount of money. However, Ms. Block proceeded to make awards (the project was split into pieces) to the Tribe for the full construction project.

The Tribe used part of the funds to establish and staff a new construction management office. The ~$20 million health center and associated 62 quarters were the first construction projects to be managed by the SWO Construction Management Office and the staff had little or no knowledge of Federal laws or regulations (e.g., construction safety, environmental, or Federal acquisition) prior to this project. I was very concerned about this. My concerns were well founded.

CONTRACT NONCONFORMANCE

I was the Federal PM for the new Sisseton Health Center. In this role Kathy Block had asked me to check the Tribe's contract folders during my monthly on-site visits to ensure general conformance with Federal Acquisition Regulations (FAR). I did same and began to notice a number of things, including the lack of evidence of any kind of competitive bidding for the work being performed. I asked the Tribal PM about this and he told me that they had placed copies of the construction documents in various plan exchanges (places where organizations with projects to bid bring their plans and specifications for contractors to view and potentially use in developing bids) throughout the area. I asked him where the plan exchanges were and he provided a list of three communities in North and South Dakota. I called the exchanges in those communities and they were each unaware of having any construction documents for work in Sisseton. One can draw their own conclusions as to how these contracts were being awarded without a procurement office and without advertisement. This went a long way toward explaining the continued delays (and subsequent requests for extensions and more money) and lack of basic construction knowledge of issues such as construction safety.[22]

The first sign of problems with safety on the job site came in the form of digital photos innocently taken and sent by Alan Labelle, Facility Manager, IHS Sisseton Hospital, who is also a SWO Tribal Member. Mr. Labelle had simply visited the new health care facility site as the Tribe was beginning work on the site. The photos showed laborers working in a trench near heavy equipment who were not wearing hard hats. It was actually other staff within our office who picked up on the safety issue, but it was decided that it had to be addressed. A letter expressing concern for construction safety was sent to Lisa Losano, SWO attorney and Tribal Contracting Officer for the new health center and associated quarters. The letter indicated a need for the SWO to address the obvious safety issues. The SWO promptly banned Mr. Labelle (the person who would be responsible for all the newly constructed facilities) from the site until the project was complete.

The next major safety issue involved trench safety. During one of my regularly scheduled site visits I arrived to find a contractor installing a deep section of sewer main. One section of the trench was 18-20 feet deep. That section had an extension ladder extending to the bottom and a spade planted at the bottom of the ladder. The trench did not have any of the requisite Occupational Safety and Health Act/Administration (OSHA) safety features designed to protect workers (i.e., no benching, shoring, sloping, or trench box) and had water pouring into it at the bottom of the near shear face opposite the ladder. As an added bonus the pile of removed material, which was on the same side as the flowing water, had no setback from the edge of the trench to protect workers below from having material fall onto them and there was a large bulldozer working the upper surface of the pile. This site had numerous major OSHA violations and was screaming for someone to die within the trench. I asked one of the nearby individuals who the competent person (person possessing the requisite training and authority to recognize and correct safety issues with that type of work) was on the job site. He had no idea what I was talking about. I then asked who the supervisor was and he pointed to an individual several feet away. I went to speak with him and asked him if he was the supervisor and got a vague response. I asked him if he was the competent person and he had no idea what I was talking about. I told him that I did not want anybody going down into the trench and proceeded to call Kathy Block. Ms. Block is a strong individual and she actually backed me up as I informed the contractor they were not to perform any further work on the site until they received further instruction from the Tribe.

During nearly every site trip performed by either me or another civil engineer from DES there were safety violations noted. This concerned me a great deal since it was always known well in advance when we were going to be on-site. Therefore, I wondered what kind of things occurred when they knew we were not in the area. Ultimately, I called OSHA twice to the site. However, Ken Harper required that the Tribe be first notified that OSHA was going to be on-site. I should have realized this was a setup by him that he would later use against me. I had also noted the Tribe was not following a number of environmental protection requirements and advised the new Contracting Officer (Kathy Block accepted a leadership position at IHS headquarters during the performance of this contract) of same. Of course, the Contracting Officer was not going to demand environmental compliance since it would not have been politically correct and, from his perspective, I was already riding them very hard on safety issues as I tried to keep people alive and healthy.

Things came to a head during a site visit in December 2006. We were performing a pre-final inspection and I noticed staff climbing into a utility vault (an OSHA confined space[23]) without any kind of confined space safety precautions. I advised them they should not be in there (they knew better, but did it anyway) and then Dan Donnell asked me what the issue was with the vault. This surprised me since he was the Tribal construction inspector and should have known not only the valve vaults were confined spaces, but also the manholes. He did not seem to understand what a confined space was so I explained it to him and it became clear to me there had been no confined space protections provided for the numerous confined spaces on the site. Proper protection requires specialized equipment and a construction inspector would have been well aware of the use of such equipment. I noted this in my site visit report along with another unknown safety hazard associated with a worker I had seen working within a false ceiling area without a hard hat. The latter was the only one with a photo and, therefore, got the greatest attention.

Ms. Losano responded with a letter (see Appendix 10) which included a threat of banishment from the reservation if I didn't quit finding safety issues on the job site.[24] Mr. Harper and CAPT Weaver responded by placing me on notice that my efforts were not appreciated[25] (the notes from meetings with Mr. Harper and CAPT Weaver are included in Appendix 11).

FAILURE TO NOT COMMUNICATE

During a routine weekly project update meeting Mr. Hardnett made a comment suggesting he thought it was inappropriate for me to mention a safety violation for someone who was simply installing ceiling tile. I responded I was not aware when I took the photograph as to what type of work he was performing, only that he was on stilts and was performing overhead work within the ceiling.

It did not strike me until the next day that Mr. Hardnett had information (the person I photographed without a hard hat was installing ceiling tile) he did not have access to through official channels. It should be noted Ms. Losano had been very strict throughout the contract regarding compliance with the formal communication protocol which is duly incorporated into the Tribe's construction contract. Mr. Hardnett is not included within the communication protocol. All PM communication was to come through me and I distribute same to the appropriate parties within the IHS. I presented this to CAPT Weaver and suggested that I suspected Mr. Hardnett may be conducting unauthorized communication with the Tribe. He agreed to discuss this with Mr. Hardnett and me later in the day.

During the subsequent meeting between Mr. Hardnett, CAPT Weaver, and me I asked Mr. Hardnett how he came to know the individual pictured in my trip report was installing ceiling tile since nobody had been aware of this until the response letter from Ms. Losano. His initial claim was it was mentioned in my trip report. I stated it was not and produced my copy of same and he promptly left to retrieve his copy and after verifying his was a copy of the same document he admitted that he had been discussing various project issues with Ms. Losano the previous week. I asked him why this communication was occurring since he is not authorized for such communication. He initially claimed Ms. Losano was calling him to relay information on to Mr. Harper. CAPT Weaver noted Mr. Harper had been in the office the previous week. I asked Mr. Hardnett again why Ms. Losano would call him if both Mr. Harper and I were in the office at the time. He then indicated it may be because she feels more comfortable talking to him since he is a person of color (he is African-American) as she is (she is Hispanic). I then asked Mr. Hardnett what he and Ms. Losano had been discussing and he first indicated they had discussed safety issues. He added that he did not understand why I was so persistent on finding fault with the project. I advised him it was our job to illuminate problems with the project. He responded he believed our function was to find things that have been done right on the project. I asked him how he expected to correct problems with that perspective. He responded problems can still be resolved. I responded you have to find the problems before you can resolve them.

I asked Mr. Hardnett if he and Ms. Losano had discussed anything else and he said there were some personal issues he would not share. I asked why he would not share them and he suggested they were of a personal nature. I asked Mr. Hardnett if he realized his communication was outside the communication protocol. He acknowledged this and suggested I was too strict with the protocol. I reminded him it was Ms. Losano who had been demanding strict conformance with the communication protocol. I then commented I thought it was very strange she would abandon her own demands for conformance to the protocol by contacting Mr. Hardnett.

Mr. Hardnett then began opening up and stated Ms. Losano cannot understand why I keep bringing up safety issues when the OSHA has not found anything and suggested perhaps the reason for this is that I am a racist. I then asked Mr. Hardnett what his response to this was and he indicated he had suggested to Ms. Losano I might be. I was shocked by this and asked Mr. Hardnett to confirm this which he did by reiterating he thought I might be a racist. I asked him what would make him think that and he indicated it was based on my disposition on the safety issue. I advised him construction safety is not something I feel we should compromise and I did not understand how upholding Federal construction safety regulations could possibly be equated to racism. I asked Mr. Hardnett how many times he had these conversations and he suggested at least twice in the recent past. Mr. Hardnett seemed to be cavalier with his statements and indifferent toward the impact of his actions or the gravity of what he had just said so I asked him if he understood same. He began speaking about various people he thought may be racist, including CAPT Weaver, and then stated he was a racist. I then asked him to confirm what he had stated and he reiterated he was a racist and he thought I may be also. I then indicated to CAPT Weaver I no longer trusted Mr. Hardnett to be on my project team and I did not want any further communication between Mr. Hardnett and the Tribe. CAPT Weaver acknowledged my "preference" but made it clear he would make the decision. It should be noted there was no contrition expressed by Mr. Hardnett toward me during the meeting regarding his conduct (the notes from the meeting with both Mr. Hardnett and CAPT Weaver are included in Appendix 12).

SEE NO EVIL, HEAR NO EVIL, SPEAK NO EVIL ... DO EVIL

Following the above meeting I suggested to CAPT Weaver I believed Mr. Hardnett's conduct should be addressed as an equal opportunity employment (EEO) issue. I also sent an E-mail to CAPT Weaver asking him to advise me as to what action would be taken regarding same. He responded appropriate action would be taken. On January 31, 2007, while I was on leave, I called our travel planner to coordinate another planned site trip to Sisseton and was advised Mr. Hardnett had already scheduled his flight to the area. I then left a message for CAPT Weaver to discuss this with him. He called me back shortly thereafter and I asked him why Mr. Hardnett was traveling to the site and he indicated there was a rupture of a sprinkler line within the building over the weekend and Mr. Hardnett was going to look at same. I suggested Paul Ninomura, mechanical engineer, was already planning on going to the site and he should be able to check this out. CAPT Weaver suggested he still wanted Mr. Hardnett to visit the site. I asked about my stated mistrust for Mr. Hardnett based on his previous conduct and CAPT Weaver stated he had addressed this and Mr. Hardnett assured him it would not happen again. I suggested it was unwise to place Mr. Hardnett in a position to be able to continue his inappropriate activities and we had other architects within the office who could go in lieu of Mr. Hardnett. CAPT Weaver insisted Mr. Hardnett go. I stated I had not seen any sign of contrition on the part of Mr. Hardnett for his conduct and I still did not trust him and did not want him on my team. I then advised CAPT Weaver, if he was going to insist on having Mr. Hardnett not only involved in the project but placed into a leading role for this planned visit, he should consider removing me as the PM. That is exactly what happened.

CAPT Weaver sent me an E-mail later in the day on January 31, 2007, transitioning me out as the PM effective the following day. At 8:00 am on February 5, 2007, upon my return to the office following my leave I was called into a meeting with Mr. Harper and CAPT Weaver. CAPT Weaver introduced the meeting by suggesting I have performance and behavior issues and suggested I pursue counseling and officially requested I do so immediately. He stated a Dr. Caserta with the Medical Affairs Branch (MAB) wanted to speak with me about an assessment of me and the MAB can order me to be involved in same. For the record I asked Mr. Harper if he agreed with this and he responded in the affirmative. I then asked what the performance and behavior issues were. The only example I was given was my unwillingness to continue to work with Mr. Hardnett on the Sisseton project. I stated I did not understand why they were handling the situation in the manner they were as it appeared to me that I was the aggrieved party and that Mr. Hardnett, who had shown no contrition for his conduct, should not only have been precluded from traveling to the site but should also have been removed from the project. CAPT Weaver responded that was the reason why I should be evaluated (apparently because I didn't understand the manner in which the situation was being managed). I also stated I could not believe everything I had been exposed to because I would not compromise Federal construction safety regulations and was simply trying to save the lives and limbs of people working on the site. I advised Mr. Harper and CAPT Weaver I did not see how my stand on construction safety related to a mental health issue and I had no intention of contacting Dr. Caserta. I was told by Mr. Harper to date I had always been provided with positive Commissioned Officer Effectiveness Reports (COERs) but my behavior could threaten future COERs. I received a call following the meeting from Dr. Caserta. He said that he had just received a call from Mr. Harper and I explained my perspective to him. He seemed to understand but said, since both Mr. Harper and CAPT Weaver felt as if I was angry about how they were managing the situation, he would have to order me to be assessed.

I believe the above responses by Mr. Harper and CAPT Weaver were a form of reprisal against me for my recent claim of discrimination against the agency based on Indian Preference and/or for my firm stance on Federal construction safety regulations (which they both agreed with until the situation was made political by the Tribe). I had been repeatedly told by Mr. Harper, CAPT Weaver, and Abram Vinikoor, Contracting Officer, it was the Tribe's responsibility to ensure the OSHA requirements are met. They were aware and agreed there had been repeated violations and were apparently comfortable not taking action since they believed the Tribe would be solely liable for any deaths, dismemberments, etc.

I believe the IHS has a fundamental obligation to eliminate or at least try to mitigate the possibility of those deaths, dismemberments, etc. by ensuring Federal construction safety regulations are followed (several of those working on the site were also Tribal members). I also believe as part of the contract with the Tribe the IHS is entitled to construction safety in accordance with Federal regulations just as the agency is entitled to all the features of the actual building structure (if we didn't get windows we would advise the Tribe of the need to provide windows). I also believe the above response by Mr. Harper and CAPT Weaver were a form of reprisal against me in part for my strong suggestion that Mr. Hardnett's conduct be addressed as an EEO issue and their unwillingness to do same. They apparently addressed this as unprofessional conduct. CAPT Weaver apparently never reported this incident of discrimination nor did Mr. Harper report the acts of reprisal (premature removal of me as the PM for the Sisseton project and "recently identified behavior and performance issues") as required by the USPHS Commissioned Corps Personnel Manual, Subchapter 26.1.

All of the above information was shared with RADM Gary Hartz, Director, OEHE, IHS, who was Mr. Harper's supervisor and well as the Acting Surgeon General Steven Galston. I followed up with a phone call to RADM Hartz during which he advised me that he "would, of course, have to side with management." I asked him why this was the case and he tried to walk it back. I believe the real reason was simply because it was the easiest thing to do since the path to do the right thing would require admonishing a couple of ranking managers and a Tribe— nobody would want to do that, not even an admiral.

So, I had to endure the humiliation of being subjected to a mental health exam because I tried to keep people safe on a construction job site. I later found out the medical provider who eventually ordered the evaluation approved it based on Mr. Harper and CAPT Weaver fabricating a story that I had office violence tendencies because I had desired to bring a weapon into the workplace (which is only partly true, as explained above, since I had requested one time to store a weapon in my locker in the fitness center—just trying to be above board). I believe the real reason they were so terrified of me was because they both knew they were destroying my career for no good reason.

At this point it should be noted all of the hostility exhibited toward me by CAPT Weaver and Mr. Harper came on the heels of a performance evaluation wherein I was provided a near perfect score and CAPT Weaver described my performance as "outstanding" (see Appendix 13).

LET THE EEO COMPLAINTS BEGIN

Just prior to the development of the various reprisal actions described above all IHS employees were offered their first exposure to the provisions of the Notification and Federal Employee Antidiscrimination and Retaliation (NoFEAR) Act of 2002. The Act was passed due to chronic problems within the Federal government with discrimination and reprisal actions being taken by Federal managers against their employees. However, even with these special protections now being finally promulgated by the agency (nearly five years after passage of the law) the old behaviors were apparently still engrained within agency officials. I had filed an EEO complaint based on the numerous positions I had not even been considered for throughout my career because I was not of the "preferred race." Following the above described actions taken by Mr. Harper and CAPT Weaver I filed another EEO complaint of retaliation (see Appendix 14).

The processing of my complaints was supposed to be performed by the IHS headquarters EEO office run by Pauline Bruce, a Native American from South Dakota, and roots in management of the Aberdeen Area IHS (the Area for whom we were providing the services in Sisseton). However, neither of my complaints was processed in accordance with published requirements including timelines. Her office had missed every one of the published timelines. However, ironically, they used timeliness as a reason to attempt to summarily dismiss one of my complaints (I was outraged by this since I had met each and every deadline and several of their responses were egregiously late, one by nearly two years).

As expected Ms. Bruce found no evidence of discrimination or retaliation and, as expected, then Acting Surgeon General Steven Galson simply accepted the agency recommendation as his final decision (and there was no recourse). It was clear that the process is a joke. My first complaint took over 2 years to process (with no litigation) and it was clear right from the start that the EEO office viewed themselves simply as an advocate for management (probably one of the reasons it took so long to process). I guess IHS management understood this EEO office incompetence and/or clandestine support for their actions as it seemed to simply emboldened them to continue to perpetrate gross discrimination and retaliation against employees (at least those not of the "preferred race").

LESSONS LEARNED

The rule of law seems to have little or no meaning for certain agencies within the US Government. Abiding by Federal law is only something which they follow when it is either easy or necessary (i.e., others with power are watching) to do so. Politics is everything and bureaucrats with power seem to feel as if they can do as they please. This includes destroying those around them if they get in the way, even if they are trying to do the right thing—Machiavelli was right.

ABERDEEN AREA INDIAN HEALTH SERVICE

LEADERSHIP

Figure 25. Charlene Red Thunder, Director,
Aberdeen Area IHS (2008-present)

Charlene Red Thunder became the Director of the Aberdeen Area IHS during my tenure within the Area. She is a member of the Cheyenne River Sioux Tribe and has a master's degree in education from Northern State University in Aberdeen, South Dakota. At first I believed her to be competent in her position (this is usually my default position for anyone). However, as I was made to suffer at the hands of her subordinates for my sins of trying to do the right things it appeared to me Ms. Red Thunder could be considered the Don (or, more appropriately, the Donna) of a network of administrative thugs who have a history of abusing certain employees and protecting those who are connected. They seemed to have no hesitation in doing whatever they pleased irrespective of morality, agency regulations, or Federal law (and if they got called on it they could simply play the victim card as she did during a Senate hearing where she was called to testify in response to a number of chronic issues affecting the Aberdeen Area).

Her chief lieutenants included Rick Sorensen, Deputy Director, Aberdeen Area IHS, and CDR Jon Fogarty, Associate Director, OEHE. As mentioned above Jon Fogarty was a former COSTEP who worked under me. He had risen quickly through the IHS ranks due to his fractional Native American heritage.

Helen Thompson is a long-time friend of Ms. Red Thunder's and also worked under Ms. Red Thunder as the Administrative Officer after she was asked to be removed from the same position at the Sioux San IHS Hospital in Rapid City, SD by a new CEO. Ms. Thompson later returned to the Sioux San IHS Hospital as the Acting CEO before returning to her original position as the Administrative Officer.

Lorraine Jewett was the CEO of the Sioux San IHS Hospital who hired me. She is highly intelligent and well educated and began her career as a nurse. Ms. Jewett's tenure at Sioux San was short-lived and her official replacement was Fred Koebrick. Mr. Koebrick is from Oklahoma and, as a civil service employee, has worked at a number of facilities in Oklahoma and elsewhere in the IHS system (this is a red flag as most civil servants do not transfer if things are going well for them).

CDR Ron Keats was the Commissioned Corps Liaison for the Aberdeen, Bemidji, and Billings IHS Areas. As such he was responsible for assisting USPHS commissioned officers located in those Areas with administrative issues. However, I later found out that he did not look at his function as one of assistance to commissioned officers as he described himself as a "tool for management."

Gail Martin is/was the EEO Compliance Manager for the Aberdeen Area IHS. As such she was responsible for ensuring that Area EEO issues were duly processed in accordance with Federal law. However, it appeared she was simply another pawn under the control of Ms. Red Thunder. EEO compliance was one of the key issues the Senate wanted to know about during its hearing on the Aberdeen Area.

It should be noted that all of the above persons are fractionally Native American with the exception of CDR Ron Keats.

SIOUX SAN IHS HOSPITAL[26]

In 1896 Congress allocated $25,000 to purchase 160 acres of land near Rapid City, South Dakota to build a school to serve Native American students from Minnesota, Montana, Nebraska, North and South Dakota, and Wyoming. The school opened in September 1898 providing primarily elementary level education. By 1925 the school had grown to include 50 buildings and an additional 1400 acres and was also providing instruction on vocational skills (e.g., farming, ranching, carpentry, nursing, etc.). Despite the success of the school the Office [Bureau] of Indian Affairs converted the school to a tuberculosis sanatorium for Native American children in 1929. After only one year the sanatorium was closed and the facility converted back to the Rapid City Indian School which was maintained until 1934 when the school was closed.

A hospital was later constructed on the main Rapid City Indian School campus in 1938. The bulk of the land which was procured to support the vocational school was no longer needed with the change in mission for the facility. Therefore, the Bureau of Indian Affairs gradually divested same to institutions within the area which serve the common good (e.g., National Guard Camp, churches, geriatric centers, schools, parks, etc.). The hospital is still in existence. However, in 1955 ownership was transferred to the USPHS due to the establishment of the IHS. The campus today is still known as Sioux San.

FIRST SIGN OF TROUBLE

As in any new position I enjoyed a honeymoon period during the first several months of my tenure as the Facility Manager at Sioux San. The work was challenging but I seemed to have the support of Ms. Jewett who had in common with me a strong orientation to customer service. However, it was clear she was under a great deal of stress from the Area office. I believe this was due to her removal of Helen Thompson, Administrative Officer. Apparently the Area was looking for any excuse to remove her as the CEO at Sioux San. Unfortunately, I would be the one to hand her over to the Area.

I was approached by the father of a potential student extern who was an engineer at nearby Ellsworth Air Force Base. The father told me his son was an electrical engineering student and he was looking for summer employment in the Rapid City area so he could stay at home with his parents for the summer and get some engineering experience. I thought this was a God send. We had significant electrical system distribution issues on the campus and I had been looking for a way I could get an analysis and recommendations for same which could then be utilized to justify project funding for corrections. This would have been a perfect summer project for an electrical engineering student.

I went to speak with Ms. Jewett about hiring the electrical engineering student as a summer COSTEP. After listening to my explanation her first and only question was, "Is he Indian?" I responded I did not know since I didn't ask. She then directed me to find out since she was only willing to hire Indians. I was very surprised and disappointed in this racist exchange from someone for whom I had held in high esteem.[27]

I am an intensely loyal individual. However, I am also a big believer in following the rules and laws that we are all supposed to live within. I struggled a great deal with the idea of reporting Ms. Jewett's comments to the local EEO counselor. In the end I determined it was something that I had to do due to my commission and the fact I was a ranking officer (i.e., it was incumbent upon me to do the right thing regardless of the potential consequences).

BE CAREFUL OF WHAT YOU ASK FOR...

I reported Ms. Jewett's comments to the EEO counselor. A report was taken. However, apparently it was lost somewhere in the Aberdeen Area Office black hole. Several weeks passed and I was approached by the EEO counselor to redevelop my complaint against Ms. Jewett. Ms. Jewett was quickly and quietly removed from her position at Sioux San and detailed to the Aberdeen Area Office. She was reportedly tucked away into a cubicle (and probably performing work which was far below her pay grade).

Helen Thompson was returned to Sioux San as the Acting CEO. It was clear to me Ms. Thompson was ill prepared to be in such a leadership position since she did not seem to possess the demeanor, intelligence, or training to hold such a position.

During one of our early Executive Team meetings with Ms. Thompson at the helm we were discussing a recent threatening incident I had with a Native American person who was a known campus agitator. This prompted Ms. Thompson to share a story about a similar incident she had with the same individual. Apparently this individual had presented himself to her within her office doorway at Sioux San so she could not leave and began making veiled threats. She called Security (as I had in the more recent incident) and this apparently incensed the individual (as it also did in my case). Ms. Thompson then shared with the Executive Team that following the incident she had shared the story with her son at home about what happened to her at work. Apparently her son then went to the individual's home (it was unclear from Ms. Thompson's presentation as to whether or not she encouraged him to go there) and threatened him with violence if he ever did that again to his mother. Ms. Thompson seemed quite proud of her son's response. I was quite embarrassed that she was our new (Acting) CEO.

The Aberdeen Area had a habit of transferring their problem employees to other locations. One of those the Area decided to transfer was Michelle Keith. Ms. Keith is a Native American with an extremely strong personality. She came to Sioux San from the Pine Ridge IHS Hospital. I was told by a ranking officer from that hospital that she was a low level employee (i.e., limited education) who had been consistently promoted through the ranks due to her overbearing personality. When she arrived at Sioux San she became my new supervisor.

RACISM AT ITS WORST

At the time of the arrival of Ms. Thompson and Ms. Keith I was managing campus maintenance, housekeeping, and the fleet of government (GSA) vehicles. The last two functions were not in my billet (job description). However, I've always been one to try and help out and I assumed that the extra duties would be recognized when it came time for my performance evaluation. I guess that assumption only holds when you are being evaluated based on what you actually did and not on your parentage.

Managing housekeeping at Sioux San was difficult at best. For starters most people do not grow up wanting to be a housekeeper. Therefore, there's an automatic edge within at least the older housekeepers. In addition to that they were all Native American (they had all been awarded their jobs due primarily to their race and some took this to mean they were owed their job). In addition to the protection related to their race (i.e., ability to pull the "race card" at any time if a manager dared suggest they were not performing), they had the full suite of protections associated with being civil service workers as well as being union members. The bottom line was it would be nearly impossible to remove a poorly performing worker, and some knew it and took full advantage of it.

There were several poorly performing workers and two of them happened to be female (the only two female housekeepers at the time which made a nearly impossible situation even more difficult). One of the housekeepers had a chronic medical condition which she believed precluded her from performing her work. Therefore, she took it upon herself to sit in the break room and do nothing. When I discovered this and started requiring her to perform work (after consulting with personnel specialists in Aberdeen) I received a fax from Senator Tim Johnson's office on behalf of the employee. Ultimately I assisted the employee in getting hired into another position within the hospital where she was deemed capable of performing the required work. However, she maintained a strong dislike (hatred?) for me (must have been due to my unreasonable expectation that she should actually do something to continue to get paid, or maybe it was simply because I am a white guy).

I had 14 written customer complaints regarding the remaining female housekeeper's (lack of) performance. I had included a specific number of written complaints within her last performance evaluation requirements which would deem her performance unacceptable and she was well beyond the number. Therefore, under the guidance of personnel specialists in Aberdeen I placed her on a performance improvement plan (PIP).

The PIP required she receive no further written complaints during the performance period and she received several. Therefore, she was not going to be successful in the performance of her plan. Ms. Thompson and Ms. Keith seemed to adopt the problem employee and believed I had not given the problem employee adequate opportunity to be successful (keep in mind she had been performing at a subpar level for years prior to my arrival).

About the same time I was also having issues with two employees from the maintenance department. They had both been spotted by another employee from the department (while the other person was on leave) at one of the local scrap yards in a GSA vehicle and it was suspected they were involved in selling scrap. One of the two was also consistently implicated in stealing tools and equipment from the maintenance department and pawning same. The same employee was also caught red-handed by me trying to defraud the Government by claiming that he had been called back to work one night to check on a maintenance issue. He worked up the form for monetary reimbursement which included a description of the work he reportedly performed. However, the work was located within a mechanical room which had a security camera trained on the only door in and out of the room. I asked the security guard to review the recorded video from that camera and he did same. The employee was not seen in the video for a window of 12 hours before to 12 hours after he claimed to be there. When confronted he started trying to walk it back by suggesting he was supposed to get paid as long he started driving in to check on the problem. This was not true and he knew it. I contacted the Aberdeen Area human resources office and was told I should provide him with a written reprimand which would only be placed in his local file and maintained for up to one year at which time it would be removed unless he had another similar incident. I thought this was a joke, but if I went beyond the recommendation I knew there would be nobody there to support me and my work environment was already very uncomfortable.

The problem employees from Housekeeping and Maintenance were both shopping for allies and found same in Ms. Thompson and Ms. Keith. In addition they had been complaining about me to the campus agitator previously mentioned above (the one who had previously threatened both me and Ms. Thompson). This Native American campus agitator was now presenting these employee complaints to Ms. Thompson who was a willing participant in hearing them. The only reason I can think that she would even entertain such a discussion with someone who was not an employee and had a proven history of violence with her was simply because she was also searching for a means to harm me (I guess it is consistent with the old proverb "the enemy of my enemy is my friend").

Michelle Keith was the perfect partner for this and the two apparently went on a fishing expedition to find whatever they could to harm me (keep in mind this was my management chain—I thought they were supposed to help me). They then gave me the double team during a meeting which was supposed to be about their concerns over how I was treating my staff. The presentation was they had spoken with ALL of my staff and they ALL had issues with me. However, that was not true, it was only the problem employees. They also suggested there were complaints from members of the community. However, when I pressed them it became clear it was probably one and that one was the known campus agitator. I tried to interject during the rant but they objected at each turn because I was interrupting them. After they had talked themselves out I asked again if I could respond and was told there was no need since they had already spoken with ALL my staff who were ALL saying the same thing (this was not true as several members of my staff later told me they knew what was going on and provided positive comments on my behalf). Therefore, it must be true. I responded to each of their issues and they were both quiet for awhile.

During the meeting Ms. Thompson and Ms. Keith seemed emboldened by each other's strong personalities and racial prejudices. Ms. Keith asked me how my assistant got hired since he is not Native American and then proceeded to explain to me her perception that all positions within the IHS are supposed to be filled by Native Americans and not … (she hesitated at this point since she was apparently unsure how to refer to white guys like me in a politically correct manner). Ms. Thompson proceeded to tell me she found me very irritating and didn't like the way I looked (I was known for wearing my service dress blues to work, and was on that day, so this comment did not relate to my dress). I found myself apologizing to them for the way I look by explaining this was simply the way I came from the factory.

I filed grievances over the way I was treated by these two individuals. However, this seemed to only make them more determined than ever to make my work life as difficult as possible. Their racial prejudices apparently blinded them with rage against me. This rage culminated in a poor performance evaluation based on fabricated data. It seems over the course of the time Ms. Thompson and Ms. Keith were at Sioux San there were two separate door closers (out of scores of them on the campus) that were discovered by two separate inspectors on two separate occasions separated by several months that required replacement. One of them was replaced within minutes of the finding and the other was replaced within a couple of days. However, in the search by Ms. Thompson and Ms. Keith to find something to pin on me they seized upon this issue and featured it prominently within my performance evaluation suggesting I had allowed one door closer to not be repaired for several months. When confronted with the completed maintenance requests which clearly showed there were two separate door closers and both had been repaired very soon after each finding they still held fast to their assertion I was delinquent.

The whole thing was asinine, especially that year, since I had kept everything running and within code despite being short staffed in Housekeeping and Maintenance for significant periods, having no secretary for nine months of the year due to bureaucratic red tape, having significant personnel issues, and not being able to spend money (i.e., no ability to pay for anything due to a changeover to a new procurement and payment system) for four months. During the procurement and payment blackout period I had garnered volunteer assistance for groundskeeping, housekeeping, and welding services from various campus employees and non-campus entities willing to help. I had also been deployed in response to Hurricanes Gustav and Ike and was performing work far in excess of what was included within my billet. However, apparently none of that amounted to anything in the minds of Ms. Thompson or Ms. Keith.

As they continued to try to harm me I continued to file grievances (see Appendix 15).[28] However, I was not one of the "Cartwrights" so I got little or no support from anybody at the Aberdeen Area Office (supervised by Ms. Thompson's long-time friend Ms. Red Thunder) or from the national EEO office, which I later discovered was being supervised by a former management official of the Aberdeen Area Office. I felt like a man in the wilderness with no place to go for help—literally nobody cared, except my wife.

BUTTERFLY RASH

My wife Susette and I try to walk every evening. For us it is more than simply exercise. It is a way for us to share time and download the day's events. Unfortunately, in hindsight, I would share my work experiences with Susette. Whenever I mentioned something she understood perfectly, because she had "been there" by virtue of her experiences with the Apaches in Arizona (they seemed to hate her simply because she was a cute young white girl). This seemed like very much the same situation. I was doing the best I could at internalizing it. However, racial hatred is something that cries out for rebuke (and **I** certainly would have been severely rebuked if the situation had been reversed). I would speak to my limited circle of friends about it, but would only get a quizzical look and a non-reassuring nod of the head as they tried to comprehend this politically uncomfortable concept—Native Americans, long propagandized as the ultimate American victims, being actively involved in racial discrimination against non-Tribal persons. I am very thankful that my wife had the experiences she did in Arizona, because she was one of those who just didn't understand until she stepped in it and then all the crap came home. However, when I shared my daily experiences with Ms. Thompson and Ms. Keith it affected her in a way I did not intend, and I still feel terrible about it to this day.

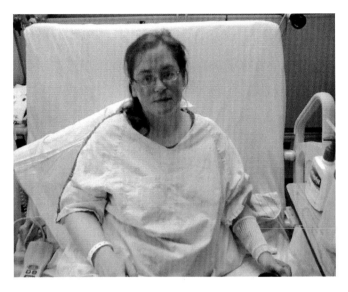

Figure 26a-b. Susette Gjovik in Hospital for Lupus Flare (2009)

Susette has systemic lupus erythematosus (SLE or lupus), a disease that can be triggered by stress. I have known about her disease since before we got married. However, I had not known her to have any symptoms of the disease because it had only really affected her as a child following the sudden and unexpected death of her father just before her 12th Christmas. Her 30-year relapse came to an end, due at least in part, to the constant pounding

I was receiving by these two Native American management officials and the lack of any kind of response, much less support, I received from any member of the IHS management chain. I guess to them I was simply expendable, but it was my beautiful wife who paid the price. She developed a "butterfly rash" on her face (the quintessential sign of a lupus flare) and had to be hospitalized and placed on strong medications to get her immune system under control (and may now have to be on them the rest of her life).

I documented the fact that my wife had been hospitalized within my complaint responses to the various discriminatory actions by Ms. Thompson and Ms. Keith in the hope that this might move some member of the IHS management team to take action. Ms. Keith was eventually detailed to another service unit. However, Ms. Thompson continued to stay on and create problems as the next CEO entered the scene.

HONEYMOON II TO IRRECONCILABLE DIFFERENCES

The new CEO came to Sioux San from White Earth, MN (White Earth Indian Reservation). His name is Fred Koebrick and he is originally from Oklahoma. I viewed his arrival as a positive development since I had spent so many years in Oklahoma and had generally found Native Americans from Oklahoma to be much less hostile than others because Oklahoma does not have any reservations.[29] We are also both Oklahoma Sooner fans and I found out later we had both worked at the Oklahoma City Area Office at the same time in the past. He had been a property specialist and I was an engineer. However, he was a member of the "preferred race" and, thus, found himself to be my supervisor even though his credentials for same were probably not comparable to mine. Be that as it may he was a breath of fresh air and things seemed to be going well until the politicos starting getting involved.

Eventually the usual Native American suspects—poorly performing staff members, the campus agitator, and Ms. Thompson—started leading the new CEO down the path of racial hatred. Around this same timeframe there was a fire at the local sweat lodge. The sweat lodge was not an officially sanctioned facility. It was allowed on the Federal campus as a means to allow our Native American customers the opportunity to practice their form of holistic medicine. I wholeheartedly agree with the concept. However, the facility was not operated responsibly and we had another major fire incident (the second major fire event by the same group at the sweat lodge facility since I had been there) which resulted in the loss of the sweat lodge and threatened nearby campus buildings for which I was responsible, one of which being a Headstart facility for Native American children. I was not pleased with the manner in which the sweat lodge was being operated and suggested we should ban the offending group from further use of the facility. This was deemed unacceptable. It was determined by Mr. Koebrick that a policy should be put into place to protect users of the sweat lodge facility as well as the campus (nearly all Native Americans).

I drafted a policy and Mr. Koebrick agreed with the draft and asked me to work with two individuals associated with the sweat lodge. Both individuals worked on campus and are militant when it comes to issues related to Native American rights (I did not know that at the time). We scheduled a meeting to discuss the policy and it was clear from the start neither of the Native American participants were supportive of the policy and neither wanted to have any sort of accountability associated with the sweat lodge. They snickered as I read the policy and then started suggesting this sounded like "prison" and I would be the "warden" and then suggested I "need codependency counseling." These two individuals were supposed to be professionals, one a substance abuse counselor[30] and the other a health educator. However, I felt as if I was working with children and the meeting was frustrating for everybody.

I believed the behavior of the health educator was highly inappropriate, and she was a fellow employee of the hospital (the other meeting attendee was an employee of the Oglala Sioux Tribe [OST] who were provided space on the campus for their substance abuse program) and sent an E-mail to her which was copied to Mr. Koebrick. Of course, she responded in kind and accused me of racism and asked the other party to likewise respond. He did in a barely coherent E-mail message (see Appendix 16). Mr. Koebrick seemed unhappy with me at the lack of results from our joint effort and caved to the desires of the Tribal activists and a new policy was put into place which did little to address accountability for anyone using the sweat lodge facility.

Shortly thereafter Mr. Koebrick visited me in my office within the maintenance garage. He looked around my office and noticed my clock with the Cherokee Nation logo and their syllabary numbers shown on the face. He asked if I was part Cherokee. I do not look at all as if I am Native American. However, having worked in Oklahoma for many years I understood why he would ask the question since many "Native Americans" from Oklahoma have only a small fraction of Native American ancestry and therefore, look as Caucasian as I do and are still Tribal members. I responded facetiously that I was northern Cherokee and he looked at me quizzically. I smiled and explained that I would use that line when I worked for the Cherokees. He asked if I was Chickasaw because he thought someone had told him so. I reluctantly divulged that I am of Scandinavian heritage. He said his wife is Chickasaw and left my office shortly thereafter (and never visited again) and his demeanor toward me took an abrupt change in direction.

Mr. Koebrick began making demands of me and my program. I understood some of these were because he wanted things to look nice, as I did. He wanted me to start dumping various chemicals on the campus to make things look good. Normally I would not have an issue with this. However, we had our own potable water well on campus that probably had a compromised surface seal (i.e., it would be very easy to contaminate not only water being consumed by patients and staff but also water being consumed by others utilizing the same aquifer). I explained my concerns about this with Mr. Koebrick and he dismissed them out of hand (I guess his position made him more knowledgeable than me on the subject—I was merely a registered professional environmental engineer and a registered environmental health specialist) and directed me to do it.

Mr. Koebrick also directed me to get all of the hallway walls painted within the hospital right away. I explained to him that we had a stimulus project which had been funded for that work and the funding was due to arrive at any time, we had already had painting contractors look at it, and we had the procurement package ready once the funding arrived. He didn't care. He wanted it done right away. I continued my protest by explaining to him I did not have the budget to support overtime (my personnel budget was already in the red with no training, no travel, and no overtime) and the purpose of the stimulus was to get people working. He would have none of that and continued with his demand and added it needed to be done in two weeks. I got the hospital painting completed just as the stimulus funding arrived. Maintenance had to forgo performing several of the routine preventive maintenance work orders, which was in violation of Center for Medicare & Medicaid Services (CMS) requirements (Federal entity that inspected our facility periodically), and enlist the assistance of security staff (who loved the overtime but were not professional painters). It didn't look as nice as it would have with a professional contractor and no jobs were created (or saved), but the work got done within two weeks. It was clear that the honeymoon period was over and something had changed between Mr. Koebrick and me.

REMEDY

Apparently between all of the grievances and all of my documentation regarding my 2008 performance evaluation by Ms. Thompson and Ms. Keith it was determined the evaluation would be reworked, by Mr. Koebrick. The evaluation itself was good, not great, but at least it was better than what had been previously provided. However, the written comments were glowing and my performance was described as "exceptional." It should be noted Mr. Koebrick was not even working within the Aberdeen Area during the indicated 2008 performance period. Therefore, his frame of reference was only the several months we had worked together and he even mentioned activities with which he was familiar and I had been involved during his short tenure within the Aberdeen Area within the written comments.

However, Mr. Koebrick is the proverbial scorpion[31] and the kind words were not meant to last and soon thereafter I provided him with my first of several grievances. Despite the rhetoric provided by the agency in regard to reprisal actions being illegal in response to a grievance it was my experience this was common and nobody did anything about it. However, Mr. Koebrick saved his best licks for last.

WASTE, FRAUD, AND ABUSE[32]

I was approached by an Acting Director of the OST substance abuse center to construct needed fire and smoke partitions within their facility so they could resume in-patient treatment for their customer base (it had been suspended several months prior due to this structural deficiency). She showed me funding documents which indicated that a project had been funded through another IHS program to perform the work via a contractor. I had been involved in helping her get this project funded so I was glad to see it got funded. However, I explained to her the IHS had already provided the OST with the necessary funds to perform the work via a contractor. She explained the funds had disappeared once they were placed in the OST's general account and she was now unable to get them. I responded that I would not be able to perform the work with my IHS forces since would be double funding the project (once with cash and then once with materials and labor to perform the work that was supposed to be performed with the cash), but I could help her find a contractor. She was not happy with my response and left to speak with Mr. Koebrick.

Mr. Koebrick sent me an E-mail soon thereafter directing me to complete the construction work on behalf of the OST. I advised Mr. Koebrick the OST had already been provided funding to perform the construction via a contractor and he responded he had already made the decision and I was "to proceed as instructed." I believed, and still do, that Mr. Koebrick did not discuss this with me because of the EEO complaints I had pending against him and he had no compunction to ask me to perform work which may be considered inappropriate, improper, or even illegal.

Following the receipt of Mr. Koebrick's directive and subsequent E-mail I hand delivered a station leave request for time to develop another EEO complaint. Upon delivery he stated, "There must be something wrong with you." I responded, "No, there isn't." He replied, "There is definitely something wrong with you." He then advised me in a loud voice that he will decide as to whether or not leave will be granted. I advised him the request was for that Friday. He responded if leave was granted it may not be for Friday.

Following the directive from Mr. Koebrick discussed above and on the same day there happened to be a special agent from the Office of the Inspector General (OIG) visiting the campus. He was introduced during an Executive Team meeting which I was attending. I asked to speak to the special agent before he left and he accommodated me. I discussed the directive from Mr. Koebrick with him and he asked me to provide him with copies of the pertinent funding documents. I attempted to do same. However, IHS management must have been aware of this potential criminal activity and I was not provided with copies of the documents which were shown to me by the acting OST director.

The following morning the special agent contacted Mr. Koebrick to arrange for a conference call to discuss the situation. Within three hours of the call from the special agent Mr. Koebrick completed my performance evaluation for 2009. The performance evaluation was designed to end my career and is filled with unsubstantiated negative innuendo and vitriol.[33] This performance evaluation was performed approximately one month after the performance evaluation in which he provided glowing written comments about my performance and described it as "exceptional." I'm not sure how much more obvious a reprisal action would have to be before action is taken, but no action was taken to stop it.

Following the review of my 2009 COER I felt physically ill as I knew that, if allowed to stand, it would harm my career and I thought of how this would impact my family. I worked up a sick leave request for the remainder of the afternoon and hand delivered it to Mr. Koebrick. He seemed to relish in the fact that I was suddenly not feeling well as evidenced by the smirk he had on his face as he signed the leave slip and chided me about the need to leave if I wasn't feeling well. I asked him about my leave request for the following day. He expressed in a loud and arrogant voice that he "will decide if and when [I] will be allowed leave and, if so, how much." I reminded him that I was leaving for the day and the request was for the following day. He responded, "Nate, you will be the first to know if I approve your leave request!" I inquired as to how this would be done if I was leaving and he implied that he would send me an E-mail. I heard nothing further on this leave request and there was no reason given as to why it was not approved.[34]

The following day I sent another E-mail request to Mr. Koebrick and copied Gail Martin, Aberdeen Area EEO Manager. I explained I believed he was attempting to suppress my ability to participate in the complaint process which is, by definition, reprisal. I also explained I would now be in need of seeking legal counsel and addressing a host of other issues which were outlined on the leave request. The leave request was for the week of November 9-13, 2009 (exclusive of Veteran's Day). The only response I received to this leave request was Mr. Koebrick sternly advising me of the need to report to duty as required until he authorizes leave. However, he again did not authorize leave and, again, no reason was given as to why he did not.

Mr. Koebrick had apparently decided to make an example of my whistleblower activity concerning the double funding of the OST project by directing the entire hospital Executive Team to attend the associated conference call with the OIG special agent and also invited most of the ranking members of the Aberdeen Area management team to also participate. In his invitation for the call he made a special point of calling out my name and my allegation of possible illegal activity to be the reason for the call.

During the conference call Mr. Koebrick had a highly confrontational demeanor toward me and was pressing me to provide evidence that something illegal had taken place. Of course he knew I did not have copies of the funding documents because he was probably involved in scrubbing the situation clean. However, each time he asked the room went silent and as I tried to explain he would interrupt and ask me to provide the evidence. I eventually got the story out and had provided all the names and funding amount (nearly $13,000) and the Aberdeen Area managers admitted they had provided the funding.

I guess the management team then had to fall back on plan B which was to minimize the double funding activity. Each seemed to have their rehearsed lines for consumption by the OIG special agent who was on the call (not a great deal of money, Tribe was able to do whatever they desired with the provided funds, etc). The clincher for the OIG special agent was the suggestion by one of the Area management team members there would be an audit performed on the Tribe's finances at some future unknown date at which time the additional funding would be discovered and returned to the Aberdeen Area IHS. I highly doubt this actually occurred, but it sounded like a way out for the Area managers and OIG special agent and they took it.

On the morning of November 12, 2009, I received an odd E-mail from Mr. Koebrick suggesting I was to meet with him at 1130 in the Lakota Lodge conference room. I responded with a query as to what the meeting was about. He would not tell me, responding only he would advise me at that time. I reported to the Lakota Lodge conference room at 1130 as requested. Two security guards were also present. Mr. Koebrick entered and immediately handed me a document advising me I had been detailed to the Aberdeen Area Office of Environmental Health and Engineering effective November 15, 2009. Nothing like this had been discussed or even suggested to me previously. There was no reason provided for the sudden detail. I noted for the record that was a reprisal action for the EEO complaints and whistleblower activity. Mr. Koebrick asked the two security guards to escort me to my office to retrieve my personal effects and we all proceeded to do same.

On the way out of the Lakota Lodge one of the security guards placed a comforting hand on my shoulder in support of me in the situation and then stated they would hang back a little way "so it didn't look so bad." Mr. Koebrick admonished him they were to proceed since there is a "safety and security risk." I couldn't believe what I thought I heard him say so I asked him to confirm same and he repeated it. I stated I objected to his statement and we proceeded to my office. I will note for the record there was never even the slightest suggestion of a threat to Mr. Koebrick by me at any time. As a matter of fact, earlier that same morning I was personally helping housekeeping staff move and arrange furniture within his refurbished office (the one that I had ensured was refurbished to suit his needs). I was walking by them in the hallway in the basement of the Lakota Lodge and saw they were struggling with some large pieces and were not adequately protecting the furniture for the move to the "new" office. I intervened by personally physically moving the pieces and providing guidance on protecting the furniture. I then visited twice with Mr. Koebrick to discuss how he wanted the furniture arranged and how to repair a glass desktop surface that had been damaged. The interactions were constructive and professional and I assigned a maintenance worker to repair the glass desktop. This was a typical interaction with Mr. Koebrick when I would initiate same—constructive and professional.

When the security guards, Fred Koebrick, and I arrived at my office Mr. Koebrick confiscated my keys and then advised I was only to take what I absolutely must have from my office. I began collecting my personal effects which included various folders containing personal information I have accumulated over the course of my career. Mr. Koebrick promptly snatched them up and stated I would not be allowed to bring any documents with me. He then sharply advised me that I had two more minutes to finish. The security guards assisted me with loading boxes one of them had provided to me and various Native American art and other personal effects. Mr. Koebrick then advised them to escort me off the grounds. I shook hands with the security guards and thanked them for being decent. I then left the campus with the lead security guard following me in the security vehicle.

I was made to feel by Mr. Koebrick as if I had done something terrible when, in fact, all I had done was what the regulation demands of me—reported discriminatory activities and brought forward a funding irregularity. This was very embarrassing for me and resulted in a tarnished reputation and subsequent sleep disturbances for both my wife and me. The transmittal letters for the various subsequent EEO complaints are included in Appendix 17.

LEFT HIGH AND DRY BY THE IG

After a series of reprisal actions were taken against me I contacted the OIG special agent about seeking assistance from them in addressing the issues. However, they were of no assistance other than to refer me to the Office of Special Counsel (OSC)—thanks for nothin'. I did and the OSC also advised me that they could not help me since I was a commissioned officer—nice.

THE BEATINGS WILL CONTINUE UNTIL MORALE IMPROVES

Following my removal and forced detail to the Aberdeen Area office I was served with personnel orders that also reduced my billet grade from an O-5 to an O-4. The official reason as to why I was detailed was because my skill set was needed in the Aberdeen Area Office. I was a registered professional in both civil and environmental engineering, registered environmental health specialist, registered professional sanitarian, and a registered paramedic. I had also earned three master's degrees and several certificates. However, when I arrived they had nothing for me to do and I was asked to perform secretarial duties associated with project document development. Understand, I do not think I am above performing secretarial duties. I only mention this because it is an indicator of the lack of integrity of the management chain under which I was working. During my banishment to the Aberdeen Area Office I was treated like a pariah by management. However, I got along well with my colleagues and my morale did improve despite the repeated beatings.

EVIL INCARNATE

I was ordered by CDR Jon Fogarty, my new supervisor, at approximately 5:00 pm the night before to report to Aberdeen by 8:00 am the next morning. It was approximately five straight hours of driving between our home and Aberdeen and it was the middle of November. When I arrived the next morning I wondered why I had to risk my life driving through rural South Dakota during a winter night when they had nothing important for me to do. However, this was a pattern as I saw a callous disregard exhibited by nearly all of the Aberdeen Area management chain for my health and safety or that of my wife.

During one of the first days of my punishment tour Susette called and told me she thought her lupus might be flaring again due to the stress associated with all of the events. I went up to the EEO office to see if Gail Martin, EEO Manager, could assist me with my situation. She reluctantly agreed to call the EEO attorney they had on staff in IHS headquarters who suggested we might be able to work up a flexible workplace arrangement plan (FWAP) schedule which would allow me to work from my home office. When I returned to my desk I was met with an E-mail from CDR Fogarty that I was not to visit with the EEO counselor again since she had complained that I had arrived with a red face (I had run up the stairs after hearing that my wife could have a potentially fatal health concern) and that I had imposed on her time—she had absolutely no compassion whatsoever for my situation.

I worked up an FWAP proposal and forwarded it on to the Aberdeen Area management team as well as the EEO attorney we had spoken with. I heard nothing. I guess the idea was to make my situation as miserable as possible

That winter there were a number of vicious blizzards. One of them was setting in one Monday morning as I was leaving home for Aberdeen. I was not notified in any way that the Aberdeen Area office had already closed so I was left trying to drive through whiteout conditions. Luckily I was able to make it to a motel to wait it out, but again the callous disregard for my health and safety was obvious.

During one of my long drives to Aberdeen I received a call from Susette. She had just finished a medical appointment during which they had presented some very concerning test results. She was crying hard and I wanted and needed to be with her, but I was already four hours down the road. For some reason my commitment to work kept me going and I arrived in Aberdeen later that afternoon. A woman who worked in our office who I had been assisting with data processing was the first person I saw upon arriving. I needed someone to talk to. I started telling her about the phone call I had received from Susette and wondered why I was there (five hours away from home). I tried talking, but unfortunately the tears started flowing. I found out later the woman was simply another lieutenant for Ms. Red Thunder so I'm sure my tears only served to embolden the Aberdeen Area management team to continue in their evil ways and continue to make my life as miserable as they possibly could.

Then *CDR* Jon Fogarty (he has since been promoted to Captain—O-6) was another of Ms. Red Thunder's lieutenants and I learned about his sense of integrity through my personal interactions with him as well as what I observed. In one instance I was sitting in the audience at the annual Aberdeen Area OEHE conference as he explained he had been approached by congressional delegations seeking information on the status of the spending of the stimulus funds. He relayed to the audience he "told them something that worked" with a smirk on his face (i.e., he was aware the information he provided was not true, but apparently had no problem with it). I logged my interactions with CDR Fogarty, and other Aberdeen Area staff, since many of them were very negative (see Appendix 18).

THEIR FIRST CASUALTY

As I was enduring a very difficult work environment created by various management officials of the Aberdeen Area I was seeking assistance from anyone and everyone, including now *CAPT* Ronald Keats, Commissioned Corps Liaison. However, CAPT Keats was working as a "tool for management" as he described himself during a discussion we had. I had been trying to contact him for over one week concerning a downgrade of my billet, an action that occurred without any discussion with or warning to me. I sent him an E-mail, tried to reach him by phone but could not even reach an answering service, checked his office several times and knocked on his office door, and left a written note on the dry erase message board on the outside of his office door. He did not respond. Finally, one Friday afternoon in late December 2009 I saw CAPT Keats talking to another officer within the office where I was working and approached him and asked if I could speak to him. He said he would be over in a couple of minutes. He arrived at my work station 30 minutes later.

CAPT Keats and I went into a conference room and I asked him why my billet had been recently downgraded. He responded my supervisor requested the action and his responsibility was to simply process it. I was surprised by this response as I thought perhaps there should be some "value added" by this O-6 officer. I suggested to CAPT Keats perhaps there should have been some form of communication with me other than simply sending me the completed downgraded billet and I thought that was the primary function of a liaison. I mentioned I had worked as a liaison officer on deployment and understood the function to involve communication in both or every direction. CAPT Keats then indicated he did not appreciate being made to feel defensive when he speaks to me and he is simply of "tool for management—management tells [him] to do something and [he] do[es] it." Again, I was surprised by this response as it implies no advocacy for commissioned officers. I further asked CAPT Keats as to what else was being planned or developed as far as actions related to me and he responded he did not know. CAPT Keats was obviously perturbed by our conversation and asked if there was anything else. I thanked him for his time and he left immediately.

I documented the meeting and included this along with other documentation from previous discussions[36] and forwarded same in a strongly worded E-mail (see Appendix 19) to his supervisor, RADM Richard Rubendall. Several months later CAPT Keats was gone.

I thought the reason for CAPT Keats' sudden departure was due, at least in part, to my exposure of his activities. However, it was actually due to his activities associated with the exposure of others—children. It seems that in May 2010 CAPT Keats accidently left a data CD in the elevator within the Federal building in Aberdeen. On the CD was at least one document authored by him along with child pornography. Upon further investigation he apparently had more of the damning files. CAPT Keats was recently sentenced to 44 months in prison and fined $100,000 for possession of child pornography (see Appendix 19)—how's that for karma?

SENATE COMMITTEE ON INDIAN AFFAIRS INVESTIGATION

The Aberdeen Area eventually came under the scrutiny of the Senate Committee on Indian Affairs (SCIA). The Chairman at the time was Senator Byron Dorgan, D-ND who had already announced that he was retiring so he had nothing to lose in addressing the issues with the Aberdeen Area during a special session to address the problems in the Aberdeen Area.

The 2010 report by SCIA Chairman Byron Dorgan., found that the IHS Aberdeen Area is in a "chronic state of crisis."

"Serious management problems and a lack of oversight of this region have adversely affected the access and quality of health care provided to Native Americans in the Aberdeen Area, which serves 18 tribes in the states of North Dakota, South Dakota, Nebraska and Iowa," according to the newspaper reports (see Appendix 20). However, to my knowledge, not one person was fired or even reprimanded—must be nice to be of the "preferred race."

LESSONS LEARNED

Evil can take many forms. I'm sure all of the people who were perpetrating these various acts to harm my wife and me had people at home and work who believe them to be good people and protect them. I'm sure many of those people will stand by the perpetrators even after reading this book and discovering the evil done by their loved one. People need to have the courage to recognize and stand against evil acts, even if it takes an unexpected form. "The world is a dangerous place; not because of the people who are evil, but because of the people who don't do anything about it."—Albert Einstein

ADDENDUM

Almost two years after I retired from the USPHS I became aware of another USPHS commissioned officer who was having a similar experience to mine with the Aberdeen Area IHS. CDR Michael Tilus is a former Army chaplain who dared to speak out against apathetic Native American leaders in order to protect children on his service reservation. Despite his strong reputation he was suddenly transferred to the Aberdeen Area Office, removing him from his clinical psychology practice on the reservation (during a time when there was deep concern over the high rate of teenage suicides on the reservation), and issued a letter of reprimand (see Appendix 21).

I am unaware of any turnover in the Aberdeen Area management team. Therefore, many of the same people that were involved in my similar situation would have been involved in these actions against Dr. Tilus.

TRANSPORTATION SECURITY ADMINISTRATION

DEADLY TOOL

When I was stationed in Seattle I was flying out to South Dakota on a regular basis as I was involved in various IHS new construction and maintenance and improvement projects. It was clear that the Transportation Security Administration (TSA) workers in the Midwest were much more thorough than those in Seattle. On one occasion I was returning to Seattle from either Sioux Falls or Rapid City. I had the same items inside my carryon bag as what I had when I left Seattle. As they were running my bag through the X-ray at the checkpoint they stopped the belt on my bag and I saw the X-ray operator starting to point something out to another Transportation Security Officer (TSO).

They asked whose bag it was and pulled me off to the side and then started digging and re-running my bag at different angles. After several iterations of this I finally asked them what they were looking for. The response was, "You've got a Leatherman® in there!" I thought for a minute and could not for the life of me think of what they were seeing. Finally they pulled a fold-up micro-pliers out of an internal pocket. The TSO held it up in front of me and I looked at him and advised him that it did not have a blade. He responded by stating that it didn't matter because it was a tool. I asked him what I could possibly do with it and he responded, with a straight face, that I could remove a panel from the aircraft. I almost responded I could also probably empty the contents of Lake Superior with a teaspoon if given enough time, but I thought better of it. I found it ironic that, following my retirement from the USPHS, I later accepted a position as a TSO, possibly in the same airport, as where this happened years earlier.

LEADERSHIP

Most of the leadership, and many of the coworkers, I worked with at the TSA were prior military. The management cadre included Bob Baker, Assistant Federal Security Director; David Mundell, Transportation Security Manager (TSM); and Dean Pelofske, TSM. All of these individuals have only the highest level of integrity and it was clear they were all fully engaged in their jobs and making decisions with the best interests of their customers, the traveling public, in mind. In my experience this was unusual in the public sector and I was impressed.

TRAINING

The training regimen at the TSA was also very impressive. It was very formal and comprehensive and included mentoring and verification testing for competence all the way through the entry on duty process as well as annually thereafter.

THE SLEEPER

On the morning of my first day of on-the-job-training (OJT) my mentor and I walked past an airline ticket counter which was not in use. Under the TSA work area behind the ticket counter one could barely make out the shoes of a TSO who was sleeping on the floor. I was shocked and wondered what I had gotten myself into. My OJT mentor and I walked by there again sometime later and the TSO was still there. We reported the issue through the chain of command and were asked to write up exactly what we saw. We both did and were subsequently interviewed by management and the TSO was summarily dismissed. In the 21 years I had worked for the IHS I had only seen one person fired, and that was someone I fired. I had been at the TSA only a few weeks and they fired someone who obviously had no business working there. Again, I was impressed.

The removed TSO had at least one powerful friend, a lead TSO (LTSO), who found out I was involved in the removal of her friend and she began to make it very clear she was not happy with me. She took every opportunity to make me feel highly uncomfortable, but mostly completely ignored me. This surprised me and I expected more from a person who had become an LTSO.

TEAMWORK?

I have always been a person who tries to keep busy. If I am not doing something productive I feel as if my time is being wasted. As is with any team we had a mix of people with varying personalities and work habits. However, there was one person in particular who seemed to be unwilling to perform even the primary work that was expected of all of the other TSOs. I was surprised he was able to get away with it. I guess at least one supervisory TSO (STSO) was unwilling to say anything. This was probably due to the offending TSO's status as a Native American, a racial status he took every opportunity to share with all who would listen. He knew of his protected status and was apparently going to milk it for everything it was worth. The team needed him but he was more interested in spending his time involved in small talk with the one STSO. I believe this was recognized by the TSMs and they were planning on moving the offending (lazy) TSO to another shift so he would be working under an STSO who would have higher expectations for his performance.

LESSONS LEARNED

The TSA is the agency that everybody loves to hate. It certainly has its share of problems which seem to take center stage when they come forward. However, it is the most well managed agency

with which I had the experience of working. Therefore, the
lesson learned was the natural tension created by a high profile
and high expectations (e.g., the need to be 100% successful
24/7/365) creates the need for a high level of competency. This
need for a high level of competency may help to ensure merit-
based selections, at least for upper-level management. However,
the pay for the entry-level TSO positions is not sufficient to
attract many high quality candidates. This, combined with ever-
changing guidelines (needed to address dynamic security threats),
creates problems and it is those problems that typically make the
nightly newsreel.

Figure 27. TSO Gjovik on Last Day with TSA (2011)

DEPARTMENT OF VETERANS AFFAIRS

APPLICATION HELL

The TSO work environment at the TSA was not desirable for me (partly due to the hostility from the LTSO) so when I received an E-mail from a former colleague about a GS-12 General Engineer position with the Veterans Administration (VA) Health Care System (HCS) in Fargo, North Dakota I applied. This application marked the beginning of a tortured path. During this time the USAJobs.gov web site, where one applies for Federal positions, was having technical issues (which were apparently exposed publicly in a "60 Minutes" episode). I did not see the episode but know that the web site should have forwarded my resume which I had built within the web site (along with one which I had uploaded) to the VA to accompany my application. However, it did not and I was casually disqualified because of this.[37] I appealed to several ranking VA officials regarding this determination, because I knew I was qualified. However, I received no response.

I later found out that I qualified for reconsideration due to my status as a disabled veteran. However, the personnel specialist would still not accept my resume as evidence of my qualifications. Therefore, I forwarded copies of all of the last several billets (job descriptions under which I had worked while on active duty which was approximately 20 pages of data). The personnel specialist found it within her to grant me the opportunity to interview for the position based on this.[38] I kept a log of the various interactions of this hellish application process (see Appendix 22). I believe it should not be so difficult to apply and be considered for positions with the Federal government (or any entity).

LEADERSHIP

Michael Murphy was the Director of the Fargo VA health care system. He is very intelligent and very formal, probably due to his past history as an O-6 officer (however, I was as well). I was actually granted an audience with Mr. Murphy to discuss my concerns over safety. He listened and took copious notes and then later responded with a follow-up E-mail. However, I feel as if he handled the situation like a military commander who was fully involved in a fierce battle which required immediate executive decisions. The issues I brought forward were worth investigating and getting right. His right-hand man was Dale DeKrey, Associate Director.

Mr. DeKrey is also a retired military officer and a registered professional engineer. Mr. DeKrey had previously been the Chief Engineer and, during the occurrences described below, was the Director of Operations and, as such, was responsible for all safety issues within the hospital.[39]

Dennis Langevin is a relatively young mechanical engineer. He has spent no time in uniformed service and had spent most or all of his working life within the VA system, most of it at the Fargo VA. Therefore, he was considered the resident expert on the mechanical systems at the Fargo VA. However, he was not professionally registered and had only recently been promoted into the supervisory role as the Chief Engineer (presumably in a supervisory role for the first time).

AN UNWELCOMING WELCOME

I recall the morning of my first day of work at the Fargo VA. I arrived early so I could find my way to the engineering office. However, I got lost (the hospital is an aggregation of several buildings which have been morphed together and added onto over the decades). I stopped at the environmental services break room and asked if they knew how to get to the engineering office.

They decided to call Mr. Langevin for me. He arrived down the hall and I approached him. There was no handshake and no welcome aboard, only a cold silence which I broke by thanking him for hiring me to which he replied, "You're welcome."

I was escorted to my new office and given a 30-minute briefing on the facility. I guess I was then expected to be off and running. The rule of thumb in previous assignments was that staff did not start becoming truly productive in their positions until they had been in an assignment for approximately two years. I guess the superior "VA way" has reduced that expectation down to less than two hours—amazing.

SAME OLD SONG AND DANCE

As I began performing my work it became obvious we were having significant construction safety issues with one of the contractors working on the campus, some of which could have resulted in significant injury or death to patients or VA/contractor staff. One week into my employment, after seeing a number of smaller safety violations (e.g., extension cords with compromised sheathing, tools with compromised cords, etc.), I witnessed the contractor having something delivered via a boom-mounted fork to a fourth floor scaffold platform. The work area was nearby the main entrance into the hospital and immediately adjacent to a smoking shelter for veteran patients. There were neither barricades nor a spotter around the truck during the delivery (or pickup) activities. Following the material delivery I witnessed one of the contractor's workers toss a bundle of long metal rods onto the fork from the fourth floor scaffold platform. After bouncing around on the forks the rods started falling off about 10 feet off the ground and struck glancing blows to a nearby pickup truck (presumed to belong to the contractor or supplier) before crashing onto the concrete driveway. I notified the safety officer and together we spoke with the contractor's superintendent. He assured us they would do a better job on safety and we all went about our business.

I continued with my construction inspection rounds and found my way to the fourth floor renovation project. As I was walking through one of the large open areas a temporary light fixture which was being installed came crashing to the ground and shattered right next to another worker who was not wearing a hard hat. The same superintendent I just spoken to was standing nearby and tried to pretend like nothing had just happened. I let him know that I was not happy, but I got the same (hollow) assurances and I worked up a safety memo—the first of many.

While I was getting adjusted to my new employment situation the facility was undergoing its annual workplace evaluation (AWE) which was being conducted by a couple of VA safety specialists. They found a number of significant safety violations associated with the scaffold platform located near the hospital's main entrance which had, in all likelihood, been present since the scaffold was placed into service several weeks or months before the inspection. I started becoming educated about scaffold safety since the contractor had expanded the scaffolding around the entire north face of the hospital which is above the main entrance to the hospital. I was finding very basic safety issues including use of old, rotting planks; lack of guardrail protection to keep workers from falling off; lack of toe board protection to keep loose items (e.g., dried pieces of brick mortar, hardware items, soda containers, etc.) on the planking from falling off the scaffolding; missing cleating (to keep planks from sliding off the ends of the scaffold frames); poorly supported scaffold bases; etc.

Federal regulations require that "…scaffolds and scaffold components shall be inspected for visible defects by a competent person before each work shift, and after any occurrence which could affect a scaffold's structural integrity." A competent person is defined as "one who is capable of identifying existing and predictable hazards in the surroundings or working conditions which are unsanitary, hazardous, or dangerous to employees, and who has authorization to take prompt corrective measures to eliminate them."[40]

It became obvious that the contractor did not have a competent person providing daily inspections of the scaffold system as required by the OSHA. It was also obvious this was placing not only the contractor's staff at risk, but also patients and staff at the facility since the scaffolding was located in close proximity to the main entrance of the hospital.

The perpetrating contractor had been working at the Fargo VA for many years and, reportedly, noncompliant with OSHA regulations for some time (by their own admission when times were better with the contractor's PM). Therefore, based on what I was experiencing, it was clear construction safety had not been a priority at the Fargo VA for a long time. The documented safety violations continued to grow in number (see Appendix 23) and all were shared with the chain of command as well as the contracting team. Mr. Langevin and the contracting staff provided superficial support. They even temporarily suspended work after the safety concerns had become so numerous and egregious as to suggest somebody could be killed at any time.

However, the contractor was soon back in the saddle after providing assurances his staff had received scaffold safety training. Contracting required no proof of this and I later found out the claims of specialized scaffold training were not true. I continued noticing the same issues and, at one point, challenged the contractor's and his subcontractor's "competent persons" to make a call on one particular scaffold plank which I believed to be unsafe. They both stated unequivocally they believed it to be safe and the contractor's "competent person" proceeded to demonstrate this empirically. He removed it from the scaffold system and set it on the floor with one end propped up and applied a force to the center. After the second application of the force a loud crack was heard and it was clear that any further demonstration would have resulted in complete failure of the plank and the "competent person" quickly discontinued the demonstration.[41]

I shared this information with Mr. Langevin and the contracting staff and it was clear they had had enough of me. This was exacerbated by the continued pressure from the contractor's PM, with whom they had a long term relationship. We had a meeting with contracting to try and clear the air. After hearing a variety of propaganda statements by the contractor's PM, I made a statement that the contractor had been placing everyone in the facility at risk and that everyone in the room should be concerned about this. The room went silent and it was clear the line had been drawn and I was on the other side of it.

Mr. Langevin was on leave soon thereafter and I continued to see significant safety issues. The contractor's PM kept asserting he had competent person(s) and then wrote in an E-mail response that OSHA had been contacted by his subcontractor. I thought about the situation overnight and sent an E-mail to the Contracting Officer (and copied Mr. Langevin, the Safety Officer, and others) concerning my desire, since the contractor had reportedly already contacted OSHA, to contact OSHA and request a targeted inspection of the job site. I also verbally discussed my desire to contact OSHA regarding my concerns over safety on the job site with the Contracting Officer. He advised me it sounded like a good idea and I should proceed. I did. However, during my telephone discussion with Keith Thompson, OSHA Construction Safety Inspector, either the Safety Officer (whom I had been directed by Mr. Langevin not to involve in construction safety issues) or the secretary had been listening to my conversation and reported it to Dale DeKrey. The secretary then advised me that she was instructed to instruct me to discontinue my discussion with the OSHA. Mr. DeKrey appeared in my office soon thereafter.

I explained the history of safety violations to Mr. DeKrey and he instructed the secretary to draft a memo directing contracting to suspend the contract with the general contractor until such time as they could prove they had a competent person managing their site. I delivered the memo to the Contracting Officer who made the decision to disregard the memo from Mr. DeKrey and have a third party verify the safety of the scaffolding.

Earlier I had paused my conversation with the OSHA. After meeting with Contracting I called Mr. Thompson back and explained to him what had transpired. I also explained that the facility was highly desirous of not having their presence on the campus. He suggested an alternative of having the Workforce Safety Insurance (WSI) program inspect the scaffolding. I thought this was a good idea and I called Mr. DeKrey and the Safety Officer to participate in the call. They both did (along with the Emergency Manager Intern in the office who has a strong safety inspection background[42]). I set my phone to speakerphone mode so we could all participate in the conversation. Mr. Thompson explained that OSHA could provide a targeted inspection under their fall protection program and then mentioned the WSI inspection option. Both Mr. DeKrey and the Safety Officer agreed that the WSI option was the correct path. I implemented this plan to have the WSI inspect the scaffold system for the general contractor.

The WSI inspection was held soon thereafter and was handled with kid gloves. There were several deficiencies noted on the scaffolding, but the contractor's "competent person(s)" were not even present for any questioning to be made of them. This was my primary issue—the contractor did not have a competent person on the job site. However, the WSI staff did provide the requirements for a scaffolding competent person (see Appendix 24), none of which were met by the Contractor. A punch list of safety deficiencies, some of which could have resulted in serious injury or death, was developed and provided to the contractor. WSI returned several days later for a re-inspection and several of the punch list items had not been corrected and the contractor's "competent person(s)" had still not been tested in any way. However, this was good enough for the VA management and contracting teams and the contractor was again green-lighted to continue unabated.

BEEN THERE, DONE THAT

My discussion with OSHA was not received well by my supervisor as he immediately began to treat me with open hostility and served me with a performance counseling memo (this was outside any regularly scheduled performance review and was provided after being employed for only two months). The performance counseling memo was filled with vagary and innuendo. I responded to each item he had listed, essentially requesting clarity or examples of the litany of issues he had found with me. However, I never received a substantive response (i.e., no clarification or examples were ever provided).

I called Keith Thompson from OSHA back to discuss this new development. He advised me that this sounded like reprisal and then he paused our conversation to discuss this with his supervisor. When he came back he advised me that Federal employees were exempted from Whistleblower Protection Act protection—unbelievable! He then asked me about the contractor and advised me that he was familiar with the offending contractor and that he was surprised that particular contractor would have been allowed to work at the VA. He also advised me of a section of the OSHA web site where one could find past violations. As it turned out this contractor had a fatality incident, which resulted in ten OSHA citations, four years prior associated with very similar activities to what I was documenting at the Fargo VA. Again, I made my chain of command and the contracting office aware of this and, again, got nothing but apathy.

I also continued to document construction safety violations even as the contractor became emboldened due to his knowledge that I did not have the support of my supervisory chain. Mr.

Langevin told me that he had been asking the contractors about their perception of my performance and logging same—unbelievable. It should come as no surprise they were not happy with me. I had also noticed Mr. Langevin taking copious notes any time I spoke during meetings where we were both in attendance. The verbals and nonverbals were coming through loud and clear—he was going to rid himself of that thorn in his side. The contracting staff followed Mr. Langevin's lead and the three of them conspired on a memo which they knew was misleading in order to document a justification for their collective lack of action (see memo along with my response memo within Appendix 25). They apparently believed they were safe in their false attestations as long as they stuck together (maybe they're right).

As a result of my performing my new job at the Fargo VA HCS in accordance with all of my past and current (Mr. Langevin and I completed a VA construction safety training program together while all of this was unfolding) construction safety training and professional experience (over 21 years working in construction as an engineer), I was subjected to a hostile work environment by professional staff who banded together and made false and misleading statements to cover up their apathy to an issue which should have been of utmost importance. Even the VA safety specialists were unwilling to take any action because after speaking with the Fargo VA chain of command they believed the body of evidence did not support the need for them to look at it again (it was their AWE which started the ball rolling on scaffold safety concerns). It was clear to me that the apple was rotten to the core and I wanted none of it. Therefore, I resigned my lucrative and potentially rewarding job (I was, after all, serving America's heroes) at a time when jobs were difficult or impossible for me to come by. However, I had been there and done that and was unwilling to go through it again.

I shared my story with the veteran issues advocates with every elected official from North Dakota. I received only lukewarm support from Senator John Hoeven's and Representative Rick Berg's office (the two Republicans) and nothing from Senator Kent Conrad's office (the only Democrat). The two Republicans obtained letters from VA management in Fargo and St. Paul, Minnesota. The letters (one from each office sent to both Representative Berg and Senator Hoeven at different times) were designed to present me as a zealot and to provide misleading information which was suggestive the VA had gone above and beyond in their efforts to satisfy my unreasonable expectations (see letters along with my response letters in Appendix 26). The letters to Senator Hoeven came after those provided to Representative Berg and were essentially the same letters. The advocate from Senator Hoeven's office was apparently satisfied and advised me I was now on my own. As I told the advocate in Senator Hoeven's Fargo office, I expected more.

LESSONS LEARNED

There were at least two individuals who I worked with at the Fargo VA who are both smart individuals. I'm sure they performed very well in their previous capacities. However, as is often the case in the public sector they got promoted into positions they have no business being in (Peter Principle—they got elevated to the level of their incompetence). However, any manager above them worth his/her salt should have known they should not have been promoted to their respective positions. I believe they were promoted as rewards for many years of faithful service to the Fargo VA. However, time in service does not a manager make, but in the public sector it seems that one's proven ability to successfully manage people (via training or experience) is secondary to chronyism and the personal reward desires of upper level management. The success of the organization as a result of a promotion decision may only be an afterthought (assuming it is even in the thought stream). Therefore, one could strongly argue public sector management places greater importance on service to certain employees than the organization's customers (assuming they even understand they have customers and know who they are).

I also learned even those who are supposed to be the standard bearers for Government integrity, Contracting Officers, are easily compromised within the VA system.

DEEPER REFLECTIONS

THE FALLACY OF NATIVE AMERICANS BEING GOOD CARETAKERS OF THE LAND

The public service commercial from the 1970s shows a Native American paddling his canoe through a litter infested lake which is surrounded by industry. It ends with the Native American standing next to a highway as a white person who is driving by tosses a bag of litter at his feet and the camera zooms to the Native American face as he turns to expose a tear emanating from one eye.

In my experience this presentation was about as far from reality as one could possibly get. I recall one site we served within the Cherokee Nation. The person(s) living in the residence apparently never hauled garbage or arranged for garbage pickup. They would simply throw it outside on their yard. The ground was literally spongy as I and another coworker approached the home while walking on several inches of compacted trash. Illegal dumpsites (common places where people would go to throw their garbage away which were typically down an embankment and/or in a remote area) were also a very common problem on Tribal lands and I was involved in several projects specifically designed to address same.

While I was stationed in Toppenish, Washington I was asked by the Yakama Nation to help address illegal wastewater outfalls into irrigation ditches. We located a couple and I authored a strongly worded letter to Tribal leadership on recommendations to resolve the problem. The Tribe had their own environmental protection program for which they received Federal funding to operate. However, it appeared the office actually performed very little and the Federal funds were spent almost entirely by the well-connected director to support his salary and junket trips to exotic locales. To my knowledge nothing was done to address the illegal wastewater disposal outfalls which were dumping raw sewage into local irrigation ditches within the Yakama Nation.

While I was stationed in Seattle one of my projects was located in Pine Ridge, South Dakota. My brother wanted to meet me in the area and we arranged same. One of the places we visited was the city park in Pine Ridge. It looked very much like the Oklahoma project site described above with garbage strewn everywhere which required one to walk on garbage when traversing the site. The odd part of this is the unemployment rate in Pine Ridge is very, very high (i.e., there are many people who have a great deal of time on their hands). You would think that Pine Ridge should be the cleanest community in the US with all those people available to perform work for the community. My brother made a spoof video of the 1970s public service commercial mentioned above. His wife videoed the Pine Ridge litter-strewn park and then focused on my brother's face and panned in to the mock tear (spit) rolling down his cheek.

Also, as noted above, while I was working as the Facility Manager at the Sioux San Hospital in South Dakota I was asked by my supervisor, Fred Koebrick, a Native American, to circumvent State and Federal regulations pertaining to groundwater wellhead protection. Mr. Koebrick directed me to use various herbicides and fertilizers to beautify the campus. When I explained to him that the areas were within wellhead protection zones around two potable water wells he showed callous disregard for same and directed me to utilize the chemicals as needed to beautify the campus (implying that he cared little for the possibility of contamination of the associated aquifers).

I'm sure there would be many who would read this and find it to be unacceptable. However, it is the truth. Somehow Native American people and tribes have garnered the politically correct image of being the ultimate guardians of the land. However, the truth is that many Native American people and tribes need to do a better job of caring for the environment.

BASIS FOR PROVISION OF SERVICES TO NATIVE AMERICANS

To read through the IHS web site one would arrive at the conclusion that Native Americans are guaranteed health care courtesy of the American taxpayer. This is due to the use of language such as the Federal government's

> "trust relationship [which] establishes a responsibility for a variety of services and benefits to Indian people based on their status as Indians, including health care. This relationship has been defined in case law and statute as a political relationship that further distinguishes Indians from racial classification for purposes of affirmative action laws and other Federal statutes that establish Federally funded programs for the general public."

The web site also states that

> "The Snyder Act of 1921 (25 USC 13) and the Indian Health Care Improvement Act (25 USC 1601) of 1976 provide specific legislative authority for Congress to appropriate funds specifically for the health care of Indian people. In addition, numerous other laws, court cases, and Executive Orders reaffirm the unique relationship between tribal governments and the federal government."

and

> "Treaties between the United States Government and Indian Tribes frequently call for the provision of medical

services, the services of physicians, or the provision of hospitals for the care of Indian people."[43]

However, while I was working for the IHS I grew tired of hearing the constant banter of how the Federal government (i.e., American taxpayers) owed the Native Americans of today. Therefore, I started performing my own research and read the treaties of the various tribes to which I was providing services. As it turned out some of the treaties did contain provisions for health care. However, those provisions were limited in scope and duration and they all expired in the latter part of the 19th century (i.e., well over 100 years ago). One example is the treaty signed with the Yakama Nation in 1855. Among the many very specific provisions made to the Tribal members of that time it provided for one physician and six assistants for a period of 20 years. Therefore, the treaty requirement for the provision of any health care to the Yakama Nation ended in 1875. However, today the Federal government through the IHS operates a 40,000 square foot health center for Yakama Nation members which is located near their Tribal headquarters (and across the street from their casino) in Toppenish, Washington. The health center was newly constructed in 1990 (to replace an older, smaller clinic) and houses various health care programs including:

> a full range of ambulatory primary care, public health, dental services, mental health, optometry, and audiology and internal medicine, women's health care, elder care clinic & pediatrics

In addition to the services provided at the IHS's Yakama Nation Health Center in Toppenish, Tribal members can also receive free health care at the local private hospital facility (in-patient contract services) and a satellite IHS clinic in White Swan, Washington which is deeper into the reservation.[44]

Reference is made to the discussion of the Winnebago Health Center above and bronze plaque which was unveiled at the dedication ceremony. The Winnebago Tribe of Nebraska designed the plaque to simply feed the populist myth of the continued victimization of tribal people. In reality the reverse is true.

Most or all of the tribal people have no treaty right to nearly all of the full suite of every imaginable advantage they currently have in the US today. The provision of the new Winnebago Health Center and Drug Dependency Unit (renovated old hospital) is a microcosm of the national guilt which has been foisted upon taxpayers of today as they are expected to pay enormous sums of money for wrongdoings which were perpetrated on both sides of the proverbial fence and, in most cases, neither they nor their great ancestors were involved. The beneficiary populations present the services as a right to which they are entitled[45] and most simply accept that. However, I have read most of the treaties of the Tribes with which I served throughout the western US and have not seen a situation where a Tribe was entitled to any health care services beyond the late 19th century. It should be noted that this belief in their right to the services creates a certain militance in their expectation of the services and a complete lack of appreciation for same.

A NEW DECLARATION?

I experienced significant ill will from the local non-Tribal population associated with the Sisseton Health Center project and for seemingly good reasons. The city of Sisseton had two hospitals—one for everybody and one for only Tribal members (IHS hospital). Rather than working to strengthen the health care facility for the benefit of everyone in the community Senator Daschle and the IHS decided that a brand new, state-of-the-art, 86,000-square foot health care center should be built that only Tribal members could utilize. Non-Tribal members of the community would have to continue utilizing the Coteau des Prairies Hospital which was originally built in 1967. Their only involvement with the new facility would be the expectation they help pay for it through their Federal taxes.

To add salt in the wound the local Tribe, the Sisseton-Wahpeton Oyate (SWO) of the Lake Traverse Reservation, has wildly successful casino operations (businesses that non-Tribal members are not allowed to have) and, consequently, a great deal of expendable income (which begs the question of why the Federal taxpayer is providing, free of charge, a new health care facility to this population). This income is reportedly used to purchase every scrap of available land in the area. Once the land is purchased it is converted to "trust" status which means it is held in trust by the Federal government via the Bureau of Indian Affairs on behalf of the Tribe. This new status removes the land from the local tax base which further compounds the situation for non-Tribal members of the community and county.

Perhaps we need to rewrite our Declaration of Independence to better reflect today's American reality: We hold these truths to be self-evident, that **NOT** all men are created equal…

THE FACES OF MODERN DISCRIMINATION

Reference is made to the chapter above on President Clinton's DOL and its impact on Security National Bank in Norman, Oklahoma where my wife worked in the human resource department. I sometimes wonder what happened to that little old man who wanted that mail handler job so desperately but could not get it due purely to his race (he is/was Caucasian) and gender. However, there was another example we were aware of in Oklahoma where opportunity was withheld from white persons in order to satisfy some sort of government mandate. My wife applied to the Nutritional Science (dietetic) program at the University of Oklahoma Health Sciences Center in Oklahoma City (OUHSC). In preparation for same she had to take a variety of prerequisites. As she was taking the prerequisite coursework she came to know several other students, including one young man who had made application to the same dietetic program. Unfortunately, he was denied a slot in the program. However, an African American male was allowed into the program. It was clear to all who worked with the African American student that he was not properly prepared for the program and should not have been given one of the very valuable program slots. His lack of preparation ultimately culminated in his removal from the program after the first year.

I wonder how many people's pathways have been inexorably changed by the heavy hand of Government as it determines winners and losers based on some sort of populist paradigm. What people don't seem to realize by these actions are the impacts they have on the disenfranchised (the losers). There are real people being adversely impacted by these actions.

Imagine what it would have meant for that little old man to have been selected for the mail handler position at Security National Bank or for that young male student to have been given the opportunity to study dietetics at the OUHSC. These would have been life changing events for both individuals. However, they were not allowed those opportunities because of their affliction—they were born with white skin at a time when white-skinned people were not favored by the Government. Therefore, they were expendable and whatever lives they were able to muster for themselves following the loss of opportunities stripped from them due to their affliction would be relegated to the scraps of whatever opportunities remained after the favored populations received theirs.

What those who promulgate these racist and discriminatory policies don't realize is that the damage is not only done to the innocent citizens of today who are forced to pay the perceived bill of generations past, but so do the intended recipients of the policies. The IHS was borne in 1955 as a result of the gross incompetence of the BIA in providing health services to their Native American clientele. The IHS is currently traveling down that same path due to the policy of Indian Preference. This should not be construed to imply that I believe Native Americans are generally incompetent. Nothing could be further from the truth. However, this practice of racial preference fosters mediocrity as the most qualified individuals are not necessarily hired, promoted, etc. It has also created apathy toward high performance because it simply affords opportunity to Native Americans who meet the minimum requirements and provides another level of protection to nonperformers. This is obviously contrary to the needs of the Native American population being served by this agency and the taxpaying public and complaints among the IHS customers are common (and many or most of the worst performing employees are Native American, because they were hired due to their race rather than qualifications, and they know it).

FEDERAL OBSESSION WITH RACE

The Federal government work force seems to be dominated by those of a liberal perspective. I watched a discussion on a news program while writing this section of the book which made the assertion there are two groups in America which are obsessed with race—Nazis and liberals (I guess the Black Panthers must fall within the liberal category). After reflecting on this I believe it is true. I have long known the Federal government has a preoccupation with race. I became sensitized to this preoccupation shortly after being commissioned with the USPHS and going to work for the IHS. It was clear there were limited opportunities for me due to my unfortunate parentage resulting in my being born white (and, unfortunately, male).

I worked harder on my career than anybody I knew. However, I was routinely surpassed along the career ladder by minority and female officers who had far less in terms of credentials or experience. In my last assignment I worked under the supervision of a former extern who had worked for me. He had risen through the ranks simply due to his race (he is fractionally Native American). Even though I had sacrificed far more over the course of many years to build my résumé and breadth of experience by uprooting my family every few years to move to a new duty station, none of it mattered in the eyes of the IHS masters. I am not Native American. Therefore, I was not worthy.

The Federal government's preoccupation with race seems to permeate nearly every Federal action including hiring, promotions, contracting awards (white males are at a distinct disadvantage for any Federal contracting action unless they have veteran preference), willingness to uphold Federal law (i.e., far less willing to take a negative action against a minority person or group). This preoccupation can even be seen in the census process. During the last census effort the second question after asking me how many people lived in our home was, "What are their races?" Most people probably simply answer this question without even wondering as to why such a question would be appropriate in a land of supposed equals. However, I have been repeatedly victimized by my own government due to my race and gender and am now very aware of how this information is used— to determine the winners and losers.

FEDERAL DOUBLE STANDARDS

The Federal government passes an endless litany of laws which it expects the citizens of the country to follow. However, it routinely exempts itself from those same laws (see Been There, Done That section above which includes a discussion on Whistleblower Protection for Federal workers pertaining to construction safety at the VA). However, as has also been discussed above, even if the laws do apply to the Federal work force they may not be enforced due to the race or gender of the offending party(ies).

There is a debate currently being promulgated by Federal government related to being "fair"—each American paying their fair share and people being treated fairly, etc. However, the Federal government appears to be the greatest offender of the proposition of fairness—with gross double standards that are so numerous as to block one's ability to see what is fair and what is not.

BIRDS OF A FEATHER STICK TOGETHER

During my various trials and tribulations with the various Federal Departments I tendered formal complaints through the entire chains-of-command up to the respective Secretary and including the Surgeons General. I also tendered formal complaints to the agencies which were charged with the responsibilities of at least investigating the complaints and then taking action to correct any findings. These included agency, department, and Federal EEO offices, DOL, OIG, OSC, OSHA, and several Congressional offices in North Dakota, Oklahoma, South Dakota, and Washington. With the notable exception of the Rapid City office of Senator John Thune (R-SD) nothing was ever done. In each case staff and officials sought the path of least resistance which was to either ignore my complaints or "throw me under the bus" by seeking a means to not have to perform their oversight function (e.g., find or fabricate an interpretation of a law or legal opinion which would preclude their involvement) and/or by supporting those with whom they shared some form of hierarchical or racial bond (i.e., management supporting their fellow managers and/or racial minorities supporting other racial minorities). In one case where I presented a senior executive service level manager with overwhelming evidence of wrongdoing by subordinate managers he responded with, "Of course, I have to support management." When I asked for clarification on his statement he started trying to walk it back, but his perspective was clear and, once again, nothing was done to correct the wrongdoing.

PROPOSED SOLUTIONS

One of my engineering mentors by the name of Bill Reid trained me to avoid coming forward with only problems. He also wanted to know I had given thought to potential solutions. This section of the book is offered in that engineering spirit of finding solutions to sometimes seemingly intractable problems.

The most obvious solution to the problems noted above is to revert back to the vision of our founding fathers—small central government with limited authority and responsibility. Many of the agencies noted above would simply vanish under such a scenario (and over time a freer, happier, and more future-oriented American populace would wonder why we ever felt as if we needed such burdensome government overhead).

However, given the fact a large percentage of our citizenry are now dependent upon the Federal government for some or all of their day-to-day existence and would probably be unwilling to sacrifice this for the betterment of the country (or, in many cases, themselves) I offer the following potential solutions.

EVALUATE PROGRAM NEED

There are many, many programs within the Federal government which are in serious need of evaluation to determine whether or not they are actually performing in accordance with their original mandate, or if there is still a need for same. The IHS and USPHS (and possibly the VA) are good examples of this. At the time when both of these organizations were established there were significant numbers of medically indigent persons who were congregating in certain areas (and sharing their various diseases with surrounding populations). In the case of the USPHS it was medically indigent seamen affecting port cities. In the case of the IHS it was Native Americans on reservations.

Most or all American port cities now have adequate medical infrastructure to address medical issues which may present within those coming to their port city. President Reagan understood this and, while he was President, attempted to do away with the USPHS commissioned corps. He closed all USPHS hospitals which were still in operation in port cities and turned them over to the local communities. However, the USPHS commissioned corps lived on as officers found homes in Federal agencies (e.g., the IHS).

Approximately half of all USPHS commissioned officers work for the IHS. This is used as a justification or rationalization of the need for this service since, it is argued, it is difficult to fill professional positions on some of the more remote Indian reservations.[46] However, nobody seems to ask why we are still providing services to this population when there is no treaty obligation to do so, especially after nearly every tribe has been given the advantage of earning revenue via means unavailable to other Americans (i.e., gaming and off-shore banking). This advantage has made some tribes wildly rich and, yet, they continue to receive free health care (and a suite of the other free services, cradle to grave).

The situations which created the justifications for the establishment of various agencies like the IHS and the USPHS have changed. There should be a real review of the need for such programs and real decisions made as to the continued existence of such programs.

FORCE CREATIVE TENSION

One of the most powerful lessons I learned during my career with the USPHS can be found in the Contracting Cutbacks section above. This section discusses how a dramatic reduction in resources for the Oklahoma City Area IHS contracting office resulted in an improvement in service. This was a direct result of the need for the Director to evaluate how he could continue to perform the required work far more efficiently. The private sector automatically has that pressure. However, in the public sector, this can only be achieved through artificial means by deliberate and dramatic reductions in resources (funds and/or FTEs). I'm sure if this became a common practice the agencies would find new and interesting ways to game the system (probably why they never give funds back at the end of the fiscal year—they simply burn them up). This practice of forcing a creative tension on Federal government agencies should be expanded and perfected.

MANDATE MANAGEMENT TRAINING AND/OR EXPERIENCE

The Federal government has a propensity of rewarding long-time employees with management positions even though they may be underprepared for same. It is my contention that this creates significant issues across the Federal government. It is also my contention that it should be incumbent upon any person selected for a management position they have the requisite training and/or experience for such a position (and it's not the Federal government's responsibility to provide it to them). I earned an MBA on my own time with a combination of my own resources and those I had earned and paid for through the Montgomery GI Bill. I thought this would help my career wherever my career ultimately took me. However, I am convinced that my MBA harmed my career with the Federal government as many managers were simply afraid to hire someone who had superior management credentials to theirs (which may very well have been nothing prior to their being selected for the position).

CONSTITUTIONAL AMENDMENT(S)

Due to the Federal government's dual propensity to exempt itself from the very laws that it passes as well as its desire to determine winners and losers based on various categories of Americans there should be a new constitutional amendment (or two) which prohibits these practices. The amendment should mandate all Americans live by the same rules across the board in respect to any and all legislative activity (i.e., the Federal government would be precluded from carving out exemptions for themselves, or anybody else, for anything). The amendment should also preclude the Federal government from collecting any information on Americans which would allow them to categorize Americans in any way. If we are truly a nation of equals then we *all* should be treated as such. If some sort of categorization is needed it can and should be developed by the non-Federal entity requiring same. The current American situation is more akin to the South African apartheid situation I heard so much about in the 1980s and early 1990s (with a reversal of the racial roles). I have done nothing to cause harm to the groups on behalf of whom the Federal government has resolved itself toward correcting past perceived wrongs. However, I have been expected to pay the price for the perceived wrongs. This needs to end.

The current system of reverse discrimination, which goes by various euphemisms (e.g., affirmative action, Indian preference), requires some twisted logic as some try to rationalize the correction of past discrimination by discriminating against those who were not involved in the discrimination—not sure how anybody could have determined this was a good idea at any level. Nearly all of the living American citizens of today have little or nothing to do with having either perpetrated or been victimized by any wrongdoings which occurred in the past. The current situation would be akin to a car pileup which occurred on a bridge in Alabama in 1965 and a Federal judge in 2005 in his/her courtroom in Washington DC deciding all current residents in Alabama, and every other state in the country, should pay damages into perpetuity to the children, grandchildren, great-grandchildren … of those who *may* have been involved in the pileup on the Alabama bridge some four decades earlier. The damages should have been paid by the involved parties in 1965 (and probably were).

It's high time our Federal government began to exist in the real world, not the Netherworld.

APPENDICES

APPENDIX 1.
ABBREVIATIONS AND ACRONYMS

AANHS	Alaska Area Native Health Service
ACLU	American Civil Liberties Union
ACOE	Army Corps of Engineers
ADM	Admiral
AGC	Associated General Contractors
AI/ANCOAC	American Indian/Alaska Native Commissioned Officers Advisory Committee
AWE	Annual Workplace Evaluation
CAPT	Captain (O-6 officer)
CDR	Commander (O-5 officer)
CEO	Chief Executive Officer
CMS	Center for Medicare & Medicaid Services
CNB	Community National Bank
CO	Commissioned Officer
COER	Commissioned Officer Effectiveness Report
COO	Chief Operating Officer
COSTEP	Commissioned Officer Student Training and Extern Program
DES	Division of Engineering Services
DFM	Division of Facilities Management
DHHS	Department of Health and Human Services
DHS	Department of Homeland Security
DHUD	Department of Housing and Urban Development
DOE	Department of Energy
DOL	Department of Labor
DSFC	Division of Sanitation Facilities Construction
EADO	Eastern Arizona District Office
EEO	Equal Employment Opportunity
EMT	Emergency Medical Technician

ENS	Ensign (O-1 officer)
EOC	Emergency Operations Center
ESF	Emergency Support Function
FAR	Federal Acquisition Regulations
FEMA	Federal Emergency Management Agency
FRP	Federal Response Plan
FTE	Full-Time Equivalent
GSA	General Services Administration
IHS	Indian Health Service
INEL	Idaho National Engineering Laboratory
LG	Love Gun (Love Gums)
LCDR	Lieutenant Commander (O-4 officer)
LNO	Liaison Officer
LT	Lieutenant (O-3 officer)
LTJG	Lieutenant Junior Grade (O-2 officer)
LTSO	Lead Transportation Security Officer
M&I	Maintenance and Improvement
MSPB	Merit Systems Protection Board
NEAR	National External Audit Review
NoFEAR	Notification and Federal Employee Antidiscrimination and Retaliation
NOLA	New Orleans, LA
OEHE	Office of Environmental Health and Engineering
OIG	Office of Inspector General
OJT	On-the-Job-Training
OPDIV	Operating Division
OSC	Office of Special Counsel
OSHA	Occupational Safety and Health Act/Administration
OST	Oglala Sioux Tribe
OU	University of Oklahoma
OUHSC	University of Oklahoma Health Science Center
PFO	Principle Federal Official

PCS	Permanent Change of Station
PIP	Performance Improvement Plan
PM	Project Manager or Preventive Maintenance
RV	Recreational Vehicle
SCIA	Senate Committee on Indian Affairs
SeaDO	Seattle District Office
SERT	State Emergency Operations Center
SG	Surgeon General
STRAC	Standing Tall Right Around the Clock
STSO	Supervisory Transportation Security Officer
SWO	Sisseton-Wahpeton Oyate
TSA	Transportation Security Administration
TSM	Transportation Security Manager
TSO	Transportation Security Officer
UND	University of North Dakota
USCG	United States Coast Guard
USPHS	United States Public Health Service
VA	(Department of) Veterans Affairs
VP	Vice President
WTP	Water Treatment Plant

APPENDIX 2.
ARTICLE ON RADM HARRY

The following article appeared in the *August 2003 Vol. XVII, No. 8 Commissioned Corps Bulletin Page 11:*

RADM Robert Harry, Jr. Receives the AI/ANCOAC 2003 Flag Officer Award

RADM Robert Harry, Jr. is the Executive Advisor to the Indian Health Service (IHS) Director and the IHS Representative to the Surgeon General's Policy Advisory Council in Rockville, MD. RADM Harry is an outstanding Public Health Service Commissioned Corps officer who exemplifies leadership to present and future American Indian/Alaska Native community members. He has a distinguished career spanning more than 26 years with IHS. RADM Harry served as Acting Director for the Office of Public Health at IHS Headquarters. He also served on the Indian Health Leadership Council and on the Executive Leadership Group. He was assigned the responsibility for the recent IHS-wide implementation of the requirement for the Health Insurance Portability and Accountability Act (HIPAA) of 1996. RADM Harry's leadership in this area of health reform has directly resulted in tremendous progress in a relatively short period of time. His efforts have enabled the HIPAA Program to work more efficiently and to fully meet the requirements established by the Secretary of the Department of Health and Human Services (HHS). RADM Harry has also been given the responsibility of establishing the Continuity of Operation Plan for IHS and has achieved great success in the area involving national impact and accomplishing a HHS priority. He has also been heavily involved in commissioned corps activities. His knowledge and ability to analyze and solve difficult problems as well as his creative and critical thinking has made his expertise extremely valuable. As an example, his work has been instrumental in contributing to a total review of the entire commissioned corps promotion system.

APPENDIX 3.
MEMO ON SEADO
OFFICE MANAGEMENT

The following is the text from a memo dated 5/12/1998 to my supervisor CDR Michael Weaver requesting assistance/support of me in managing a difficult office environment:

I am providing this memo to formally request your assistance in rectifying the adverse situation I have been placed in within the Yakama Field Office. On May 11, 1998, I expressed during our telecon that I feel as if I have experienced very little, if any, supervisory support from you (the kind that provides confidence in my knowing that I will be supported when I have to make a call prior to approving it through you) since my transfer to this office. Upon my arrival I was involved in overseeing the construction of the new water storage tank south of White Swan, WA. During construction I experienced several problems associated with the contractor Northwest Permastore out of Dallas, OR. The problem(s) primarily involved a highly confrontational demeanor when inspection indicated tank elements were either not being constructed properly (e.g., attempt to construct tank footing with approximately 25% less reinforcement than required) or quality assurance/control checks not performed (e.g., footing fill compaction testing and concrete slump and cylinder break tests). Some of the break tests were eventually performed, but only through the direct intervention of this office (when this was clearly the contractor's responsibility). The 28-day break of the laboratory cured cylinders showed one barely achieving and the other significantly less than the minimum required ultimate strength written in the contract. The 28-day break of the cylinder left on site was never performed. Based on this I desired to require further testing of the footing. Despite your knowledge of the problems I had experienced with this contractor, and of similar past difficulties from this contractor with this agency, additional testing was not supported by you and I was made to feel as if I was out of line. Therefore, I was forced to abandon my request to the contractor for further testing. I have since been made to feel by you as if my efforts in getting this tank constructed properly went too far.

At a meeting in Seattle on March 20, 1998, with Judi Jzyk, Mike Peterson, Dayton Newbrough, and yourself we discussed the format of bid schedules for our contracts which would be administered through Engineering Services. My contention was (and still is) that if we were to do anything with our present format that it should be to add further detail (e.g., a line item for labor costs noting required use of Davis-Bacon wage rates) to our schedules. This would force contractors to think through the actual costs they would incur and, therefore, provide for more responsible bids. It might also preclude award to the contractor who had spent the least time developing their bid (as they often tend to be the low) and, therefore, mitigate future problems. It would also provide us with more information on contractors' cost structure. This could then be used in developing better engineer's estimates for subsequent projects or to highlight problem areas where costs were much different than the engineer's estimate for rebidding purposes. This was not viewed favorably (because philosophically it is the contractor's responsibility to determine the cost line items in his bid) and I had to relinquish in favor of a single line item for all work to be completed on a contract. Despite the fact that I did yield, this meeting has been used as an example by you of my inflexibility.

For the past several months I have experienced conduct and performance problems with both Wanda Jimenez, Secretary, (unwillingness to perform office duties, extended conversations unrelated to work, and a negative disposition toward office staff) and William Thompson, Engineering Technician, (poor productivity, tardiness, insubordination, and belligerence toward supervisor) in this office. I have discussed these problems with you on several occasions. You have been involved in redirecting unfinished work on more than one occasion from Mr. Thompson to another employee in order to get it completed.

Shortly after my arrival at this duty station you had commented to both Dayton Newbrough[47] and myself during a return trip from Pendleton, OR, on Ms. Jimenez's poor performance and some of the difficulties that the previous engineer, Dan Williams, had in dealing with her (essentially the same that I now have). At that time I defended her as I was attempting to give her the benefit of the doubt and because I had not seen the negative side of Ms. Jimenez. Since then I have experienced Ms. Jimenez's unwillingness to perform anything she perceives as beyond the minimum required of her (using the excuse that she had been somehow exploited by Dan Williams and was, therefore, unwilling to perform anything she perceives as extra) to the extent of literally stopping dead in her tracks on two occasions to provide a sigh and a look suggesting that she absolutely did not want to perform the clerical tasks I had requested of her (which by her own later admission were reasonable). At the same time she had abundant time to engage in extended non-work related discourse with Mr. Thompson and other friends on the telephone. In the absence of any supervision from her former supervisor, Margaret Bolte, Sanitarian, I discussed both issues with Ms. Jimenez. These discussions precipitated a clandestine campaign to assassinate my character. She found a willing partner in Mr. Thompson (she was "poisoning" him as related by Kevin Sutton) with whom I had also discussed the extended non-work related discourse and his chronic tardiness (i.e., beyond five minutes) to the Monday morning meeting (approximately five times over the span of approximately three months).

During the period when interpersonal relations were positive with Ms. Jimenez, she had made several comments to me suggesting a very negative demeanor toward other coworkers.

The comments included, "William and I don't consider Kevin [Sutton] a real Indian" and, "I didn't think I could hate anyone as much as I hated Dan [Williams]."

On April 10, 1998, an incident occurred whereby every individual in the office, except for myself, was invited to a farewell luncheon for her former supervisor. The luncheon was organized by Ms. Jimenez and special effort was made by her, including misrepresentations, to ensure that I would not attend. I addressed the luncheon at our Monday morning meeting on April 13, 1998, from the perspective of functioning as a team. Ms. Jimenez implied that she did not believe in the concept of teamwork which is consistent with my past discussions with her where she referred to it as that "team thing." She also made comments that she is "only accountable to Jesus Christ" and that what is needed in this office is prayer because "Satan is at work in this office."

On April 15, 1998, I met with Ms. Jimenez in my office to attempt again to improve our working relationship. I asked her several times to please let bygones be bygones and to move on with a positive attitude. Ms. Jimenez was unwilling to do this as she was bent on uncovering "the truth" about who said she was poisoning Mr. Thompson (this was relayed to her by Ms. Bolte with whom I had discussed this issue during what I thought would be a discreet problem solving meeting). (It was also during this meeting that Ms. Jimenez made the comment that Mr. Thompson was like a little brother to her and that she "would back him up even if she knew he was wrong.")

On April 22, 1998, you and I met with Ms. Jimenez, Mr. Thompson, Don Newquist, and Kevin Sutton.[48] The purpose of the meeting was to discuss the interpersonal relationship difficulties experienced within the office (similar to what had been done in the past with the previous engineer, Dan Williams). You were to lead the discussion. I presented the facts as I saw them (essentially that my relationships with Ms. Jimenez and Mr. Thompson began to deteriorate after I had discussed the conduct

NATHAN D. GJOVIK

and performance issues with each individual) and then saw the meeting turn to my character and management deficiencies. There was no focus or any further mention by you of the root problems of conduct and performance by Ms. Jimenez and Mr. Thompson or of my responsibilities as office manager. Rather, the focus, according to our post-meeting discussion, was on how I needed to adjust my "style" in order to become more flexible.

One of the examples used of my inflexibility was the phone answering policy I had recently implemented. The policy (which outraged Ms. Jimenez) is simply that she is to answer all phone calls while she is in the office. The reasoning as I had explained to you is because 1) it is in her (and only her) job description to perform such duties, and 2) time spent answering the phone was used as an excuse on more than one occasion by Mr. Thompson of why he was not able to complete his work (which to a degree I understand as I have also had to answer the phone innumerable times when Ms. Jimenez was also in the office which siphoned significant time from my schedule). Ms. Jimenez's attitude toward this policy caused her to push the envelope on more than one occasion in order to demonstrate how unreasonable the policy was. The example heralded by Ms. Jimenez and supported by you of the unreasonableness of the policy was a phone call which was missed (the day of the implementation of the policy) due to Ms. Jimenez being in the copy room and, therefore, being unable to hear the phone ringing. However, you did not bother asking her why she had to wait in the copy room for the completion of 20 sets of our new scattered site application during the time the call was missed.

Your administration of the meeting was sympathetic to the excuses and negative propaganda presented by Ms. Jimenez and Mr. Thompson, two individuals with a known and documented history of conduct and performance problems. This legitimized their belief that they have been victimized by my supervision of them for their conduct and performance deficiencies and has completely undermined my authority. I have asked you to help to correct the situation and you have declined claiming that it is simply up to me "to become more flexible."

Your handling and interpretation of the meeting of April 22, 1998, and our dealings over the past year (specific symptomatic examples detailed above) clearly indicate a lack of support for me. Because of the personnel issues involved (and the implied intent of Ms. Jimenez and Mr. Thompson to pursue some sort of future discrimination action by their maintenance of written notes of my alleged wrongdoing) and the immense amount of construction, and therefore problems, I will be responsible for this summer, this is unacceptable to me. I am now extremely apprehensive about any interaction with either Ms. Jimenez or Mr. Thompson and am concerned about the pending construction due to the lack of support from you. Therefore, I am asking that one of the following be performed (listed in order of preference):

1. Assist me in rectifying the personnel management problems in the Yakama Field Office. This can be accomplished by you having sincere discussions with both Ms. Jimenez and Mr. Thompson about why they have been verbally and orally reprimanded for their conduct and performance problems and that it is my job to perform such legitimate actions. Then allow me to manage the program as I am supposed to and **support** me in doing so.

2. Allow and arrange for another individual to supervise me.

3. Assist me in transferring to another position outside the Seattle district of equal or greater billet.

Cc: Richard R. Truitt, PE, Director, OEHE
     Kelly R. Titensor, PE, Director, DSFC
     Michael E. Peterson, PE, Deputy Director, DSFC

APPENDIX 4.
LETTER TO PHOENIX ON
RETIREMENT PLAN ERROR

The following is the text from a letter dated 3/31/2003 demanding correction of retirement funds erroneously placed in the CSRS :

Mr. Richard Gerry, Associate Director, Office of Human Resources
Two Renaissance Square
40 North Central Avenue, Suite 600
Phoenix, Arizona 85004-4424

Re: Erroneous CSRS Deduction

Dear Mr. Gerry:
    I am a registered dietitian. In April of 2001 I gained employment with the U.S. Public Health Service Hospital in Whiteriver, Arizona following a transfer with my husband to the area. I was erroneously placed in a retirement system which has not been available for many years (the Civil Service Retirement System or CSRS). A total of four payments totaling $384.40 were deducted from my first four paychecks into this incorrect retirement system before I questioned the local personnel office about this deduction on my earnings and leave statement. I requested to get this corrected and to provide me with documentation informing me how the monies were allocated. After nearly 22 months I still do not have resolution as to the whereabouts of the funds erroneously deducted from my pay and transferred to the CSRS.
    Through the assistance of Congressman J.D. Hayworth's and Senator Jon Kyl's offices I have received a response letter from Dr. Charles W. Grim, Assistant Surgeon General (see enclosed copy). However, there are several misrepresentations in the letter.

The letter suggests that "the Human Resources Department, Phoenix Area IHS, corrected the error on June 13, 2001." I wish this were true. Your department did place me in the correct retirement system. However, based on my follow up conversations with you and/or your staff on 2/13/2003, 2/25/2003, 3/6/2003, 3/21/2003, and 3/25/2003 it is clear that this issue has not been resolved. During our conversations it was clear that neither you or your staff had reviewed the documentation from the payroll audit referenced in Dr. Grim's response letter which claimed that "the enclosed documentation outlines how the money was distributed and shows the final outcome of the appropriate transfer of monies." As we discussed and your staff agreed during our conversations the audit simply reveals that there is a discrepancy and there is no documentation indicating that the discrepancy has been corrected. This has been exactly my premise now since I first received a copy of the audit report over one year ago. If you or your staff had cared enough to provide a simple cursory review of the documentation you would come to the same conclusion immediately.

The letter from Dr. Grim goes on to say that I expressed that "the signed error notice and supporting documentation from the Central Payroll Office was not acceptable proof that [my] money was transferred appropriately. This was due to the fact that the erroneous $384.40 CSRS contribution was still showing on the earnings and leave statements [I] was receiving at the time." The letter further says that "payroll officials … provided [a] corrected earnings and leave statement." This portion of the letter suggests that I have been unreasonable and that I am so shallow as to think that simply removing the $384.40 from my earnings and leave statements implies that the issue has been corrected. Again, by the admission of your own employees the documentation provided simply indicates that there is a discrepancy and not that it has been corrected. **For nearly 22 months I have simply requested a statement indicating the disposition of my money.**

This request is not unreasonable and I do not appreciate being treated as though I am simple. Simply "whiting out" the values on my earnings and leave statement doesn't cut it. I want a clear and concise statement showing the disposition of these funds.

The letter from Dr. Grim then goes on to indicate that I "was provided with the required documents to have [my] retirement money refunded to [me]." This again is inaccurate. During the final weeks of my employment with the Indian Health Service I requested on several occasions guidance and any necessary forms from your Whiteriver staff as to my options for both my Thrift Savings Plan (TSP) and FERS accounts. I was provided only with a general booklet on the TSP (without any guidance) and nothing whatsoever for my FERS account.

This letter was literally riddled with inaccuracies and spin. I do not blame Dr. Grim for this as I believe the letter had to be written by your department for his signature. The tone and inaccuracy of this response letter do not surprise me based on my past experiences with your department and my telephone conversation with you and your staff on 2/13/2003 where you arrogantly insisted that you would only consider following up on the $43.92 listed for FERS in the "DIFFERENCE" row of the audit report rather than considering all of the data.

Since I received the response letter from Dr. Grim I have been working in good faith directly with you and your staff via phone conferences (mentioned above) in the hopes that this issue would be resolved. Prior to the phone conversation on 3/25/2003 I was required to provide your office with copies of my earnings and leave statements (because your Whiteriver staff had destroyed their file copies within six months of my departure when you are legally required to maintain them for at least six years) so your staff could total the FERS contributions made through individual payroll deductions. Prior to this you had made the assertion that the amount in my FERS account was due to a transfer of the CSRS funds into my FERS account. Based on my provision of the requested earnings and leave statements and the review by your staff it is clear that the amount in my FERS account came entirely from individual payroll deductions and does not reflect any transfer of CSRS funds. At the end of the phone conversation with your staff on 3/25/2003 I was requested to again put in writing what it is that I want to get this issue resolved.

Let me make this crystal clear, **I want a clear and concise statement showing the disposition of the CSRS funds in the amount of \$384.40 which were erroneously deducted from my pay nearly two years ago**. If you cannot provide this statement I want a return of the funds in the form of a check payable to me. Since your department has proven itself over and over again to be inept I am placing a timeline on this request of 5/1/2003. If I do not hear back from you by that time and am forced to write one more letter I will issue this letter and all my prior correspondence along with additional damning information on the experiences I had while an employee of the Whiteriver Indian Health Service hospital to local and national media outlets. I have had enough of this never ending loop of my having to expend my resources to try to correct the error that your department made. *I WANT THIS ISSUE RESOLVED NOW!*

Cc: Congressman J.D. Hayworth
        Senator Jon Kyl
        Senator John McCain
        Dr. Charles Grim, Assistant Surgeon General, Interim Director, IHS
        Mr. Don Davis, Director, Phoenix Area IHS

APPENDIX 5.
MEMO TO PHOENIX ON
EADO MANAGEMENT

The following is the text from the memo dated 12/19/2002 to my supervisor CDR Constant for his use in forwarding it on up the chain of command for their use in making necessary changes:

There are several issues with two employees working in our office which I feel should be addressed for the general betterment of the office. I have numbered the issue-oriented paragraphs below for ease of any future discussion:

1. Shortly after my arrival it became apparent that there were tensions within the office between these two individuals (and another who has since left) and the professionals in the other office division. These tensions manifested a lecture by one of the individuals directed to me on how I need to be "more professional." I was also chastised by the same individual for not consulting with him during the initial inter-office E-mails intended to determine how many officers within our district may be interested in participating in the new USPHS field deployment uniform evaluation. Yesterday I was chastised by the other individual for working up an award recommendation for his employee who provides a great number of services to others in the office, including me. It seems that others within the office need to "walk on eggshells" around these two individuals in order to avoid making them angry. This creates an unhealthy office environment for staff. It also creates communication issues between parties who should be working together for our customers. For

example, I have no idea as to what activities either of these individuals is involved and how it may affect my work or vice-versa. There are also examples of how these two individuals seem to try and isolate themselves (and prevent betterment of office relations) from at least the other office division. Examples include:

- nonparticipation in office gatherings

- nonparticipation in the USPHS field deployment uniform evaluation

- driving a separate Government vehicle when traveling to the same field office on the same day as staff in the other division

2. It seems that these two individuals have ample time to converse with each other and the office secretary about issues unrelated to work. Each morning when I arrive at the office around 8:00 am they are heavily involved in conversation. They generally arrive at the office for their work day between 7:00-7:30 am each day. The conversations generally go until 8:00 am. Therefore, these sessions appear to last for between 30 and 60 minutes each day. I understand that we are all people and, therefore, have a need to socialize with each other. However, there should a limit to the amount of time (say a few minutes per day) spent in such activities. These sessions appear to be habitual and they last for extended periods of duty time (i.e., time for which they are being paid). Also, because of this activity the individual I supervise apparently believes that this activity is acceptable. I have now had to formally discuss it with him at least twice as I believe it has noticeably affected his productivity and I believe my admonishments may leave him with the impression that I am an over-zealous supervisor.

3. There appears to be a double standard within our office with regard to the need to be in uniform. These two individuals are rarely in uniform. Even during the period following 9/11/2001 when we were required by the Area Director to be in uniform daily they were rarely in uniform. Since they are ranking officers with our service and one is a supervisor of many individuals (i.e., someone who should be setting the example for subordinates) I believe this should be corrected.

4. Our current office manager does not appear to be up to the task of properly managing the office as evidenced by the recent activities associated with our evacuation of the office. It was unclear to some within the office, including myself, as to his whereabouts during the initial day(s) of the emergency. He seemed to show callous disregard for securing Government vehicles telling one person that they belonged to GSA and were, therefore, not our vehicles suggesting that we should not be concerned with their removal from the area even though we had the manpower available to do so. He was also not involved in any way that I am aware of in preparing the office for evacuation and possible loss from fire.

As you and I have discussed in the past I have a general management philosophy that "everyone brings something to the table" meaning that each member has knowledge, skills, and/or abilities to offer to the group. These two individuals certainly do appear to have strengths, including their tenure in this geographic area. However, I also believe that any strength taken to an extreme can be a weakness. It may very well be that these two individuals have been in their positions long enough to now take them for granted. Also, they may be very comfortable in their present situations and see only a limited need to apply themselves.

I believe the solutions to these issues are through active management. Specific recommendations would include:

a. Transfer office manager responsibilities to the District Engineer.

b. Supervisors of these two individuals should closely monitor their productivity, require conformance with uniform wear instruction, and encourage them to consider transferring or retiring in order to allow "new blood" to enter the district.

The outcome of not addressing the above issues will most assuredly be continued frustration by individuals such as you and me and turnover of same.

APPENDIX 6.
THE ILL-INFORMED WALRUS

The following fable appeared in Management Review, published by the American Management Association:

"How's it going down there?" barked the big walrus from his perch on the big rock near the shore. He waited for the good word. Down below, the smaller walruses conferred among themselves. Things weren't going well at all, but no one wanted to break the news to the Old Man. He was the biggest and wisest walrus in the herd, and he knew his business and they didn't want to disappoint him or put him in a foul mood.

"What will we tell him?" whispered Basil, the walrus XO. He well remembered how the Old Man had raved at him the last time the herd caught less than its quota of herring, and he had no desire for that experience again. Nevertheless, for several weeks the water level in the nearby bay had been falling constantly, and it had become necessary to travel farther to catch the dwindling supply of herring. Someone should tell the Old Man. But who? And how?

Finally Basil spoke up: "Things are going pretty well, Boss," he said. The thought of the receding water line made his heart grow heavy, but he went on: "As a matter of fact, the beach seems to be getting larger."

The Old Man grunted. "Fine, fine," he said. "That will give us a bit more elbow room." He closed his eyes and continued basking in the sun.

The next day brought more trouble. A new herd of walruses moved in down the beach, and with the shortage of herring, the invasion could be dangerous. No one wanted to tell the Boss, though only he could take the steps necessary to meet the new competition. Basil approached the Old Man. After some small talk, he said, "Oh, by the way Boss, a new herd seems to have moved into our territory." The Old Man's eyes snapped open, and he filled his great lungs in preparation for a mighty bellow. But Basil added quickly, "Of course, we don't expect any trouble. They don't look like herring-eaters to me. More likely interested in minnows. And as you know, we don't bother with minnows ourselves."

The Old Man let out the air with a long sigh. "Good, good," he said. "No point in our getting excited over nothing then, is there?"

Things didn't get any better in the weeks that followed. One day, peering down from his rock, the Old Man noticed that part of the herd seemed to be missing. Summoning the XO, he grunted peevishly, "What's going on, Basil? Where is everyone?" Poor Basil didn't have the courage to tell the Old Man that many of the younger walruses were leaving to join the new herd. Clearing his throat nervously he said, "Well, Boss, we've been tightening up things a bit. You know, getting rid of some of the dead wood. After all, a herd is only as good as the walruses in it."

"Run a tight ship, I always say," the Old Man grunted. "Glad to hear that all is going so well."

Before long, everyone but Basil had left to join the new herd, and Basil realized that the time had come to tell the Old Man the facts. Terrified but determined, he flopped up to the large rock. "Chief," he said, "I have bad news. The rest of the herd has left you." The Old Walrus was so astonished that he couldn't even work up a good bellow. "Left me?" he cried. "All of them? But why? How could this happen?"

Basil didn't have the heart to tell him, so he merely shrugged helplessly.

"I can't understand it," the old Walrus said. "And just when everything was going so well."

MORAL: What the Boss likes to hear isn't always what he needs to know.

APPENDIX 7.
LETTER TO SG CARMONA
ON INDIAN PREFERENCE

The following is the text from a letter dated 3/27/2004 advising the Surgeon General of the issues associated with Indian Preference promulgated by the IHS and suggesting the means to address same :

Surgeon General Carmona
Office of the Surgeon General
5600 Fishers Lane, Room 18-66
Rockville, MD 20857

Re: Indian Preference

Sir:

Yesterday I attended the Evergreen Chapter of the Commissioned Officer Association luncheon meeting in Seattle, WA where you spoke and entertained questions. I asked you a question about your opinion on the Indian Preference policy promulgated by the Indian Health Service (IHS). You suggested that it is a difficult issue and told me that if I have any recommendations to forward same. That is the purpose of this communiqué.

As I stated in my question at the luncheon meeting I have been employed by the IHS for my entire USPHS career (nearly 15 years). During that time I have not been considered for seven positions for which I applied due to Indian Preference. Note that this does not include those positions for which I did not apply because I knew of one or more Native American applicants who would be tendering their application. Having experienced this I have found my career within the IHS extremely frustrating and cannot in good conscience recommend this agency for employment to anyone without Native American ancestry.

In past conversations with agency leadership (including your former chief of staff) regarding this issue I believe I have been tagged as a "whiner" as I relayed my personal experiences. Therefore, I welcome the opportunity to be heard by someone of your rank and distinction.

During my career I have been detailed directly to a Native American tribe who had contracted (Title 1) the sanitation facility construction program from the US Government (Indian Health Service). The Tribe had a policy of hiring only Native American employees and non-Natives only if a Native American could not be found (similar to the Indian Preference policy of the IHS). I understand that this is their right as a sovereign entity to fashion such employment policies.

I believe it is the responsibility of the US Government to provide truly equal opportunity to all of its citizens when they apply for US Government positions. I also believe that it is the responsibility of the US Government to hire only the best qualified candidates when staffing agencies such as the IHS in order to provide the best possible service to agency customers. I believe the Indian Preference policy promulgated by the IHS to be antithetical to these responsibilities.

I understand the original intent of Indian Preference to be the noble ideal of increased participation within the agency for Native Americans. However, as stated above that exists in the form of Public Law 93-638 which allows tribes the opportunity to contract/compact the agency programs that serve their constituencies. Once programs are contracted/compacted the tribes have control over the program including whatever employment practices they deem appropriate.

From my perspective the best solution for the long term health of the IHS is to abandon the policy of Indian Preference. I recognize that this solution is simple to author and may be difficult to implement. Based on my research the policy has its roots in 25 U.S.C. 472 which took a major shift in 1979 as a result of litigation involving a Native American from Oklahoma named Don Tyndall (I do not have a cite for this case, but it is probably called Tyndall v U.S.). Therefore, I believe the means to address the issue would be through statutory law.

If you believe the premise that any service organization is only as good as the people which make up the organization then you have to believe that high organizational quality is a function of attracting and maintaining the best qualified people. I propose that the IHS has already fallen deep into the abyss of mediocrity (a natural byproduct when the best qualified applicants are not necessarily hired and the larger candidate pool is disenfranchised).

I believe the stakes are enormous for the IHS and have been grossly underestimated (or perhaps ignored) by past leadership. Since the IHS has traditionally been the agency from which many in other agencies begin their careers the stakes are also high for the entire USPHS. However, I also believe that dissolution of the Indian Preference policy and strong leadership can right this ship and put it back on course to be the premier health care agency that our customers expect.

I can be reached at 206-615-2454 if you have comments or questions regarding this communiqué.

Sincerely,
CDR Nathan D. Gjovik, PE, RS, MS, MBA, MPH

APPENDIX 8.
BRIEFING ON HURRICANE
KATRINA DEPLOYMENT

The following is taken from a briefing I provided on 3/16/2006 during a presentation to DHHS Region X Government staff:

My name is CDR Nathan Gjovik. I was deployed on 9/25—10/9/2005 to assist in relief efforts following Hurricanes Katrina and Rita. I was initially told that I would be part of a forward element moving into Lake Charles, LA. I was provided airline tickets for a red-eye itinerary to Baton Rouge and told to contact the State Emergency Response Team (SERT) once I arrived. Upon my arrival I tried a couple of times to call the SERT on my cell phone, but nobody answered the phone. Having no instruction I thought it would be wise to rent a vehicle, preferably a four wheel drive since the roads may be pretty rough between Baton Rouge and Lake Charles. I did same and was eventually able to reach someone at the SERT. They gave me directions to the SERT and I proceeded to report there. Upon my arrival the situation seemed very chaotic and it was clear that they were not expecting me nor did they seem to have any idea what to do with me. I spent a couple of hours attending a conference call with one of the special needs shelters in Alexandria, LA.

Following the conference call it was decided that I should report to CAPT Michael Milner in New Orleans. I assisted CAPT Debra Lewis in collecting her bags and she and I drove together down to New Orleans while following a lead vehicle with other PHS staff. The roads coming into New Orleans were generally pretty good. However, once we arrived in the city driving became a bit dicey as several streets were blocked or partially blocked by debris, abandoned cars, boats, downed power and telephone lines, etc. I dropped off CAPT Lewis at Ochsner

Hospital where she would be spending the next two weeks as the commanding officer for PHS assets assigned to the hospital.

I then proceeded to the Hyatt Hotel in downtown New Orleans where the city's emergency operations center (EOC) was located. There I met several PHS staff who were working directly with city officials. One of them was CAPT Paul Wagner. He had a room at the Omni Royal Orleans Hotel in the French Quarter, a 4-star hotel, and offered to share his room with me until I could find other lodging arrangements.

The following morning I briefly met CAPT Michael Milner, who was also staying at the Omni, and followed him down to the Principal Federal Official (PFO) headquarters which was located in the cruise ship terminal. This was the nerve center for the Federal response to the hurricane relief effort. CAPT Milner advised me that I would be serving as a liaison officer (LNO) there at the PFO along with another individual. CDR Sharon White arrived shortly thereafter to serve as the other LNO. CAPT Milner provided us with a briefing on hot issues and then introduced us to a few of the staff before leaving to catch a flight home for some R&R. His replacement Dr. Dalton Paxman arrived the following day. Much of his time over the week he was available to us was spent trying to get a handle on what HHS assets were present in the greater New Orleans area and what they were doing.

CDR White and I immediately set out trying to get a handle on what was going on around us. We formulated a plan and began getting ourselves "plugged in" by making contacts and asking questions. We fell into a routine dictated by the twice daily update meetings, one in the morning and one in the evening, which were led by the US Coast Guard who had command of the PFO.

Our responsibility at the PFO was to report on emergency support function 8 (ESF-8) activities and to ensure coordination of those activities with other ESFs. This was very challenging since we had no knowledge of some of our assets and there did not seem to be any central authority over all of our assets. However, we did the best we could by closely monitoring all E-mail traffic, reports, and reaching out to those we knew were in the area. We started a database containing a listing of HHS personnel in the greater New Orleans area and were continually adding and updating same as staff rotated in and out and new information became available.

After a few nights at the Omni Hotel all Federal response workers were asked to vacate in order to allow room availability for residents returning to the area. Alternate quarters were setup for us in one of two cruise ships berthed just outside the PFO. All rooms were shared and seemed very small and crowded with all of our gear. However, the beds were comfortable and the food was great and I was very thankful to have such nice accommodations on a deployment. My last night in the area was spent at Camp Phoenix in Baton Rouge. There I slept on a cot in the gymnasium with several other COs.

During my tour at the PFO I typically reported each day by 6:00 am and worked until anywhere between 6:00 pm and 10:00 pm. By the end of my deployment I was very exhausted. However, other services like the Coast Guard had their people on 4-week rotations (twice as long as what most PHS staff were working). It was nice getting back to my regular job and working hours.

Highlights for me during my deployment included a helicopter tour of the city and learning from the exemplary leadership and organization by the US Coast Guard command.

Areas where we could improve include:

- better organization of our entire response effort (e.g., deployment and tracking of assets, greater communication, establishment of a chain of command, etc.)

- better use of available resources (e.g., create complimentary and diverse teams)

- improve response quality via longer deployments and better rotation management (e.g., ensure overlap with departing and backfilling staff)
- provide stronger leadership

APPENDIX 9.
TREATY WITH THE WINNEBAGOES

The following treaty was included within the "Winnebago Treaty Hospital Blessing & Dedication" ceremony program dated 4/8/2004:

TREATY WITH THE WINNEBAGOES September 15,1832

Made and concluded, at Fort Armstrong, Rock Island, Illinois, between the United States of America, by their Commissioners, Major General Winfield Scott of the United States' Army, and his Excellency John Reynolds, Governor of the State of Illinois, and the Winnebago nation of Indians, represented in general Council by the undersigned Chiefs, Headmen, and Warriors.

ARTICLE I. The Winnebago nation hereby cede to the United States, forever, all the lands, to which said nation have title or claim, lying to the south and east of the Wisconsin river, and the Fox river of Green Bay; bounded as follows, viz: beginning at the mouth of the Pee-kae-tal-a-ka river; thence up Rock river to its source; thence, with a line dividing the Winnebago nation from other Indians east of the Winnebago lake, to the Grande Chute; thence, up Fox river to the Winnebago lake, and with the northwestern shore of said lake, to the inlet of Fox river; thence, up said river to Lake Puckaway, and with the eastern shore of the same to its most southeasterly bend; thence with the line of a purchase made of the Winnebago nation, by the treaty at Prairie du Chien, the first day of August, one thousand eight hundred and twenty-nine, to the place of beginning.

ARTICLE II. In part consideration of the above cession, it is hereby stipulated and agreed, that the United States grant to the Winnebago nation, to be held as other Indian lands are held, that part of the tract of country on the west side of the Mississippi, known, at present, as the Neutral ground, embraced within the following limits, viz: beginning on the west bank of the Mississippi river, twenty miles above the mouth of the upper Ioway river, where the line of the lands purchased of the Sioux Indians, as described in the third article of the treaty of Prairie du Chien, of the fifteenth day of July, one thousand eight hundred and thirty, begins; thence, with said line, as surveyed and marked, to the eastern branch of the Red Cedar creek, thence, down said creek, forty miles, in a straight line, but following its windings, to the line of purchase, made of the Sac and Fox tribes of Indians, as designated in the second article of the before recited treaty, and thence along the southern line of said last mentioned purchase, to the Mississippi, at the point marked by the surveyor, appointed by the President of the United States, on the margin of said river; and thence, up said river, to the place of beginning. The exchange of the two tracts of country to take place on or before the first day of June next; that is to say, on or before that day, all the Winnebagoes now residing within the country ceded by the, as above, shall leave the said country, when, and not before they shall be allowed to enter upon the country granted by the United States, in exchange.

ARTICLE III.   But, as the country hereby ceded by the Winnebago nation is more extensive and valuable than that given by the United States in exchange; it is further stipulated and agreed, the United States pay to the Winnebago nation, annually, for twenty-seven successive years, the first payment to be made in September of the next year, the sum of ten thousand dollars, in specis; which sum shall be paid to the said nation at Prairie du Chien, and Fort Winnebago, in sums proportional to the numbers residing most conveniently to those places respectively.

ARTICLE IV.   It is further stipulated and agreed, that the United States shall erect a suitable building, with a garden, and field attached, somewhere near Fort Crawford, or Prairie du Chien, and establish and maintain therein, for the term of twenty-seven years, a school for the education, including clothing, board, and lodging, of such Winnebago children as may be voluntarily sent to it: the school to be conducted by two or more teachers, male and female, and the said children to be taught reading, writing, arithmetic, gardening, agriculture, carding, spinning, weaving, and sewing, according to their ages and sexes, and such other branches of useful knowledge as the President of the Unites States may prescribe: Provided, that the annual cost of the school shall not exceed the sum of three thousand dollars. And, in order that the said school may be productive of the greatest benefit to the Winnebago nation, it is hereby subjected to the visits and inspections of his Excellency the Governor of the State of Illinois for the time being; the United States' General Superintendents of Indian Affairs; of the United States' agents who may be appointed to reside among the Winnebago Indians, and of any officer of the United States' Army, who may be of, or above the rank of Major: Provided, That the commanding officer of Fort Crawford shall make such visits and inspections frequently, although of an inferior rank.

ARTICLE V. And the United States further agree to make to the said nation of Winnebago Indians the following allowances, for the period of twenty-seven years, in addition to the considerations herein before stipulated; that is to say: for the support of six agriculturists, and purchase of twelve yokes of oxen, ploughs, and other agricultural implements, a sum not exceeding two thousand five hundred dollars per annum; to the Rock river band of Winnebagoes, one thousand five hundred pounds of tobacco, per annum; for the services and attendance of a physician at Prairie du Chien, and of one at Fort Winnebago; each; two hundred dollars; per annum.

ARTICLE VI. It is further agreed that the United States remove and maintain, within the limits prescribed in this treaty, for the occupation of the Winnebagoes, the blacksmith's shop, with the necessary tools, iron, and steel, heretofore allowed to the Winnebagoes, on the waters of the Rock river, by the third article of the treaty made with the Winnebago nation, at Prairie du Chien, on the first day of August, one thousand eight hundred and twenty nine.

ARTICLE VII. And it is further stipulated and agreed by the United States, that there shall be allowed and issued to the Winnebagoes, required by the terms of this treaty to remove within their new limits, soldiers' rations of bread and meat, for thirty days: Provided, That the whole number of such rations shall not exceed sixty thousand.

ARTICLE VIII. The United States, at the request of the Winnebago nation of Indians, aforesaid, further agree to pay, to the following named persons, the sums set opposite their names respectively, viz: To Joseph Ogee, two hundred and two dollars and fifty cents, To William Wallace, four hundred dollars, and
To John Dougherty, four hundred and eighty dollars; amounting, in all, to one thousand and eighty-two dollars and fifty cents, which sum is in full satisfaction of the claims brought by said persons against said Indians, and by them acknowledged to be justly due.

ARTICLE IX. On demand of the United States' Commissioners, it is expressly stipulated and agreed, that the Winnebago nation shall promptly seize and deliver up to the commanding officer of some United States' military post, to be dealt with according to law, the following individual Winnebagoes, viz: Koo-zee-ray-Kaw, Moychenum-Kaw, Tshik-o-ke-maw-kaw, Ah-hun-see-kaw, and Waw-see-nee-kay-hse-weekaw, who are accused of murdering, or of being concerned in the murdering of certain American citizens, at or near the Blue mound, in the territory of Michigan: Nau-saw-nay-he-kaw, and Tong-ro-nave-koo-ray-see-ray-kaw; who are accused of murdering or of being concerned in murdering, one or more American citizens, at or near Killogg's Grove, in the State of Illinois; and also Wow-kee-sun-shave and his son, who wounded, in attempting to kill, an American soldier, at or near Lake Koshke-nong in the said territory; all of which offenses were committed in the course of the past spring and summer. And till these several stipulations are faithfully complied with by the Winnebago Nation, it is further agreed that the payment of this annuity of ten thousand dollars, secured by this treaty, shall be suspended.

ARTICLE X. At the special request of the Winnebago Nation, the United States agree to grant, by patent, in fee simple, to the following named persons, all of whom are Winnebogoes by blood, lands as follows: To Pierre Paquette, three sections; to Pierre Pagette, junior, one section; to Therese Paquette one section; and to Caroline Harney, one section. The lands to be designated under the direction of the President of the United States, within the country herein ceded by the Winnebago Nation.

ARTICLE XI. In order to prevent misapprehensions that might disturb peace and friendship between the parties to this treaty, it is expressly understood that no bank or party of Winnebagoes shall reside, plant, fish, or hunt after the first day of June next, on any portion of the country herein ceded to the United States.

ARTICLE XII. This treaty shall be obligatory on the contracting parties, after it shall be ratified by the President and the Senate of the United states. Done at Fort Armstrong, Rock Island, Illinois, this fifteenth day of September, One thousand eight hundred and thirty-two.

WINFIELD SCOTT,
JOHN REYNOLDS

Prairie du Chien Deputation.

Tshee-o-nuzh-ee-kaw, war chief, (Kar-ray-mau-nee),
Wau-kaun-hah-kaw, or snake skin, (Day-kan-ray),
Khay-rah-tshoan-saip-kaw, or Black Hawk,
Wah-kaun-kaw, or snake,
Sau-sau-mau-nee-kaw, or he who walks naked,
Hoantsh-straw-straw, or white bear,
Hoo-tshoap-kaw, or four legs,
Mau-hee-her-kar-rah, or flying cloud, son of Dog Head,
Tshah-shee-rah-wau-kaw, or he who takes the leg of a deer in his mouth,
Mau-tree-wuk-kaw, or cloudy,
Ho-rah-paw-kaw, or eagle head,
Pash-tray-ray-kaw, or fire holder,
Eazhcok-hat-pay-kaw, or big gun
Xo-ro-ko-ro-hee-kaw, or bell,
Haun-heigh-kee-paw-kaw, or the night that meets.

Fort Winnebago Deputation.

Hee tshah-wau-saip-straw-straw, or white war eagle, De-kaw-ray sr.
Hoo-wau-nee-kaw, or little elk, (orator) one of the Kay-ra-men-nees,
Wau-kaun-tshah-hay-ree-kaw, or roaring thunder, Four legs nephew,
Mau-nah-pey-kaw, or soldier, (Black Wolf's son),
Wau-kaun-tshah-ween-kaw, or whirling thunder,
Mau-nee-ho-no-nik, or little walker, son of Fire branded,
To-shun-uk-ho-no-nik, or little otter, son of Sweet Corn,
Tshah-tshun-hat-pay-kaw, or big wave, son of Clear Sky.
Mau-wau-ruck, or the muddy,
Mau-shoatab-kaw, or blue earth,
Wee-tshah-un-kuk, or forked tail.

Rock River deputation.

Kau-ree-kaw-see-kaw, white crow, (the blind),
Wau-kaun-wson-kaw, or whirling thunder,
Mo-rab-tshay-kaw, or little priest,
Mau-nah-pey-kaw, or soldier
Ho-rah-hoank-kaw, or war eagle,
Nautsh-kay-peen-kaw, or good heart,
Keesh-koo-kaw,
Wee-tshun-kaw, or goose,
Wau-kaun-nig-ee-nik, or little snake,
Hoo-way-skaw, or white elk,
Hay-noamp-kaw, or two horns,
Hauk-kay-kaw, or screamer,
Ee-nee-wonk-shik-kaw, or stone man.

Signed in presence of, R. Bache, Captain Ord. Secretary to the Commission. Jos. M. Street, United States Indian Agent. John H. Kinzie, Sub Agt. Indian Affairs. Abrm Eustis. H. Dodge, Major U. S. Rangers. Alexr. R. Thompson, Major United States Army. William Harvey, Capt. 1st Infantry. E. Kirby, Paymaster United States Army. Albion T. Crow. John Marsh. Pierre Paquette, Interpreter. P.H. Galt, Assistant Adjutant General. S W. Wilson. Benj. F. Pike. J.B.F. Russell, Captain 5th Infantry. S. Johnson, Captain 2nd Infantry, John Clitz, Adj. 2nd Infantry. Jno. Pickell, Lieutenant 4th Artillery. A. Drane, A. Qr. U.S.A. J.R. Smith, 1st Lieutenant 2nd Infantry. H. Day Lieutenant 2nd Infantry. William Mayradier, Lieutenant and A. D. C. P. G. Hambaugh, S. Burbank, Lieutenant 1st Infantry. J.H. Prentiss, Lieutenant 1st Artillery. E. Rose, Lieutenant 3rd Artillery. L.J. Beall, Lieutenant 1st Infantry. Antoine Le Clure.

To the Indian names are subjoined marks.

APPENDIX 10.
TRIBAL LETTER ON
CONSTRUCTION SAFETY

The following is a letter from Lisa Losano, SWO attorney and Contracting Officer for the new health center and associated quarters project, dated 1/10/2007:

247

Sisseton ~ Wahpeton Oyate
OF THE LAKE TRAVERSE RESERVATION
LEGAL DEPARTMENT

OLD AGENCY BOX 509 • AGENCY VILLAGE, SOUTH DAKOTA 57262-0509
PHONE: (605) 698-3966 • FAX: (605) 698-7844

January 10, 2007

Via Facsimile @ 206-615-2466 and Electronic Mail

Nathan Gjovik
Technical Officer
Indian Health Service
Division of Engineering Services
2201 6ᵗʰ Avenue, M/S 24
Seattle, WA 98121-2500

Re: Safety Issues Noted in Correspondence Dated December 22, 2006

Dear Nathan:

Rather than discuss the issue ad nausea, I will simply state that the Tribe and Gordon Construction take safety issues very seriously and comply with the minimum standards of the Occupational Safety Health Administration (OSHA). You have reported the Tribe and Gordon Construction to OSHA on at least two occasions and OSHA has visited the site both times. NO violations have been issued.

The overhead work being conducted in the photograph of your December 22, 2006 correspondence is for installation of ceiling tile. OSHA has already communicated to us that this type of work does not require a hardhat.

Furthermore, those safety precautions utilized for confined space work are implemented when such work is being conducted. You did not see someone conducting work in a confined space not taking the precaution. Rather, you assumed that the Tribe and Gordon Construction would not utilize the precautions based upon a "lack of awareness" (as you put it) of a tribal employee.

Your conduct leads the Tribe to conclude that you are intentionally harassing Gordon Construction and the Tribe and are interfering with our ability to perform under our '638 contracts with Indian Health Service. The inference that the Tribe and Gordon Construction are not complying with OSHA is inappropriate and unprofessional.

BIG COULEE • BUFFALO LAKE • ENEMY SWIM • HEIPA/VEBLEN • LAKE TRAVERSE • LONG HOLLOW • OLD AGENCY

This is your last warning to cease your continual need to find something wrong with the OSHA compliance of the Tribe and Gordon Construction. The Tribe has contracted to take full responsibility for compliance with OSHA. Indian Health Service does not have any responsibility for the Tribe's compliance with OSHA.

Any further conduct on your part with regard to this issue will result in severe action being taken by the Tribe, i.e. a recommendation that a resolution be enacted by the Tribal Council requesting your banishment from Reservation lands which includes those lands leased to Indian Health Service.

Again, the Tribe welcomes your constructive comments during the construction of the Health Care Center. However, your current conduct is far from "constructive" but merely impedes the Tribe's ability to abide by its other responsibilities by unnecessarily forcing the Tribe to deal with unwarranted OSHA complaints.

If you would like to discuss this further, please contact me directly. Otherwise, I consider this matter addressed and CONCLUDED.

Sincerely yours,

Lisa M. Llosano
Legal Counsel
Contracting Officer

Cc: Tribal Council & Executives
       Abram Vinikoor, DES-Seattle, Contracting Officer
       Ken Harper, DES-Seattle

APPENDIX 11.
TRIBAL LETTER RESPONSE
MEETING NOTES

The following notes pertain to a meeting with Kenneth R. Harper (KH), Director, Division of Engineering Services, and Michael R. Weaver (MW), Project Management Branch Chief, on Thursday January 11, 2007, from approximately 1300 to approximately 1530.

Background:

I was approached by MW and asked if I could meet with he and KH in the conference room in approximately five minutes. The purpose of the discussion would be to discuss a letter written by Lisa Losano (LL), Sisseton-Wahpeton Oyate of the Lake Traverse Reservation attorney which was received by fax on Monday January 10, 2007 (see attachment 1).

Discussion Notes:

The meeting began with KH asking me why I included the reference to the hard hat in my recent pre-final inspection letter to the SWO (see attachment 2). I explained that I included same because it was something that I observed while onsite. I continued by explaining that this was the lesser of the safety issues I observed with the lack of confined space entry being the primary issue. KH asked if I witnessed someone in a confined space with no safety provisions. I responded in the negative, while noting that I had stopped IHS staff from going down into the confined space, and explained that when I identified the ground source heat pump vault installation as a confined space Dan Donnell (DD), the Tribal employee responsible for ensuring safety on the site, was not aware of what a confined space was or the required provisions which I then explained. KH suggested that since I had not witnessed an actual infraction I had no basis for the determination that there had not been any infraction. I stated that there was a chance that the contractor (Gordon Construction) could have installed the vault and all of its plumbing and electrical contents during the late night and early morning hours which would explain why DD would not be aware of confined space safety but that this was highly unlikely. KH acknowledged this but also acknowledged that LL had indicated that confined space safety was performed in her letter and, therefore, it was done. I suggested that this was probably not true.

KH & MW proceeded to advise me on how the individual noted in my photo should not be required to wear a hard hat since he was reported to be installing ceiling tile. They cited the OSHA requirement for use of hard hats and read an explanatory letter pertaining to the lack of a need for hard hats if working on a scaffold. I suggested that the scaffold letter did not necessarily pertain to overhead electrical work. I then indicated that I did not know that the individual was placing ceiling tile at the time and that as far as I knew he was performing electrical work. MW indicated that he did not know why I included the reference to the hard hat issue. I responded that he had the opportunity to review the letter before it was sent and that if he had an objection to same that he should have indicated it at that time, not now after we had received a letter from LL attacking my efforts.

KH asked me if the OSHA had cited the contractor for any infractions. I responded that he knew the answer to that was no and the reasons why—he had directed the contracting officer to provide LL advance notice of OSHA's planned first visit and that the OSHA staff responding to the second visit had every intention of citing the subcontractor depicted in my E-mail but that the sub had mobilized off the site by the time they had arrived. He then suggested that because OSHA had not found any violations there was no legitimate claim to safety violations.

I indicated that I thought I was qualified to determine obvious safety violations and that this entire discussion was improper as I was being placed on the defensive for simply noting my observations and that I felt strongly that they should be supporting me. KH suggested that they have been supportive of my efforts through the last letter issued by Abram Vinikoor (AV), Contracting Officer, regarding this issue. I indicated that the letter was not strong enough. KH mentioned that he had added verbiage regarding safety and I acknowledged same. I stated that this was better but it was still not enough to send a strong message about the importance of safety. I then advised him that AV had undermined the indicated verbiage during our last teleconference with LL by simply accepting LL's statement that she had no intention of addressing the issues included in the letter—all of them, including safety—even though a response was clearly required by our letter.

KH indicated that under the '638 regulations it is our responsibility to provide assistance to the Tribe in meeting requirements such as construction safety. I responded that I understood this and have been providing assistance all along but noted that what we were doing was not working as evidenced by the continued violations. I then stated that I believe that there are two parts to correcting any problem, the first of which being a recognition that there is a problem, and that absent this recognition it cannot be corrected. I stated that I believe this to be the case here.

KH asked what I was asking from them and I indicated that I would like a stern response letter to the Tribe indicating that we expect OSHA requirements be met on this as well as the quarters project. KH stated that he was not going to do that. I suggested that I was disappointed in both he and MW and he indicated that he was also disappointed in me. He proceeded by revealing to me that someone had indicated to him before they hired me that he should not hire me as I am a problem employee. I asked who said that and KH stated that he would not tell me but that they were "not in Phoenix, higher up."

KH suggested that I shouldn't be so inflexible and that my behavior was childish. I stated that I didn't belong there as I felt tears welling up in my eyes. I then stated that safety is an issue that we should not compromise at all and pointed to MW and advised him that he used to believe that. KH indicated that he had once buried someone in a trench and I responded that he should then be a champion for safety. He suggested that he was and I responded that he certainly was not in this case. MW suggested that there had only been a few major safety violations on this project and that no project is perfect. I then asked MW how many violations were acceptable to him and he responded that none would be the goal. KH asked how many major issues there had been on this project and I found my notes pertaining to same and noted that there had been

- three instances of trench safety violations involving a variety of issues noted by a several people,
- two instances of fall protection violations noted by two people (Hank Payne and I),
- two instances of equipment safety noted by two people (Hank Payne and I),
- several instances of lack of personal protective equipment (e.g., hard hats, safety glasses, ear protection, etc.) noted by several people, and
- this did not include the recent hard hat and confined space issues.

I then asked him for examples of how I had been inflexible in the past and he noted my efforts to get medical triage kits purchased for our building. I responded that I had brought it up a second time because I felt that it was important issue that had been quashed by one individual and that nearly everyone else familiar with the issue had agreed with me that we should purchase and pre-position them within our building. I also pointed out that both MW and KH had agreed with me as to the need. KH said that he had been expecting me to follow-up on this with a kit for our office and asked why I had not prepared same. I indicated that I had been directed to coordinate my efforts with CAPT Stevermer and that he did not support the purchase of such kits. I explained that I had provided the necessary information in my first effort to raise the issue and that I had reached my frustration threshold and was not willing to pursue it any further. I also indicated that my EMT licensure was expiring within two months and that the idea was to have these kits in the hands of those who would be medically qualified to use them throughout the building. I finished by stating that this was not an example of my inflexibility. No further examples were provided.

The meeting ended with all parties frustrated. No follow-up was planned.

The following notes pertain to a meeting with Kenneth R. Harper (KH, Director, Division of Engineering Services) on Friday January 26, 2007, from approximately 0900 to approximately 1000.

Background:

On January 16, 2007, I had sent an E-mail to KH which read as follows:

During the meeting between yourself, Michael Weaver, and myself last Thursday (1/11) to discuss safety issues at Sisseton you made a comment that very much troubled me. You stated that you had been warned against hiring me because I was a "problem employee." I asked you who had given you that warning and you responded that you would not divulge that, but that it wasn't anyone from the Phoenix Area, "it was higher up." Can you tell me why you brought this up? Also, can you tell me why the individual suggested I was a "problem employee" (i.e., what is the basis for this label)?

KH responded on January 18, 2007, suggesting that I "misunderstood his comment" and that we could discuss this further upon his return to the office if I desired. We scheduled to meet in his office on Friday January 26, 2007, at 0830.

Discussion notes:

KH was not available when I checked his office at 0830. He called me at approximately 0845 and said that he was available to meet if I still desired to do so. I responded that I did and reported to his office a few minutes later.

The substantive discussion began with KH backing away from his previous comment that the individual who made the comment about me being a problem employee was not in Phoenix and that they were "higher up." When I pressed him that he had clearly said that he then stated that he had checked with several people including those in Phoenix and had heard similar comments from others including from Phoenix. I asked who they were and he said that he would not share that information.

The rest of the meeting was spent revisiting (arguing over) my handling of the Sisseton project-related issues. I noted that KH agreed that I did the right thing in stopping some excavation work during a site visit due to an unsafe trench condition. However, he suggested that my noting of other safety issues (e.g., recent confined space safety and personal protective equipment—hard hats) was inappropriate because it is the Tribe's responsibility to address safety issues. I noted that I believe there is a gap in the logic—in one case it is appropriate for me to shut down the project and in the other the mere mention was inappropriate. He stated that it is the Tribe's responsibility to ensure construction safety. I responded that I understood that, and asked as to what we should do if they don't provide construction safety. He responded that we should simply document it. I stated that is what I was doing and he suggested that there was no proof that the items I was mentioning were legitimate since the OSHA had not issued a citation during either of their visits. I stated that he knew that was not accurate and corrected his statement by explaining that, upon his own insistence as well as that of Abram Vinikoor (AV), the Tribe had been provided a "heads-up" by AV that the OSHA would be on-site prior to their first visit and that the OSHA intended to issue citations during their second visit, but the offending subcontractor had already mobilized off the site by the time they arrived.

The meeting ended with both parties frustrated. No follow-up was planned.

APPENDIX 12.
ALTERNATE PM RACISM
MEETING NOTES

The following notes pertain to a meeting with Henry C. Hardnett, Project Manager[49], and CAPT Michael R. Weaver, Project Management Branch Chief on Thursday January 17, 2007, from approximately 1330 to approximately 1430.

Background:

During a visit to the Sisseton-Wahpeton Oyate Health Care Center on December 13-14, 2006, I discovered another potentially life threatening construction safety violation (lack of confined space safety provisions) and another lesser safety violation (no hard hat on at least one individual). I again mentioned the safety issues in my trip report to the Tribe (along with other items including a follow-up mention from previous trip reports concerning environmental regulation violations). On January 10, 2007, I received a fax copy of a letter from Ms. Losano of the same date wherein claims are made that confined space safety provisions were implemented and that there was no requirement for the individual depicted in my trip report to wear a hard hat since he was installing ceiling tile. A threat is also made within the letter that the Tribal Council is considering banning me from their reservation if I continue my perceived harassment of the Tribe and their contractor over safety violations.

The letter from Ms. Losano was copied to Mr. Vinikoor and Kenneth Harper, Director DES, and I provided a copy to CAPT Weaver. Mr. Hardnett did not receive a copy of this letter. During a normal weekly project update meeting on January 16, 2007, Mr. Hardnett made a comment suggesting that he thought it was inappropriate for me to mention a safety violation for someone who was simply installing ceiling tile. I responded that I was not aware when I took the photograph as to what type of work he was performing, only that he was on stilts and was performing overhead work within the ceiling and added that I believe that the OSHA would still require wear of a hard hat for this activity.

It did not strike me until the next day, January 17, 2007, that Mr. Hardnett had information (the person I photographed without a hard hat was installing ceiling tile) that he did not have access to through official channels. It should be noted that Ms. Losano has been very strict throughout the contract regarding compliance with the formal communication protocol which is duly incorporated into the Tribe's P.L. 93-638 construction contract. Mr. Hardnett is not included within the communication protocol. All PM communication was to come through me and I distribute same to the appropriate parties within the IHS. I presented this to CAPT Weaver and suggested that I suspected Mr. Hardnett may be conducting unauthorized communication with the Tribe. He agreed to discuss this with Mr. Hardnett and me later in the day (~1:30 pm).

Discussion Notes:

During the meeting between Mr. Hardnett and CAPT Weaver I asked Mr. Hardnett how he came to know the individual pictured in my trip report was installing ceiling tile since nobody had been aware of this until the response letter from Ms. Losano. His initial claim was that it was mentioned in my trip report. I stated that it was not and produced my copy of same and he promptly left to retrieve his copy and after verifying that his was a copy of the same document he admitted that he had been discussing various project issues with Ms. Losano the previous week. I asked him why this communication was occurring since he is not authorized for such communication. He initially claimed that Ms. Losano was calling him to relay information on to Mr. Harper. CAPT Weaver noted that Mr. Harper had been in the office the previous week. I asked Mr. Hardnett again why Ms. Losano would call him if both Mr. Harper and I were in the office at the time. He then indicated that it may be because she feels more comfortable talking to him since he is a person of color (he is African-American) as she is (she is Hispanic). I then asked Mr. Hardnett what he and Ms. Losano had been discussing and he first indicated that they had discussed safety issues. He added that he did not understand why I was so persistent on finding fault with the project. I advised him that it was our job to illuminate problems with the project. He responded that he believed that our function was to find things that have been done right on the project. I asked him how he expected to correct problems with that perspective. He responded that problems can still be resolved. I responded that you have to find the problems before you can resolve them.

I asked Mr. Hardnett if he and Ms. Losano had discussed anything else and he said that there were some personal issues that he would not share. I asked why he would not share them and he suggested that they were of a personal nature. I asked Mr. Hardnett if he realized that his communication was outside the communication protocol. He acknowledged this and suggested that I was too strict with the protocol. I reminded him that it was Ms. Losano that had been demanding strict conformance with the communication protocol. I then commented that I thought it was very strange that she would abandon her own demands for conformance to the protocol by contacting Mr. Hardnett.

Mr. Hardnett then began opening up and stated that Ms. Losano cannot understand why I keep bringing up safety issues when the OSHA has not found anything and suggested that perhaps the reason for this is that I am a racist. I then asked Mr. Hardnett what his response to this was and he indicated that he had suggested to Ms. Losano that I might be. I was shocked by this and asked Mr. Hardnett to confirm this which he did by reiterating that he thought I might be a racist. I asked him what would make him think that and he indicated that it was based on my disposition on the safety issue. I advised him that construction safety is not something that I feel we should compromise and that I did not understand how upholding Federal construction safety regulations could possibly be equated to racism. I asked Mr. Hardnett how many times he had these conversations and he suggested at least twice in the recent past. Mr. Hardnett seemed to be cavalier with his statements and indifferent toward the impact of his actions or the gravity of what he had just said so I asked him if he understood same. He began speaking about various people that he thought may be racist, including CAPT Weaver, and then stated that he was a racist. I then asked him to confirm what he had stated and he reiterated that he was a racist and that he thought I may be also. I then indicated to CAPT Weaver that I no longer trusted Mr. Hardnett to be on my project team and that I did not want any further communication between Mr. Hardnett and the Tribe. CAPT Weaver acknowledged my "preference" but made it clear that he would make the decision. It should be noted that there was no contrition expressed by Mr. Hardnett toward me during the meeting regarding his conduct.

No follow-up discussion or meeting was planned.

APPENDIX 13.
2006 COER FROM IHS DES

The following COER dated 9/30/2006 was generated by CAPT Michael Weaver and concurred by CAPT Kenneth Harper (Ret.) prior to their attempts to damage my career (following my first EEO complaint and the SWO's threatening letter regarding my continued findings of safety issues on their job site). It should be noted that the scale from A to E/F is poor to excellent (i.e., the opposite from school grades).

2006 ANNUAL COMMISSIONED OFFICERS' EFFECTIVENESS REPORT PHSNO: ▮

Officer Name: CDR GJOVIK, NATHAN	Present Position/Billet Title: SENIOR ENGINEER II
Agency/Program: IHS OD	Reviewing Official: CAPT HARPER, KENNETH
Rating Official: CAPT WEAVER, MICHAEL	How long have you supervised this officer? 1 Years, 3 Months

Questions	Values					
Q1. QUANTITY OF WORK	○ A	○ B	○ C	○ D	⦿ E	
Q2. QUALITY OF WORK	○ A	○ B	○ C	○ D	⦿ E	
Q3. PUNCTUALITY OF WORK	○ A	○ B	○ C	○ D	⦿ E	
Q4. INIATIVE, CREATIVITY, AND JUDGEMENT	○ A	○ B	○ C	○ D	⦿ E	
Q5. PLANNING AND ORGANIZING	○ A	○ B	○ C	○ D	⦿ E	
Q6. ABILITY TO ANALYZE PROBLEMS	○ A	○ B	○ C	○ D	⦿ E	
Q7. SUPERVISORY SKILLS	○ A	○ B	○ C	○ D	○ E	⦿ F
Q8. ABILITY TO WORK WITH OTHERS	○ A	○ B	○ C	⦿ D	○ E	
Q9. ABILITY TO EXPRESS SELF VERBALLY AND IN WRITING	○ A	○ B	○ C	○ D	⦿ E	
Q10. PROFESSIONAL SKILLS IN PRESENT ACTIVITY	○ A	○ B	○ C	○ D	⦿ E	
Q11. RESPONSIVENESS TO SUPERVISION	○ A	○ B	○ C	○ D	⦿ E	
Q12. RESPONSE TO CRISES	○ A	○ B	○ C	○ D	⦿ E	○ F
Q13. GROWTH IN SKILLS DURING RATING PERIOD	○ A	○ B	○ C	○ D	⦿ E	○ F
Q14. COMMITMENT TO PROGRAM GOALS	○ A	○ B	○ C	○ D	⦿ E	
Q15. MANAGERIAL RESPONSIBILITY	○ A	○ B	○ C	○ D	○ E	⦿ F
Q16. WEARING OF THE PHS UNIFORM	○ A	○ B	○ C	○ D	⦿ E	
Q17. EQUAL OPPORTUNITY	○ A	○ B	○ C	○ D	○ E	⦿ F
Q18. OVERALL JOB PERFORMANCE	○ A	○ B	○ C	○ D	⦿ E	

Officer concurrence statement: Officer concurred with ratings

Reviewing Official has concurred with your ratings

Comments.

I do not have a 2006 performance plan.	
2006 COER Officer's Duties, Accomplishments, and Goals	Nathan D. Gjovik

Current duties with the Division of Engineering Services include, but are not limited to:

- Project management of new health care and head start facilities.   Specific projects include:
    - new health center and site work for health center and associated staff quarters in Sisseton, SD;
    - proposed new health center in White Swan, WA;
    - proposed new health center in Longview, WA;
    - proposed new health center in Neah Bay, WA;
    - proposed new health center in Canyonville, OR;
    - proposed new health center in Siletz, OR;
    - proposed new head start in Savoonga, AK.
- Provision of technical assistance to other projects on civil and environmental engineering issues.

Accomplishments within the past reporting period included:

- Provided project management of construction activities associated with proposed new $40M health center (contracted by Tribe with limited construction experience).
- Provided leadership in coordinating design review and follow-up with review comments within an extremely compressed schedule for a new head start facility.
- Served as a liaison officer for ESF-8 with the Principal Federal Official in New Orleans, LA following hurricanes Katrina and Rita.
- Volunteered to serve on the regional tier 1 incident response coordination team (IRCT) and accept the responsibilities and risk associated with same.
- Provided regular briefings on emergency preparedness issues to office and building staff.
- Served as a floor warden and have provided leadership on emergency preparedness issues affecting the (high-rise office) building.
- Served as the acting president of the local COA branch (Evergreen).
- Completed a project management certificate program from the University of Washington.

Goal(s) for future assignments include:

Enter into organizational management in order to better be able to utilize related training, experience, and skills to effect meaningful change in public sector management.

I have used the rated officer's 2006 performance plan, which has been in effect for a minimum of 90 days, to complete this evaluation.	
2006 COER Rater's Comments for:	Nathan D. Gjovik

Attachment 2 - CDR Nathan Gjovik

CDR Nathan Gjovik performed well in COER year 2006. He continued his outstanding performance of PM duties for the Sisseton new health care facility. He added additional responsibilities as the PM for four new Small Ambulatory Program (SAP) health care facilities projects and added technical assistance duties to the Agency For Children and Families (ACF), for a Head Start facility located on St. Lawrence Island, Alaska. CDR Gjovik performed all of these duties at the exceptional level. He also served as the local COA chapter acting President, deployed as a Commissioned Officer during hurricane Katrina, and provided valuable leadership for emergency preparation issues for the Division of Engineering Services (DES) staff. CDR Gjovik wears his uniform daily and provides an excellent example for the Commissioned Corps of the USPHS. His dedication to the Corps is witnessed by his volunteering to be a member of the Incident Response Coordination Team (IRCT) for Region X. He can always be relied upon to get the job done and is always willing to accept additional duties.

APPENDIX 14.
EEO COMPLAINTS AGAINST IHS DES

On November 3, 2006, I completed mandatory training on the NoFEAR Act which was passed by Congress in 2002 (i.e., it took the IHS over 4 years to implement the law). The Act states that "illegal discrimination occurs when one employee is treated differently than another employee and treatment is based on race…" However, the IHS routinely treats employees differently based on race. Therefore, I filed my first EEO complaint for non-consideration for several jobs based purely on racial considerations. I provided the table presented below documenting the various positions. The response from the agency dated September 22, 2008, nearly two years after I presented my complaint, was to assert their right to discriminate against non-Tribal people based on various court rulings and to assert untimeliness in the submittal of my complaint. The issue of untimeliness is ironic since the agency had grossly missed every established deadline for the processing of the complaint.

The final decision authority is vested in the Surgeon General. As became the norm Acting Surgeon General Steven Galson upheld the right of the IHS to discriminate based on race, essentially ignoring the NoFEAR Act and the principle of equality upon which our country is founded. He also did not give due consideration to the gross incompetency exhibited by the IHS in regard to the processing of the complaint, exhibited by it taking nearly 2 years to process.

Future complaints submitted to Surgeon General Regina Benjamin (an African American) likewise took the same track with her simple acceptance of the agency/department recommended decisions, all of which were developed by minority staff members (with the agency recommended decisions developed by Pauline Bruce, a former management official from the Aberdeen Area IHS who refused to recuse herself despite her relationships with the accused managers). Coincidentally, all of the recommended decisions found no evidence of discrimination. All of the EEO staff and Surgeons General associated with my complaints completely ignored my well documented complaints of gross discrimination and incompetence by each EEO office in the processing of the complaints (each had missed many or most of the deadlines established by regulation for the processing of the complaints). Even when I was able to successfully get my complaints heard at the department level it didn't seem to matter since they had relationships with the IHS EEO staff and they all enjoyed minority status.

The following was submitted to Pauline Bruce, IHS Director, EEO, as a complaint of reprisal on April 27, 2007:

ATTACHMENT A

Complaints

I am a commissioned officer engineer stationed in Seattle, Washington with the Division of Engineering Services (DES). I have been managing construction projects for over 17 years. For the past several years I have been the Federal project manager (PM) for a new health center in Sisseton, South Dakota. The new health center is being constructed by the Sisseton-Wahpeton Oyate of the Lake Traverse Reservation (Tribe) under Title I P.L. 93-638 construction contracts. The required health center work was divided between two separate contracts: early site development package (ESDP—earthwork and utilities) and health center construction (there is also a third for employee quarters which is not included here).

The ESDP and health center contracts are the first to be managed by the Tribe's newly formed (as of 2003) Construction

Management Office and the staff had little or no knowledge of Federal construction safety regulations prior to these contracts. The Tribal contracting officer is Lisa Losano who is also one of their attorneys. The current IHS contracting officer is Abram Vinikoor. The alternate Federal PM is Henry Hardnett. Both Abram Vinikoor and Henry Hardnett work in the same office as I do in Seattle.

As part of my duties in managing this project I was responsible for monthly inspections of the work on the site to ensure compliance with the terms of the contract. One of those terms states that the Tribe is responsible for ensuring that Occupational Safety and Health Administration (OSHA) requirements are met. During many or most visits made by me and others to the site construction safety issues were observed with at least one representing an immediate threat to life. After repeated attempts to assist and advisories by me I ultimately called the OSHA to the site. The first call to the OSHA was done concurrently with a courtesy phone call by Abram Vinikoor to Lisa Losano to advise her that the OSHA would be visiting the site (this was done pursuant to local management). Consequently, there were no findings by the OSHA during this first visit. The second contact was in the form of an E-mail containing photos of the construction safety violations (trench safety and personal protective equipment— no hard hats). I understand from a discussion with the OSHA manager in Bismarck, North Dakota that upon receiving my E-mail he immediately mobilized OSHA staff to the site with the intent of citing the offending subcontractor. However, the subcontractor had completed his work and had mobilized off the site by the time the OSHA staff arrived. Therefore, there were no findings by the OSHA during this second visit. The lack of any findings by the OSHA has now been held up by Lisa Losano as proof that my concerns over safety are not legitimate. It should be noted that my supervisor, Michael Weaver, was supportive and even encouraging my efforts to continue to document any safety issues I discovered while on site and to contact the OSHA (he even laid odds that there would be a several thousand dollar fine issued by the OSHA during their second visit to the site).

During a site visit on December 13-14, 2006, I again discovered another potentially life threatening construction safety violation (lack of confined space safety provisions) and another lesser safety violation (no hard hat on at least one individual). I again mentioned the safety issues in my trip report to the Tribe (along with other items including a follow-up mention from previous trip reports concerning environmental regulation violations). On January 10, 2007, I received a fax copy of a letter from Lisa Losano of the same date wherein claims are made that confined space safety provisions were implemented and that there was no requirement for the individual depicted in my trip report to wear a hard hat since he was installing ceiling tile. A threat is also made within the letter that the Tribal Council is considering banning me from their reservation if I continue my perceived harassment of the Tribe and their contractor over safety violations. It should be noted that the Tribe banned the local IHS service unit facility manager from the site after he had snapped some photos at the start of the ESDP work and shared them with our office. The intent of sharing the photos was simply to show progress on the site. However, the photos showed workers not wearing hard hats which resulted in a safety issue which was addressed by others within our office in my absence.

The letter from Lisa Losano was copied to Abram Vinikoor and Kenneth Harper, Director DES, and I provided a copy to Michael Weaver. Henry Hardnett did not receive a copy of this letter. During a normal weekly project update meeting on January 16, 2007, Henry Hardnett made a comment suggesting that he thought it was inappropriate for me to mention a safety violation for someone who was simply installing ceiling tile. I responded that I was not aware when I took the photograph as to what type of work he was performing, only that he was on stilts and was performing overhead work within the ceiling and added that I believe that the OSHA would still require wear of a hard hat for this activity.

It did not strike me until the next day, January 17, 2007, that Henry Hardnett had information (the person I photographed without a hard hat was installing ceiling tile) that he did not have access to through official channels. It should be noted that Lisa Losano has been very strict throughout the contract regarding compliance with the formal communication protocol which is duly incorporated into the Tribe's P.L. 93-638 construction contract. Henry Hardnett is not included within the communication protocol. All PM communication was to come through me and I distribute same to the appropriate parties within the IHS. I presented this to Michael Weaver and suggested that I suspected Henry Hardnett may be conducting unauthorized communication with the Tribe. He agreed to discuss this with Henry Hardnett and me later in the day (~1:30 pm).

During the meeting between Henry Hardnett and Michael Weaver I asked Henry Hardnett how he came to know the individual pictured in my trip report was installing ceiling tile since nobody had been aware of this until the response letter from Lisa Losano. His initial claim was that it was mentioned in my trip report. I stated that it was not and produced my copy of same and he promptly left to retrieve his copy and after verifying that his was a copy of the same document he admitted that he had been discussing various project issues with Lisa Losano the previous week. I asked him why this communication was occurring since he is not authorized for such communication. He initially claimed that Lisa Losano was calling him to relay information on to Kenneth Harper. Michael Weaver noted that Kenneth Harper had been in the office the previous week. I asked Henry Hardnett again why Lisa Losano would call him if both Kenneth Harper and I were in the office at the time. He then indicated that it may be because she feels more comfortable talking to him since he is a person of color (he is African-American) as she is (she is Hispanic). I then asked Henry Hardnett what he and Lisa Losano had been discussing and he first indicated that they had discussed safety issues along with other issues that he would not share. I asked why he would not share them and he suggested that they were of a personal nature. I asked Henry Hardnett if he realized that his communication was outside the communication protocol. He acknowledged this and suggested that I was too strict with the protocol. I reminded him that it was Lisa Losano that had been demanding strict conformance with the communication protocol. I then commented that I thought it was very strange that she would abandon her own demands for conformance to the protocol by contacting Henry Hardnett.

Henry Hardnett then began opening up and stated that Lisa Losano cannot understand why I keep bringing up safety issues when the OSHA has not found anything and suggested that perhaps the reason for this is that I am a racist. I then asked Henry Hardnett what his response to this was and he indicated that he had suggested to Lisa Losano that I might be. I was shocked by this and asked Henry Hardnett to confirm this which he did and reiterated that he thought I might be a racist. I asked him what would make him think that and he indicated that it was based on my disposition on the safety issue. I advised him that construction safety is not something that I feel we should compromise and that I did not understand how upholding Federal construction safety regulations could possibly be equated to racism. I asked Henry Hardnett how many times he had these conversations and he suggested at least twice in the recent past. Henry Hardnett seemed to be cavalier with his statements and indifferent toward the impact of his actions or the gravity of what he had just said so I asked him if he understood same. He began speaking about various people that he thought may be racist, including Michael Weaver, and then stated that he was a racist. I then asked him to confirm what he had stated and he reiterated that he was a racist and that he thought I may be also. I then indicated to Michael Weaver that I no longer trusted Henry Hardnett to be on my project team and that I did not want any further communication between Henry Hardnett and the Tribe. Michael Weaver acknowledged my "preference" but made it clear that he would make the decision. It should be noted that there was no contrition expressed by Henry Hardnett toward me during the meeting regarding his conduct.

Following the above meeting I suggested to Michael Weaver that I believed that Henry Hardnett's conduct should be addressed as an equal employment opportunity (EEO) issue. I also sent an E-mail to Michael Weaver asking him to advise me as to what action would be taken regarding same. He responded that appropriate action would be taken. On January 31, 2007, while I was on leave, I called our travel planner to coordinate another planned site trip to Sisseton and was advised that Henry Hardnett had already scheduled his flight to the area. I then left a message for Michael Weaver to discuss this with him. He called me back shortly thereafter and I asked him why Henry Hardnett was traveling to the site and he indicated that there was a rupture of a sprinkler line within the building over the weekend and that Henry Hardnett was going to look at same. I suggested that Paul Ninomura, mechanical engineer, was already planning on going to the site and that he should be able to check this out. Michael Weaver suggested that he still wanted Henry Hardnett to visit the site. I asked about my stated mistrust for Henry Hardnett based on his previous conduct and Michael Weaver stated that he had addressed this and that Henry Hardnett assured him that it would not happen again. I suggested that it was unwise to place Henry Hardnett in a position to be able to continue his inappropriate activities and that we had other architects within the office who could go in lieu of Henry Hardnett. Michael Weaver insisted that Henry Hardnett go. I stated that I had not seen any sign of contrition on the part of Henry Hardnett for his conduct and that I still did not trust him and did not want him on my team. I then advised Michael Weaver that if he was going to insist on having Henry Hardnett not only involved in the project but placed into a leading role for this planned visit that he should consider removing me as the PM. That is exactly what happened.

Michael Weaver sent me an E-mail later in the day on January 31, 2007, transitioning me out as the PM effective the following day. At 8:00 am on February 5, 2007, upon my return to the office following my leave I was called into a meeting with Kenneth Harper and Michael Weaver. Michael Weaver introduced the meeting by suggesting that I have performance and behavior issues and suggested that I pursue counseling and officially requested that I do so immediately. He stated that a Dr. Caserta with the Medical Affairs Branch (MAB) wanted to speak with me about an assessment of me and that the MAB can order me to be involved in same. For the record I asked Kenneth Harper if he agreed with this and he responded in the affirmative. I then asked what the performance and behavior issues were. The only example I was given was my unwillingness to continue to work with Henry Hardnett on the Sisseton project. I stated that I did not understand why they were handling the situation in the manner they were as it appeared to me that I was the aggrieved party and that Henry Hardnett, who had shown no contrition for his conduct, should not only have been precluded from traveling to the site but should also have been removed from the project. Michael Weaver responded that this is the reason why I should be evaluated (apparently because I don't understand the manner in which the situation is being managed). I also stated that I cannot believe everything I have been subjected to because I would not compromise Federal construction safety regulations and was simply trying to save the lives and limbs of people working on the site. I advised Kenneth Harper and Michael Weaver that I did not see how my stand on construction safety related to a mental health issue and that I had no intention at that time of contacting Dr. Caserta. I was told by Kenneth Harper that to date I had always been provided with positive Commissioned Officer Effectiveness Reports (COERs) but that my behavior could threaten future COERs. I received a call following the meeting from Dr. Caserta. He said that he had just received a call from Kenneth Harper and I explained my perspective to him. He seemed to understand but said that since both Kenneth Harper and Michael Weaver felt as if I am angry about how they are managing the situation that he would have to order me to be assessed.

During the process of the administrative preparation for the comprehensive mental health examination a written description was shared with me of my alleged behavioral issues which Michael Weaver had provided to Dr. Caserta (on February 21, 2007). The description was designed to portray an unstable individual who could be involved in an act of violence. This is/was untrue. However, as far as I know nobody investigated the claims by Michael Weaver or attempted to stop the examination despite several appeals by me for same. The mental health examination was performed on April 10, 2007. The findings were that there are no concerns with my mental health. It should be noted that the form which accompanied the description of my behavioral issues by Michael Weaver states that its purpose is "to protect [uniformed service members] from referral to the mental health system as a means of 'reprisal' or control of 'whistleblowers'."

I believe the above described actions by Henry Hardnett (undermining my work efforts due to his racial prejudices) represent racial discrimination. I also believe that the above described actions by Kenneth Harper and Michael Weaver are reprisal against me, at least in part, for my suggestion that Henry Hardnett's conduct be addressed as an EEO issue and their unwillingness to do same. They have apparently addressed Henry Hardnett's actions as unprofessional conduct. It should be noted that Michael Weaver apparently did not report the incidents of racial discrimination by Henry Hardnett nor did Kenneth Harper, or his supervisor Gary Hartz (since Kenneth Harper was complicit in the reprisal), report the acts of reprisal (premature removal of me as the PM for the Sisseton project, sudden identification of behavior and performance issues, and subjection to a mental health examination) as required by the Commissioned Corps Personnel Manual, Subchapter 26.1.

ATTACHMENT B

Remedies

I am hereby requesting the following as remedies:

1. RADM Charles Grim provide a letter to me explaining why management above Kenneth Harper allowed the reprisal actions against me to continue and why no investigation was done to determine whether or not the accusations/concerns of my supervisor(s) were true/valid.*

Mr. Henry Hardnett write a letter to the Tribe (Tribal attorney and Tribal council), which is to be copied to me, acknowledging all of the conversations he had with the Tribal attorney, or others, regarding me being "a racist" and the inappropriateness of same along with a recounting of the various construction safety violations, a discussion of the importance of construction safety, and an explanation that this is, in fact, the reason for my continued concern about same.**

Both CAPT Michael Weaver and Mr. Kenneth Harper develop, sign, and provide a letter of apology to me acknowledging regret for their mismanagement of the EEO issue presented by Mr. Hardnett and their reprisal against me for same. The letter is to detail the various reprisal actions taken against me which are described in the complaint.**

Both CAPT Michael Weaver and Mr. Kenneth Harper agree that the various incidents associated with the racial discrimination will not be used by them to negatively reflect on me.

RADM Gary Hartz, or his successor, issue letters of reprimand to both CAPT Michael Weaver and Mr. Kenneth Harper for their reprisal actions. Copies of the respective letters are to be placed in each individual's official personnel file.***

* This element is modified from that originally presented in an E-mail dated February 14, 2007. The original remedy element requested that all reprisal actions immediately cease. They did not despite several appeals by me to various IHS and USPHS managers/leaders.

** Element varies somewhat from that originally presented in an E-mail dated February 14, 2007.

*** This element was not included in the remedies originally presented in the E-mail dated February 14, 2007. It is added due to the egregious nature of the actions perpetrated by these two individuals as well as to mitigate the possibility of it happening to others in the future.

APPENDIX 15.
ABERDEEN AREA IHS
GRIEVANCES-ROUND 1

The following is a formal rebuttal to my 2008 COER letter dated 12/31/2008 which incorporates the pertinent text from the series of grievances filed against the managers who developed and concurred with the COER:

CDR Nathan D. Gjovik

REBUTTAL TO 2008 COER

For those who are unfamiliar with the Indian Health Service (IHS) and who may be reviewing my COER I offer the following. The IHS often deals with problem employees via forced transfers or temporary details to other IHS locations. I believe the Rater for my 2008 COER has been detailed from the Pine Ridge IHS Service Unit because of problems she has there (based on conversations with Pine Ridge staff). The Reviewing Official (RO) for my 2008 COER had been the Administrative Officer (AO) at my current duty station (Rapid City IHS Service Unit) prior to a forced detail to the Eagle Butte IHS Service Unit by my previous supervisor, the Chief Executive Officer (CEO) from whom I received a strong 2007 COER. Both the Rater and RO are currently functioning in acting capacities, Rater as the Acting AO and RO as the acting CEO. The RO has a very assertive personality and returned to her original duty station, the one from which she had been forcefully removed, with a strong orientation to change things back to how they used to be when she was asked to leave. The Rater, likewise, has a very assertive personality and works synergistically with her supervisor, the RO, for change, even those improvements that had taken years under the previous CEO to improve.

Coincidentally with the above issues there is also a strong anti-commissioned corps demeanor within the Aberdeen Area. I sit on the hospital's Executive Team (ET), the decision making group whose function has been marginalized under the current acting leadership (Rater and RO mentioned above). I am the only non-Tribal person and the only commissioned corps officer on the ET (and aside from the clinical director who is not able to attend many meetings, the only man). I believe this plays a large role in how I am currently treated by the Rater and RO. They seem to desire to replace me with someone more of their choosing and are attempting to utilize the COER as a tool to do this. The RO has placed me under the supervision of the Rater, which is contrary to the current and past organizational chart. However, this allows the ability to keep the entire COER process, rating and review, within their control. Because of the manner in which I have been treated by the two individuals I have filed a combined seven grievances and one EEO complaint over the past several months. One of those grievances and the EEO complaint are related to my COER, the pertinent text (introductory, closing, and attachments not included) for which are included below.

Grievance against Ms. Keith (rater):
As my acting supervisor Ms. Keith was charged with the responsibility of being my rating official for my commissioned officer effectiveness report (COER) annual performance review from October 1, 2007, through September 30, 2008 (only 6 weeks of which she supervised me). The COER was due from the rating official no later than November 19, 2008. After several requests via E-mail for an update on the status of my COER and some intervention from Ms. Shelly Harris, Deputy Area Director, Ms. Keith completed my COER on December 8, 2008.

Ms. Keith included several negative comments within my COER. I will address each derogatory comment as best I can as follows:

Comment 1: This Officer may not fully understand some of the regulations which dictate procurement processes. As a result, the ability to heat various buildings on the compound may be jeopardized. This may have been avoided with good communication skills and follow through.

CDR Nathan D. Gjovik   ███████

Response 1: I have successfully completed project officer training twice over my career and have been the contracting officer project representative/project officer, project manager, and/or engineer of record for scores of projects valued in excess of $50 million. I understand very well the procurement regulations. The problem with the procurement Ms. Keith references was exactly that - my level of knowledge. I understand when a justification for other than full and open competition (JOFOC) is appropriate. The situation we had with the boiler repair was that it was both urgent and compelling (could lose all heat to the campus if work not completed prior to the winter heating season) and economically advantageous to the Government (material prices were going up ~5% every month). I communicated this to and followed-up with all those I knew to be in the loop or able to impact the decisions. This communication chain was copied to Ms. Keith and was also shared with her (and Ms. Thompson) verbally in a meeting I called to discuss the issue with them. Both Ms. Thompson and Ms. Keith agreed that this should have been processed as a JOFOC as I had strongly urged during the procurement development. For Ms. Keith to now claim this situation to be a shortcoming of mine is disingenuous.

Comment 2: Gjovik has exhibited reluctance to follow instruction outlined in Agency guidelines, sometimes leading to delays in completion of duties.

Response 2: There is no detail or explanation included with this comment. I have no idea what is meant by this.

Comment 3: This Officer appears to have difficulty performing work through others and may benefit from training in this area.

Response 3: Again, there is no detail or explanation included with this comment. I have 17 direct reports and complete an enormous amount of work through others every day.

Comment 4: CDR Gjovik does not respond well to direction from supervisors at times.

Response 4: Again, there is no detail or explanation included with this comment. I do not function well under autocratic management (nor do most or all of the other professionals I know). This is how Ms. Keith conducts her supervision.

Comment 5: CDR Gjovik has not displayed good financial planning practices in the Facility Support Account.

Response 5: Again, there is no detail or explanation included with this comment. However, I believe I know the reason for her comment. The Aberdeen Area Facility Management Deputy Director changed the non-recurring funds disbursement scheme after a commitment was already made by me to backfill a position which had been vacant for nearly nine months. This creates a deficit budget for this fiscal year. I have notified the appropriate individuals of this and have received no response other than this derogatory review comment from Ms. Keith. I am limiting to the best of my ability the costs being incurred by this account, including energy costs. This is the best that anybody, including Ms. Keith, could do.

It is clear from reviewing my COER that Ms. Keith continues to try to harm me and my career.

EEO Complaint against Ms. Thompson (reviewing official):
On Monday December 29, 2008, following my return from Christmas leave I read an automated E-mail indicating that Ms. Thompson had signed off as the reviewing official on my commissioned officer effectiveness report (COER). What I found upon a review of my COER was a reviewing official statement (ROS), crafted by Ms. Thompson, containing unfair and untrue information designed to harm me and my career. I will address each comment as best I can as follows:

CDR Nathan D. Gjovik ■■■■■■

Comment #1: Although he has written he has managed a fleet of 12 GSA vehicles this officer did not meet the reporting requirements for a year which put the service unit at risk for losing said vehicles. Did not adhere to reporting requirements on a timely basis.

Response #1: Managing the GSA vehicles is not included in my job description. Despite that I have been performing this function for over 1.5 years in order to be helpful to the service unit. I developed an on-line vehicle reservation system, coordinated all vehicle maintenance needs, and completed all mandatory GSA reporting requirements within their maintenance database. This was all done despite my not having secretarial support for over nine months of the past year. I have also communicated on several occasions with local GSA office management about the need to maintain the additional (IHS) database referenced by Ms. Thompson. I have consistently been told that it is not a GSA requirement to maintain this system. Therefore, the statement made by Ms. Thompson that the service unit was at risk for losing the GSA vehicles is not true. Also, she was aware that maintenance of the local GSA vehicle fleet is not included in my job description before placing the derogatory comment into my COER. Rather than thank me for my extra efforts she chose to try to damage me and my career with the indicated unfair and untrue information within the ROS.

Comment #2: During the Life Safety & Utilities Management Survey conducted by the Aberdeen Area Office on January 30, 2008 the hospital was cited 2.2.17.1 and 2.2.17.2, respectively for doors without positive latching and doors not self-closing or automatic closing. These deficiencies were not corrected until November 15, 2008. Deficiencies not corrected in a timely manner.

Response #2: The door authoritatively referenced by Ms. Thompson as not having been corrected is that to the soiled linen room #225. That door was corrected by Michael Gray, Maintenance Worker, on February 27, 2008. The deficiency noted during the CMS re-inspection on November 5, 2008, was for the door to room #338, a completely different door than that indicated by Ms. Thompson. The November 15, 2008, date referenced by Ms. Thompson relates to the original CMS finding related to the need for a closer on room #338 – there was none. A closer was installed in July 2007 (i.e., the CMS deficiency was corrected in July 2007). The finding from the CMS re-inspection on November 5, 2008, was because the previously installed closer was broken. Someone had opened the door too far or too fast and broken the closer sometime between July 2007 and November 2008. My department was unaware of this since a work request had not been input to repair it. However, once I was made aware of the issue by the CMS inspector it was repaired immediately (by Howard Herman, Maintenance Worker, on the same day – November 5, 2008). Therefore, a new closer was installed on the door to room #338 twice, once very soon after each CMS inspection.

Ms. Thompson was not interested in determining (comment #2) or disclosing (comment #1) the actual facts related to her derogatory comments. She was simply looking for something, even if it isn't true or fair, and no matter how insignificant, that she could hold up as an indication that I am not performing my duties correctly. She then used these in a manner which will maximize the harm to me and my career via placing it into my COER which will stay in my official personnel file (OPF) for many years. It should be noted that Ms. Thompson ignored the deficiency corrections which have been completed by me and my staff and the fact that the departments I managed may be the only ones which have resolved all CMS findings. This type of inappropriate and discriminatory behavior should not be tolerated.

I have attached the pertinent text from the early grievances (those presented prior to my COER rating) as attachments below. I respectfully request consideration by those reviewing my COER for the difficulty of my current situation. I work long hours, receive numerous phone calls at all hours of the evening, and work weekends in order to keep my campus functional and accredited for patient care. Despite this, for whatever reason, my current supervisory chain does not appreciate me.

CDR Nathan D. Gjovik

Officer Signature   31 DEC 2008   Date   Liaison Signature   Date

Attachment #1 (Pertinent Text from 10/14/2008 Grievance)

On the morning of Tuesday October 7, 2008, in response to an E-mail I sent to an Aberdeen Area human resource specialist I discovered from Ms. Thompson that she had spoken with "all of [my] staff [I] supervise and with the exception of one all of them expressed grave concerns but also fear of speaking up, threats regarding job or offering suggestions." I later discovered that this had apparently occurred during my recent deployment approximately one month prior. Ms. Thompson also indicated in her E-mail that she was also regularly receiving information "from community member(s) regarding [my] treatment/disposition towards staff." I responded that I was unaware of these issues, advised her of some reasons why she may have been receiving some negative feedback from various staff members, and asked for her support and the benefit of the doubt in working through various human resource issues. Following some additional E-mail communication and a brief discussion with Ms. Keith, it was clear to me that I was not going to receive the benefit of the doubt due to the perceptions by both Ms. Thompson and Ms. Keith as to the manner in which I am managing both housekeeping and maintenance.

On the morning of Thursday October 9, 2008, I requested a meeting with both Ms. Thompson and Ms. Keith. This occurred at approximately 9:00 am in Ms. Thompson's office. I initially asked who the community member(s) was/were that was/were discussing personnel issues concerning my staff with Ms. Thompson. She refused to tell me. I asked if it was Mr. Gene War Bonnet and she acknowledged that it could be. She would not tell me if there is more than one. I advised both Ms. Thompson and Ms. Keith of the definition of slander (an untruthful oral statement about a person that harms the person's reputation or standing in the community and that it is a tort where the injured person can bring suit against the person who made the false statement). Both Ms. Thompson and Ms. Keith apparently took great offense to this and indicated, more than once, that this was proof of my confrontational tendencies toward my staff. Ms. Thompson and Ms. Keith then proceeded to describe various issues that they have with the manner in which I am treating my staff. When I tried to explain (defend myself) they got upset because they perceived that I was trying to interrupt them. It was clear that each of their minds was made up without having discussed anything with me. When I advised Ms. Thompson of this she explained that she did not have to speak to me about it since she had spoken with all of my staff and they were all saying the same things. Therefore, it must be true. I asked for some time to explain a few of the issues that were brought up by both Ms. Thompson and Ms. Keith. Ms. Thompson granted same and they reluctantly listened. Following my explanations they were quiet and seemed to want the meeting to end. I agreed to acquiesce to their desire (one of their discussion issues) to provide Theresa Brave Eagle, Housekeeper, a nursing key which gives her access to all of the exam rooms in the hospital (she had never had one in the many years of her employment and was suddenly requesting one now that she was on a PIP and may be on a path to termination) even though it was against my better judgment. I thanked them for their time and left.

A couple of things should be noted about the meeting referenced above. During the discussion Ms. Thompson commented to me that she finds me very irritating and that I "seem to always have all the answers." Also, I was asked about what LT Craig Grunenfelder does in his job as well as how he was hired for his job. The premise was that his position should have been filled by a Native American. Ms. Keith explained to me that based on Indian preference all positions within the IHS are supposed to be filled by Native Americans and not ... (she hesitated at this point since she was apparently unsure how to refer to people like me in a politically correct manner).

Over the lunch hour on Friday October 10, 2008, I had a follow-up meeting in the Lakota Lodge conference room with Ms. Keith wherein she advised that the manner in which I was conducting the PIP with Theresa Brave Eagle was incorrect. I provided her with a copy of the PIP and advised her that I had received the template from an Aberdeen Area human resource specialist, had modified it and returned it

CDR Nathan D. Gjovik   ████████

for review, that I was advised by the same person that it looked good, and that I issued exactly that same document. Ms. Keith was not satisfied with that since the manner in which I am monitoring compliance with the PIP did not meet her expectations. During our discussion I asked Ms. Keith for the benefit of the doubt in working through the various human resource issues and she responded that I have to earn any trust since neither she nor Ms. Thompson know me. She also made a comment that my staff are "not as great as I am in my job." I took this to mean that she believes to me to be arrogant and advised her that I took offense to her statement. She did not acknowledge my response and continued advising me of the various things she thinks I am not doing correctly. I advised her that I believe I have been treated disrespectfully and that this has become a hostile work environment and that I would like to file a complaint. She responded that she believed the environment was hostile toward her and that I have treated her disrespectfully. I asked her to provide me with an example which would illustrate that and she was unable to do so. She advised me that I am a ████████████████████ I acknowledged same and advised her that I still have a right to complain. I asked her for the following Tuesday off in order to prepare a complaint. She granted same and we left the room. Ms. Keith went directly into the office of Ms. Thompson and closed the door as I walked by. Later that afternoon Ms. Keith overturned a decision I had made about disapproving annual leave for Ms. Brave Eagle. This was in contradiction to a previous discussion wherein she advised me that she and Ms. Thompson would not get involved in leave issues.

I have several concerns over the events noted above as follows:
1. I was not advised in any way about any discussions with my staff prior to receiving the E-mail referenced above which was several weeks after the discussions occurred.
2. I am not clear as to why Ms. Thompson would tell me that she has spoken to all of my staff when, in fact, she has not. She has not spoken with at least four of my staff.
3. I was not advised in any way about any issues with my staff prior to receiving the E-mail referenced above which was several weeks after issues were apparently illuminated.
4. I am not clear as to why Ms. Thompson would suggest that all of my staff provided her with the same negative comments about my management. They did not. At least two of my staff that she spoke to provided positive comments (these were unsolicited comments from two staff members that I received).
5. I am not clear as to why (a) community member(s) (there may be only one) are involved in any way with Federal human resource management issues and why that would be entertained by local leadership. This would be especially true in this case if the community member(s) was actually a known campus agitator by the name of Gene War Bonnet, whom I have had a recent encounter which resulted in a response letter from Area leadership. It should be noted that Ms. Thompson also had a past encounter with Mr. War Bonnet wherein he apparently threatened her. Her solution to this that she disclosed to me personally as well as to the Executive Team during one our regular meetings (following my encounter with him) was to have one of her sons visit Mr. War Bonnet's home and threaten him with violence if he threatened her again. Ms. Thompson apparently feels as if this was an acceptable solution for her situation.
6. I am not clear as to why both Ms. Thompson and Ms. Keith would view my comment about potential slander by (a) community member(s) as a threat to them. The only logical explanation for this is that they are, in fact, complicit in the slander and would, therefore, be subject to the same tort liabilities.
7. I am not clear as to why both Ms. Thompson and Ms. Keith would have made up their minds about my human resource management practices before discussing same with me. The only logical explanation for this is that they have an agenda of some sort that predisposes them to negative conclusions about me and/or my performance.
8. I am not clear as to why Ms. Keith (and Ms. Thompson?) believe that non-Tribal people should not be hired by the IHS (reference discussion about LT Craig Grunenfelder).
9. I am not clear as to why I am not given the benefit of the doubt in managing my departments and why I have to earn the trust of the current leadership (I think it should be the opposite - I would have to earn distrust, i.e., provide good reason for them to believe that I am not capable of performing my job).
10. I am not clear as to why Ms. Keith would mock me (see comment above) if she is trying to help me manage my departments.

CDR Nathan D. Gjovik   ████████

Attachment #2 (Pertinent Text from 10/21/2008 Grievance)

This is a follow-on grievance to that provided previously dated October 14, 2008. On October 15, 2008, I was provided with a memo requiring me to attend an administrative informal mediation with certain members of my housekeeping and maintenance staff on Friday October 17, 2008. I reported at 8:00 am as indicated in the memo and was asked by the mediator, Sheila Sonberg (?), to leave and return at 9:00 am. However, I was later told that "additional people" were being interviewed and that it was taking longer than anticipated. I returned for my individual session at approximately 12:00 pm. I requested that Michelle Keith not be involved in the mediation any further due to my distrust of her. The mediator spoke with Ms. Keith out in the hallway and then gave me the impression that Ms. Keith would not be involved any further.

During my individual session with the mediator she indicated to me that the comments from my staff "were not bad" and that many of the comments involved other people, including the past CEO. She asked me some questions that clearly indicated Belva Little Brave had been interviewed and the mediator confirmed same. I asked her why Ms. Little Brave was interviewed since I had not supervised her for nearly one year. The mediator did not have an answer. The mediator finished advising me of the various complaints from the staff that were interviewed. She boiled them down to six issues as follows:

1. My alleged intimidation of employees (still unsure what was meant by this).
2. My monitoring of employee work activities (some thought I was "spying" on them).
3. The manner in which new employees are selected (one wanted more women hired in the housekeeping department and another was upset because he was asked to participate on an interview committee for a new secretary and his selection was not the person hired).
4. My use of a personality profile tool to train employees on teamwork issues (some employees did not understand the reason for this).
5. Assignment of keys to housekeepers and maintenance workers (I was told that all of the housekeepers desired a "nursing" key which would allow access to all exam rooms).
6. Role of Vernon Grinnell, work leader, in housekeeping.

The staff that was interviewed earlier returned to the meeting room at 1:00 pm. Ms. Keith accompanied them and I was asked to address the various complaints. Several additional issues came up during our discussion and Ms. Keith was clearly advocating for the staff. One of the issues was brought up by the only female housekeeper. She claimed to be uncomfortable being alone with a group of men during our meetings. I responded that she has indicated this to me in the past which has caused me to take notice of her behavior in our meetings. I commented that I had noticed her laughing and joking with staff at our last meeting. However, one of her coworkers indicated that he had sensed her being uncomfortable. She then suggested that her uncomfortable condition in the meetings was due to a cultural issue. Ms. Keith picked up on this and began to lecture me on my need to be more culturally sensitive. I indicated that I am Norwegian and asked if the housekeeper was expected to be more culturally sensitive to me. Ms. Keith seemed incensed by this and quickly advised me that this is the Indian Health Service and, therefore, it was incumbent on me to be culturally sensitive. The purpose of the day's meetings was apparently to develop a mediated agreement. We agreed to the terms of the agreement and then I was asked to leave again while the others crafted the agreement. On my way out of the room Ms. Keith confiscated my notes that I had taken over the course of the mediation exercise.

I was asked to return around 3:30 pm. I began reviewing the agreement and noticed that there were elements within the agreement that we had not previously agreed to. One of them was that all employees apparently desire master keys (keys that would open all doors throughout the campus except for pharmacy and medical records). Ms. Keith was an advocate for this and suggested that we could simply include in the key issuance document a statement that would require employees to pay from their last

CDR Nathan D. Gjovik ██████████

check the costs associated with re-keying if they did not turn in their key upon leaving Federal service. I explained that we already have a similar statement, however, one paycheck would not cover the expense to rekey the entire campus. I also stated that I thought this would not constitute a good business practice and it would not be in conformance with our policy of limiting keys to only those that absolutely needed them, but that if I was ordered to do so in writing, I would, but that I would note it was against my better judgment. Another new term was a requirement for me to attend Lakota cultural sensitivity training. Again, Ms. Keith was advocating for this. I asked her if she was requiring all supervisors to attend this training and she realized that she was singling me out. She then suggested that everybody in my two departments, including me, needed to attend. However, the intent and effect is still the same. I believe that I am the only supervisor being required to attend Lakota cultural sensitivity training.

We completed our agreement discussions and crafted the final agreement and Ms. Keith left to print the document for us to sign. During the interlude the room, filled with approximately a dozen people, was completely silent. The mediator sensed the uncomfortable silence and tried to lighten it up. Ms. Keith returned with the agreement and we all signed same. Ms. Keith then advised the staff, more than once, that if they feel in any way retaliated against for their participation in the mediation that they should advise her immediately. Ms. Thompson came in and also signed the agreement and then she advised the staff that if they have any issues to work through the chain of command. Ms. Keith then reiterated a similar message. I then asked why the chain of command was not followed in this case. This seemed to take Ms. Thompson and Ms. Keith by surprise and they asked me to repeat my question which I did. Ms. Thompson responded that I should ask Stan. She then attempted to quickly recover by advising me that we had already discussed this and that it should not be discussed in front of the employees and that I needed to "stop right now!"

This mediation was setup by Ms. Thompson and Ms. Keith due to what I believe to be analogous to a fishing expedition with my employees during a time when I was away on a deployment. It was driven by employees who have an "axe to grind" with me due to various issues. The primary person given a platform by this exercise, the female housekeeper, is currently noncompliant with a performance improvement plan (PIP) and has 14 written complaints so far this year regarding her performance (and two regarding her conduct). Ms. Thompson herself has identified this employee as a problem employee to others in the past when she supervised housekeeping. One of the housekeepers has been chronically upset because he was not asked to assist the work leader with scheduling (an apparent indication of a track to leadership within the department). However, even when asked to assist with scheduling, he turned it down. Two of the complaining maintenance staff (boiler plant operators) are probably nervous because they have recently been identified as potentially involved in selling scrap material from the campus for cash and also because they may soon be reprimanded because of repair work (costing $50,000) on one of our boilers which may have been necessitated due to their negligent water treatment monitoring (we will soon find out, when the work begins, if the catastrophic failure was caused by operator negligence). One of the complaining maintenance staff is upset because he did not receive a successful rating last year. I have discussed this with him and gave him the specific examples again as to why, but I guess this did not satisfy him. Ms. Thompson and Ms. Keith are probably unaware of these issues because they have never even tried to discuss them with me. They have only been interested in hearing the complaints of those they believe to be disenfranchised staff. Even the mediation had no focus whatsoever on the issues that I have with the various staff members. The mediator had no idea that the primary antagonist, the female housekeeper, is currently on a PIP until I mentioned it to her in my individual discussion.

I believe that one of the primary duties of both Ms. Thompson and Ms. Keith is to help me in the performance of my job. However, they are not and their involvement has only complicated human resource issues tremendously. I am currently in a situation where I know that I have personnel issues that need to be addressed. However, if I take action now it will almost assuredly be identified as a retaliatory response for the mediation involvement.

APPENDIX 16.
SIOUX SAN SWEAT LODGE
MEETING E-MAILS

The following is an E-mail which I sent to Jacqui Arpan, Health Educator, Sioux San IHS Hospital, following a meeting with her and Thomas Ghost Dog, Substance Abuse Counselor, Oglala Sioux Tribe, on May 4, 2009, to discuss the need to implement a policy addressing accountability at the Sioux San sweat lodge following the second major fire at the sweat lodge in a year:

From: Gjovik, Nathan D. (IHS/ABR)

Sent: Tuesday, May 05, 2009 5:24 AM
To: Arpan, Jacqui (IHS/ABR)
Cc: Koebrick, Fred (IHS/ABR)
Subject: Sweat Lodge Meeting

I woke up early this morning thinking about our meeting yesterday afternoon. The purpose of this E-mail is to document the manner in which I was treated as well as your apparent special interest priority of those who utilize the sweat lodge over the interests of the service unit/agency.

During the meeting it was clear that you were frustrated by my continued insistence on the use of the new policy draft. This occurred despite the direction that we both received from Mr. Fred Koebrick, CEO, to utilize same. It appeared that the reason you were disinterested in using the new policy is due to its increased control of the site by the service unit/agency and the fact that I was the principle author of the draft. This was evidenced by the continued efforts to try to weaken the policy despite valid points raised by me as to how the policy was designed to protect the service unit/agency as well as the users of the facility.

Throughout the meeting there was animosity being directed toward me by both you and Mr. Thomas Ghost Dog. There were several comments made indicating that the new policy was establishing a "prison" and that perhaps I would be the "warden" and that maybe I "need codependency counseling." As we read through the new draft policy there were regular snickers by both you and Mr. Ghost Dog when several items were read that you disagreed with (e.g., locking the site, key deposit, liability waiver, etc.). You also indicated during the meeting that you had issues with my involvement in the draft policy because I am not a Tribal member. After putting up with this behavior for approximately two hours I made it clear to you that I did not appreciate same. Ms. Helen Thompson, who returned to the meeting at the approximate two hour mark, explained on your behalf that the reason for the manner in which I was being treated is because I am "not of [your] culture" and it appeared that I was trying to dictate the terms of the policy.

I believe that your behavior during this meeting was unprofessional at best and racist at worst. As a health educator I expect more from you. As a professional colleague I expect that when we are tasked to work together to develop solutions to problems that face our service unit/agency that we should be able to perform same without racial prejudice and with consideration given to the interests of our mutual employer (as well as Tribal members).

I look forward to the successful completion of our new sweat lodge policy.

Nathan Gjovik

The following is an E-mail response from Thomas Ghost Dog, Substance Abuse Counselor, Oglala Sioux Tribe, to my E-mail above:

From: Arpan, Jacqui (IHS/ABR)
Sent: Thursday, May 07, 2009 5:20 PM
To: Gjovik, Nathan D. (IHS/ABR)
Cc: Koebrick, Fred (IHS/ABR)
Subject: FW: FW: Sweat Lodge Meeting

Forwarding for Tom Ghost Dog

From: Thomas Ghost [mailto:tghost_dog_99@yahoo.com]
Sent: Thursday, May 07, 2009 3:50 PM
To: Arpan, Jacqui (IHS/ABR)
Subject: Re: FW: Sweat Lodge Meeting

I sent to everyone and it didn't go through so I'll send it to you ok

To: Gjovik,Nathan D.
From Thomas Ghost Dog
Cc Koebrick, Fred

I woke up this morning and thinking the worse yet, I prayed for you in not really understanding us as Native American Lakotas. I think you stated many times that you understand what we are talking about, but you don't really understand, because of your attitude we all seen it, as native americans. I feel you blew this out out control as you as you used this term to make us feel like we are all firestarters. First step in understanding is to admit you really don't understand, but willing to learn and work with us and the native community in terms it meets ther needs of our native peoples isn't that why we are all here. We all get paid for working for our native peoples needs bottom-line. We as Native American people been put down by society, and at the bottom of everything that ever happens to society, and we have you dictating to us how our Sweat Ceremonies should be run and operated. We need more input from our native american community. In pride of dealing with pain and hurt we as native Americans have a real sense of humor which keeps us in contact with whats really happening in our world it seems you don't understand that either. Thank you for your time.

—On **Tue, 5/5/09, Arpan, Jacqui (IHS/ABR)** <*Jacqui.Arpan2@ihs.gov*> wrote:

From: Arpan, Jacqui (IHS/ABR) <Jacqui.Arpan2@ihs.gov>
Subject: FW: Sweat Lodge Meeting
To: tghost_dog_99@yahoo.com
Date: Tuesday, May 5, 2009, 2:52 PM

The following is the written response from Jacqui Arpan, Health Educator, Sioux San IHS Hospital, dated May 8, 2009, to my E-mail above:

This letter is a response to the e-mail I received from Nate Glovnik on 5/5/09 following a meeting the previous day related to the discussion of the sweat lodge policy draft. I felt his behavior was intimidating in that he was not able to grasp an understanding of the cultural aspects of our sweat lodge ceremony. I expected more from him as a Facilities Manger at our Indian health services Hospital where he has been hired to serve Native people. His condescending attitude prevailed as we attempted to explain our cultural perspective related to the use of the sweat lodge. Our previous Facilities Manger was respectful in his approach to the activities on the grounds and did not give an impression that there were violations of our facility policies. To threaten me by saying I did not have the Hospital safety in mind was an attack on my integrity as I have been a loyal employee here for twenty one years and the interest of the agency is at the forefront of my Health education practice. I have been a liaison between our hospital and the community in the capacity of my position and have received commendation for the communication I have built. For Nate to impose the impression otherwise I feel is harassment. The sweat lodge provides an aspect of health care and well being for those that choose to attend the ceremony. The planetree group commended our hospital for providing alternative methods of culturally appropriate healing that were community based. The Healing Center (Alcohol and Drug Treatment Center) incorporates our Native healing ceremonies into the treatment plan and are an integral aspect of treatment.

What Nate perceives as hostility from our committee comes from his lack of awareness and understanding of our Lakota culture as he is not able to provide a policy that addresses the needs of the hospital and the community. I perceived his attitude as elitist as though he knows what is best for our community based hospital. These sweat lodges have been here on our grounds for decades without incident and despite this I endured his hostile behavior for over two hours which brought me back to the oppression we as Native people endured for centuries. Nate has called me a racist which is totally beyond my cultural beliefs. I pride myself with the ability to communicate with members of all cultures I encounter but when I feel intimidated or harassed I cannot tolerate such an attack on my well being. Members of the community has asked me why Nate called those that use the sweat lodge "rock worshippers" but in his defense I admit I have never heard him make such a reference. I do not know if that is true or not.

In our follow up meeting the May 5th, he stood across from me as I was seated at the committee table and verbally threatened me and shook his finger at me as if to bully me into submission to his self imposed policy. He does not understand that his plan does not take into consideration the input of the group, including the security department.

Resolution: Mediation to resolve the feelings of racism experienced by Nate Glovnik and myself.

- Native American Cultural Sensitivity training for Nate Glovnik

APPENDIX 17.
ABERDEEN AREA IHS
GRIEVANCES-ROUND 2

The following are various grievances/complaints, shown in chronologic order and without most attachments (to conserve paper), which were filed against Fred Koebrick:

DEPARTMENT OF HEALTH AND HUMAN SERVICES

Public Health Service

Rapid City IHS Service Unit

3200 Canyon Lake Drive
Rapid City, SD 57702

To: Shelly Harris, Deputy Area Director
         Through
         Fred Koebrick, CEO, Rapid City IHS Service Unit
From: Facility Manager, RCSU
Date: July 15, 2009
Subject: Grievance Against Fred Koebrick

I have been supervised since mid-March of this year by the Chief Executive Officer, Mr. Fred Koebrick. At first he generally treated me with cordiality and respect. However, over the past

NETHERWORLD   289

several weeks, since the completion of a mediation effort (and his discovery that I am not Chickasaw as he originally thought) to try to resolve past EEO complaints (one against another of Mr. Koebrick's current employees), I have noticed some changes in his demeanor.

Over the past several weeks Mr. Koebrick has become very demanding of my department and our activities. We have had several recent conversations about priorities—physical plant upkeep (e.g., heating, air conditioning, utilities, etc.) versus aesthetics (e.g., painting and grounds keeping). I have explained to Mr. Koebrick on each occasion that we are generally understaffed given the size of our campus and the number of buildings we have under management (42-acre campus and 30 buildings with approximately 50% being around 100 years old). Mr. Koebrick has consistently agreed with this assessment. However, he believes that there should be greater emphasis placed on aesthetics versus physical plant upkeep. I have capitulated to his wishes.

Dayton Newbrough, Area Facility Engineer, and I identified several projects that had not been funded via traditional means (e.g., carpet replacement, hospital rock veneer refurbishment, and interior painting of the hospital) using stimulus funding. Once we were notified of the availability of the stimulus funding Mr. Newbrough and I proceeded to put together delivery orders (for an IDIQ contract) for several projects, including the painting of the interior of the hospital. During a conversation with Mr. Koebrick in late June he was not satisfied with the progress of the delivery orders and established a deadline by which he wanted all of the hospital hallways repainted by July 7th. I told him we would try to get the associated delivery order out as quickly as possible and he was not satisfied. He advised me that this had to be accomplished by whatever means necessary and suggested that I provide overtime to my staff to complete the work. I explained that this was not consistent with the intent of the stimulus funding (funding passed by the Federal government to create jobs), that my budget would not support overtime, and that I would be fortunate to be able to break even by the end of the fiscal year as it was. Mr. Koebrick responded that he had just approved it (not sure how this is possible since he is not part of the approval process for my funding) and that I should simply do it. He also indicated that he would back me up from his operating funds, as necessary. I asked him how he intended to do so this since the service unit was far below collection goals. He explained that he had a good handle on his fiscal situation and that I should not worry about it.

I did worry about what Mr. Koebrick was asking of me since spending beyond your means was against everything I had learned while working for several years at a well-managed bank, been taught by my business school professors, and had practiced for many years as a relatively successful project engineer and office manager within the agency. As a result of this I sought out other solutions and discovered one which satisfied Mr. Koebrick's timeframe. This involved supplementary use of security guards to paint the hospital hallways in the evenings when patient traffic was limited or nonexistent. The hospital hallway painting was completed before July 7th, just as the delivery order was issued for the contractor to paint same using stimulus funding.

During the conversation about painting Mr. Koebrick had also demanded that the grounds be completely mowed and trimmed and sprayed for weeds. I explained that we had already applied herbicide and fertilizer (weed and feed) to the grass covered areas and we were doing the best we could on mowing and trimming and spraying the various cracks to kill vegetative growth in same. I also explained that we were soliciting a grounds keeping contract to alleviate that portion of the work load for my limited staff (something he had suggested some weeks earlier when I had lost both of my part-time volunteer grounds keepers). Mr. Koebrick was not satisfied with this and said this also needed to be completed by the July 7th deadline as well.

As a consequence of the painting and grounds keeping directives at least one full week's worth of preventative maintenance work orders (PMs) had to be forgone (not sure what future cost this might have) and one of my employees had an incident because of the pressure to perform quickly which caused him to incur an avulsion of the tip of a finger requiring stitches. That employee may also be suffering from cardiac issues which the stress of the artificial July 7th deadline certainly exacerbated.

On Friday July 10th I was asked by Mr. Koebrick to report to him immediately. I did same. Mr. Koebrick advised me that he had just had a conversation with a member of the community who he later told me was Gene War Bonnet. Mr. War Bonnet had advised him that he was unhappy with a planned contract to a non-Indian contractor to perform grounds keeping and that he was told by my staff that they could perform this work. I asked why Mr. War Bonnet was involved in this and Mr. Koebrick explained that apparently my staff had approached him to be some sort of liaison between them and Mr. Koebrick. I asked Mr. Koebrick why he was having conversations with someone who is not a Federal employee about issues related to contracting and personnel—Federal management functions. He said that he has to since Mr. War Bonnet is a member of the community. I disagreed and explained that Mr. War Bonnet is a known campus agitator and that I had a brief history with him which was unfavorable and since then he has tried to damage my career. I also advised Mr. Koebrick that he had initially suggested the idea to have a contractor perform grounds keeping. He acknowledged same and suggested that we would proceed with the contract but that I needed to somehow reconcile this with my staff. I responded that I did not think this was necessary since this was a management decision and that he had made many decisions since his arrival that were not discussed or reconciled with subordinates first. However, he was insistent about same. He also suggested that he was not happy with the condition of the campus. I responded that we had forgone at least one week's worth of PMs to complete painting of the hospital, that everything had been mowed and sprayed, and that trimming was on-going. However, he was still not happy because he "had to tell [me] to do it." I disagreed and advised him that his form of management is not motivational for me and that I feel as though I am not being treated as a professional and am frustrated. He acknowledged same and stated that he is likewise frustrated. He advised me that he better see some mowing happening on Monday when the contractor arrives and I left.

I will also note for the record that Mr. Koebrick stated to me during one of our past conversations that he knows more about facility management than I do (I believe this was prompted by how we typically manage spraying grass & weed killer—after they appear in order to limit chemical use rather than preemptively). I consider this to be arrogant and disrespectful.

I have been very respectful and supportive of Mr. Koebrick since his arrival. I believe that in general he is trying to do the right things for our patients, as I am. However, his demeanor has become very disrespectful over the past several weeks and his management style autocratic rather than participative (which tends to work better with professional staff).

I am hereby requesting the following relief:

1. Mr. Koebrick cease any and all disrespectful behavior.

2. Mr. Koebrick cease any discussion with Mr. Gene War Bonnet related to anything other than patient care he has received.

3. Mr. Koebrick make recommendations for facility work he would like to see done and have the patience to allow me to work through the various support offices (contracting, personnel, etc.) to make it happen.

Sincerely,

Nathan D. Gjovik, PE, RS, MS, MBA, MPH, NREMT-B
CDR US Public Health Service

Cc: The Honorable John Thune, United States Senator, South Dakota

Attachments: #1 (Documentation regarding Gene War Bonnet-3 pages

DEPARTMENT OF HEALTH & HUMAN SERVICES

September 24, 2008

Aberdeen Area
Indian Health Service
Federal Building, Room 309
115 4ᵗʰ Ave. SE
Aberdeen, SD 57401

Mr. Gene War Bonnett
902 Haines Ave.
Rapid City, South Dakota 57701

Attachment #2

Dear Mr. War Bonnett:

This is in response to the telephone conversation that I had with you in regards to your visit at the Sioux San Health Care Facility on August 15, 1008. You stated in our conversation that you went down into the maintenance department to see a Mr. Ken Prairie Chicken about money he had owed your wife for the purchase of Indian Tacos and that at this time CDR Nathan Gjovik, Facility Manager approached you and questioned who you were.

CDR Gjovik is the Facility Manager and Housekeeping Manager at the Sioux San Health Care Facility. I realize that you felt that CDR Gjovik did not have the right to ask you who you were or why you were in the maintenance shop however as the Facility Manager CDR Gjovik is responsible for ensuring compliance with the organizational policies and procedures.

There are many individuals that present to the facility to sell home-made crafts and home baked/cooked foods however it is imperative that the continuity of a secure environment is maintained for the patients that present to the facility for healthcare.

The Sioux San Health Care Facility has a policy entitled "Temporary Vendor Permit" that requires all vendors that enter the facility to offer goods for sale, whether it be crafts or food are required to check in with security to sign in and be issued a temporary vendor permit and wear proper identification. It is the responsibility of all hospital personnel to inform any vendor without an ID tag to the Security department to sign in and obtain a temporary ID tag.

I apologize if you felt that you were being singled out, however CDR Gjovik's asking for your identity when you were located in a location that is for "Authorized Personnel Only" was performing his duties and taking responsibility for ensuring compliance with the "Temporary Vendor Permit".

Sincerely,

Shelly Harris
Deputy Area Director

Gjovik, Nathan D. (IHS/ABR)

From: Gjovik, Nathan D. (IHS/ABR)
Sent: Tuesday, August 19, 2008 12:20 PM
To: Thompson, Helen (IHS/ABR)
Cc: Birk, Gerald L. (IHS/ABR)
Subject: Gene War Bonnet

This message is in response to an apparent complaint by the subject individual. Last week Mr. War Bonnet, who was unknown to me at the time, entered the maintenance shop. Both doors to the shop are labeled "AUTHORIZED PERSONNEL ONLY." I was the only person present within the maintenance shop at the time. He stood in the doorway to my office and asked if I knew where Ken Prairie was. I initially had my back to him since I was working on my computer which faces the other direction and turned to find someone I did not know. I asked him who he was and he responded "That's none of your business" in a belligerent tone. I asked him why he needed to speak with Ken and he again provided the same response in the same tone. He asked me if I was the person in charge and I responded that I am the Facility Manager. I asked him what he was doing in the shop and he sounded as if he was becoming hostile as he responded that this was none of my business and that I needed to get Ken. I picked up my 2-way radio and began to call Security. He immediately turned around and walked briskly toward the south (far) door of the shop. I reported to Russ Kindle in Security that we had a threatening person in the shop that was exiting the south door. I began to make my way toward the south door and was met by Ed Cutgrass from the CHR program who had also entered the shop (apparently to check on Mr. War Bonnet). Ed told me as I walked by that Mr. War Bonnet had apparently just left CHR and that they "had come this close" as he indicated a close gap between his fingers.

As I exited the maintenance shop Mr. War Bonnet was in his vehicle and starting to drive away. Russ stopped him and I approached the vehicle to brief Russ on what had transpired. Mr. War Bonnet began to shout at me that I should be in Iraq or Afghanistan rather than here (I was in uniform). Mr. War Bonnet seemed very agitated and I suggested to Russ that he should consider calling the city police if things escalated and provided Russ with the tag number off the front of Mr. War Bonnet's car. My presence only seemed to agitate Mr. War Bonnet so I left to return to my office. Russ later briefed me that Mr. War Bonnet is known for behavior like this on campus and asked if I wanted to file a complaint. I responded in the negative.

I asked Ken Prairie about this incident later and Ken was not sure why Mr. War Bonnet was looking for him. Mr. War Bonnet had mentioned something about payment for Indian tacos when he was in the car talking to Russ. It appears that Mr. War Bonnet may have been acting in the capacity of a collection agent for somebody else who had sold Ken some Indian tacos the previous day and Ken hadn't had the opportunity to pay for them yet.

It should be noted that there is a WebcIdent report written by Security for this incident (control # 2008-1X9171).

Nathan D. Gjovik, PE, RS, MS, MBA, MPH, NREMT-B
CDR US Public Health Service
Facility Manager/Housekeeping Supervisor
Rapid City Service Unit
Aberdeen Area Indian Health Service
3200 Canyon Lake Drive
Rapid City, SD 57702
605-355-2339
605-355-2509 (fax)
Nathan.Gjovik@ihs.gov

Incident Report

Print Tools:

Acrobat Reader (.pdf)
FlashPaper (.swf)

Incident Report - Control Number: 2008-1X9171
Significant Non-Injury Event / Security

General Information
Incident involving: Significant Non-Injury Event
Name of person filing report: Kindle, Russell

Date of Incident:08/15/2008
General Time of Incident:09:15
Date Report filed:08/19/2008
Time Report filed:13:20:51 PM

Facility
RAPID CITY HOSPITAL - ABERDEEN/RAPID CITY

Location
On facility grounds (outside) – Roadway/Highway
Additional Location info: street in front of the Maintenance Shop

Description of the Incident:
Was called to Maintenance about a belligerant man. As I approached the Maintenance shop Gene Warbonett was coming out of the building, Nathan Gjovik, Facility Engineer was coming out behind him. I confronted Mr. Warbonett and asked what was going on. Mr Warbonett said that Nathan from Maintenance was asking him who he was and that it was none of his business. I talked with him and explained to him that Nathan was in charge of Maintenance and it was his business to know who was in his department. Gene then tried to tell Nathan that he didn't belong here. Nathan walked away to help diffuse the situation. I talked with Gene Warbonett and calmed him down. Mr. Warbonett then left.

Suggested Prevention of the Incident:
Possibly have the doors locked with a doorbell so that unauthorized persons aren't able to wander into the shop. Maybe card readers, like the one at the Dental Clinic, could be installed and each maintenance employee given a card for quick easy access.

Security

Event Nature: Perimeter Control

Public Health Service

DEPARTMENT OF HEALTH AND HUMAN SERVICES

Rapid City IHS Service Unit

3200 Canyon Lake Drive
Rapid City, SD 57702

To: Shelly Harris, Deputy Area Director
         Through
         Fred Koebrick, CEO, Rapid City IHS Service Unit
From: Facility Manager, RCSU
Date: October 1, 2009
Subject: Grievance Against Fred Koebrick

This is the second grievance I have submitted pertaining to the arrogant and disrespectful behavior exhibited by Mr. Fred Koebrick, Chief Executive Officer, Rapid City Indian Health Service Hospital, toward me. It is my understanding based on a conversation with Mr. Koebrick on September 28, 2009, that he unilaterally decided that the first grievance did not need to be acted upon. This was in spite of my insistence that I did want it addressed. I have attached a copy of that document dated July 15, 2009, for follow-up.

Our discussions on September 28, 2009, centered on a call back protocol for maintenance staff. I had given Mr. Koebrick a "heads-up" on the issue a couple of weeks earlier as a courtesy knowing that he regularly has discussions directly with staff regarding management issues within their respective departments

(I have asked Mr. Koebrick to redirect such discussions with staff that I supervise back to me for resolution, however, it appears that these discussions continue.). Mr. Koebrick became involved in the issue during my absence from work while training and was participated in the development of a solution without any discussion with me. The solution involves reestablishing a system which had been used for several years previously and has been proven not to work. Based on this I advised Mr. Koebrick that I did not wish to implement same since it was problematic for me, for staff, and for our customers (other hospital staff). Mr. Koebrick responded that it is my attitude that is preventing me from achieving the success "that I so desperately seek." I was offended by this statement, but said nothing. He then indicated to me that this was the only solution that would be acceptable to CDR Clayton Belgarde, Aberdeen Area Human Resource Specialist. I returned to my office and sent an E-mail to CDR Belgarde to clarify the situation.

CDR Belgarde responded via E-mail that he did not know what I was referring to so I called him to discuss the situation. At first CDR Belgarde did not recall having a conversation and then indicated that he did recall having a brief discussion with Mr. Koebrick. CDR Belgarde stated that the presentation he received from Mr. Koebrick was very different from what I had provided and that he had not provided anything other than a very brief informal verbal response based on the data being presented by Mr. Koebrick. He then indicated that the situation could be handled in a different manner based on the information I was presenting to him. I then forwarded the response E-mail from CDR Belgarde to Mr. Koebrick and requested that he call me to discuss this further with him.

Mr. Koebrick called me and I returned to his office to discuss the maintenance call back protocol issue with him further. He seemed clearly irritated by my follow-up on the issue and advised me that the decision was already made and I simply had to implement it. When I reiterated my reservations about the solution he stated that I had better get over it and accept the fact that the decision had been made and that I just needed to do it. I advised him that I would appreciate the opportunity to manage my department, as I was hired to do, and that I believed his involvement in making such decisions was not necessary. He suggested that he has not involved himself to any significant degree in the management of my department. I disagreed and reminded him of the previous grievance I had tendered regarding the same issue. I asked about the status of same and he advised me that he had determined that the grievance did not require any action. I responded that I had specifically requested action be taken on the grievance and asked for time to develop another grievance. He responded that he would have to review the leave request upon receipt of same. I left for my office and immediately developed a request for leave to develop another grievance and returned to Mr. Koebrick's office. He asked if I needed the whole day since I already had a grievance prepared (apparently referring to the previous grievance which he had not taken action on). I responded that I had additional information to include and he replied "I'm sure you do."

Over the past several weeks I have been attempting to complete a paramedic program. I have been doing this using 100% of my own time—evenings, weekends, and earned leave, nearly all of which is "use or lose." Mr. Koebrick has not offered to provide me with any administrative time for the training and his hospital budget has incurred no direct cost for my tuition. However, he stated to me during a conversation on or about September 14, 2009, that he's sure the service unit will benefit in some way from my training. The implication is that he was having second thoughts about his support of approving my "use or lose" leave for my paramedic training endeavor. I am not aware of any similar hesitations associated with sending other employees to various conferences and trainings incurring travel costs and tuition fees from his hospital budget. To my knowledge the service unit has not incurred any direct expenses for any of my training since my arrival in July 2007. Mr. Koebrick has an obvious double standard associated with his support of training.

I have been very respectful and supportive of Mr. Koebrick since his arrival. However, his demeanor has become very arrogant and disrespectful since his discovery that I am not a Native American, which also coincides with the timeframe of an unsuccessful attempt at mediating an EEO claim (which is still unresolved).

In addition to the relief requested from the previous grievance I am hereby requesting the following relief:

1. Mr. Koebrick allow me to manage my departments.
2. Mr. Koebrick treat me as he does other employees (most of whom are Native American).

Sincerely,

Nathan D. Gjovik, PE, RS, MS, MBA, MPH, NREMT-B
CDR US Public Health Service

Cc: The Honorable John Thune, United States Senator, South Dakota

Attachments: #1 (Grievance Dated July 15, 2009)

DEPARTMENT OF HEALTH AND HUMAN SERVICES

Public Health Service

Rapid City IHS Service Unit

3200 Canyon Lake Drive
Rapid City, SD 57702

To: Fred Koebrick, CEO, Rapid City IHS Service Unit
From: Facility Manager, RCSU
Date: October 16, 2009
Subject: EEO Complaint Against Fred Koebrick

This EEO complaint is based in large part on two grievances dated July 16, 2009, and October 1, 2009, which were submitted to Mr. Fred Koebrick, Chief Executive Officer, Rapid City Indian Health Service Hospital on July 17, 2009, and October 2, 2009, respectively. Both grievances are included as attachments to this memo along with Mr. Koebrick's response to the second grievance.

As noted within the text of the second grievance Mr. Koebrick unilaterally determined that the first grievance did not need to be addressed. The second grievance he did not address based on a technicality. When I delivered the second grievance on October 2nd Mr. Koebrick stated that he believed at one time that I was the right man for the job, but no longer believed that and that he would like me to retire or transfer and that I "am free to leave at any time." I considered this to be a veiled threat against my employment. I believe Mr. Koebrick would not have made similar statements to a Native American employee.

Mr. Koebrick's statements of October 2nd are consistent with his demeanor toward me over the past several months in creating a ███████████████████ This demeanor began shortly after a failed EEO mediation attempt on May 26, 2009, during which Mr. Koebrick was the primary negotiator for the Department. It was soon after this failed negotiation when Mr. Koebrick came to my office asked me if I was a member of the Chickasaw Tribe. I felt uncomfortable with the question since I believe one's heritage to be irrelevant in a workplace free of discrimination. However, I responded facetiously that I am a northern Cherokee since he was looking at my wall clock with the Cherokee syllabary. He inquired further and I admitted that I am of Scandinavian heritage. Shortly thereafter Mr. Koebrick began treating me differently than he had previously.

In addition to the relief requested in the previous grievances I am hereby requesting the following relief:

The IHS compensate my wife and I in the sum of $300,000.00, after taxes or tax free and in 2009 dollars, for damages incurred via this and past agency discrimination activities.

Neither the IHS nor Mr. Koebrick does anything to compromise my ability to retire under honorable conditions from the USPHS or be gainfully employed elsewhere in the future.

In exchange for the relief sought above I will drop all outstanding EEO complaints and grievances and retire from the service as desired by Mr. Koebrick.

Sincerely,

Nathan D. Gjovik, PE, RS, MS, MBA, MPH, NREMT-B
CDR US Public Health Service

Attachments: #1 (Response Letter from Fred Koebrick Dated October 12, 2009)—1 page
#2 (Grievance Dated October 1, 2009)—11 pages
#3 (Grievance Dated July 16, 2009)—6 pages

DEPARTMENT OF HEALTH AND HUMAN SERVICES

Public Health Service

Rapid City IHS Service Unit

3200 Canyon Lake Drive
Rapid City, SD 57702

To: Gail Martin, EEO Manager, Aberdeen Area Office
From: Facility Manager, RCSU
Date: October 30, 2009
Subject: EEO Complaint Against Fred Koebrick

This is an addendum to the EEO complaint against Mr. Fred Koebrick, Chief Executive Officer, Rapid City Indian Health Service Hospital dated October 16, 2009 (see attachment #1). On Thursday October 22, 2009, Mr. Koebrick apparently forwarded the original complaint to Gail Martin, Aberdeen Area EEO Manager.

On October 23, 2009, CDR Dayton Newbrough, Area Facility Engineer, received a radio call from one of my maintenance staff to come to the second floor of the hospital. CDR Newbrough and I were having lunch in the staff dining room within the hospital at the time so I accompanied him to the second floor. Within room #230 we found Mr. Koebrick directing two members of my maintenance crew to install a framed wall within the room. They had questions about the scope whereby Mr. Koebrick apparently directed them to CDR Newbrough. Mr. Koebrick had recently input work requests (see attachment #2) to have walls installed to split two large rooms into four smaller rooms (I was unaware of this at the time). I reminded Mr. Koebrick that we had already discussed this potential project and that we had both determined that it was not something that should be done[50]. Mr. Koebrick advised me that he had an approved action plan to separate the rooms. I advised him that I had not been involved in the development or approval of the action plan and again reminded him that we had discussed this within the past several weeks and that he had decided it was not prudent given the frequency of moves within the hospital and the cost and complexity of such a project. Mr. Koebrick responded that things had changed and that "everybody was claiming that [I was] the reason for the delay in getting Social Services moved." Mr. Koebrick then advised me that this needed to get done right away. I reminded him of the complexity of the project and that it was not as simple as installing a new wall. It would first require design work to determine adequate ingress and egress to each new space as well as how to serve each space with heating and air conditioning, electrical services, IT services, lighting, sprinkler protection, etc. He stated that he did not want to hear any excuses from me and that I was simply required to perform the work. I asked Mr. Koebrick how the project was to be funded. He advised me again that I needed to perform the work right away. I responded that we would input a project funding request and that hopefully it would be approved in the next funding cycle. Mr. Koebrick sternly advised me that not only was I going to do the project, but that it would be completed within two weeks. I responded that what he was asking of me was impossible. He again sternly advised me that I had two weeks and I had better get started. He also directed CDR Newbrough to get the project completed before he left the room.

My maintenance staff, sensing Mr. Koebrick's ████ toward me, had left the room early in the above described encounter. However, CDR Newbrough remained throughout the exchange.

He was stunned by it and stood and looked at me while shaking his head in disbelief for some time after Mr. Koebrick left. I explained to him that this was typical of the manner in which Mr. Koebrick was treating me recently. CDR Newbrough indicated that he thought Mr. Koebrick's behavior was highly inappropriate and advised me that he did not think the framed wall was something that should be done. He also indicated that he had worked with the same social services staff several years ago while trying to help them move into their current space and had similar problems with them being unwilling to move (roadblocks presented at every opportunity). We estimated that the work would probably cost between $5,000-$10,000 per room. I asked CDR Newbrough to input project funding requests for the two rooms with cost estimates of ~$10,000 each. CDR Newbrough later estimated the cost for each room at $13,000.

After I returned to my office I worked up a station leave request for the following Monday, October 26, 2009, in order to work up another EEO complaint against Mr. Koebrick. On my way to deliver the leave request I walked past Luke Kochutin, Security Guard. I advised him that I was going to deliver a document to Mr. Koebrick and that he would probably not be very happy about it and if Mr. Kochutin could simply stand out in the hallway and monitor the situation I would appreciate same. Mr. Kochutin obliged me as I delivered the leave request. Mr. Koebrick became angry upon seeing the document and immediately advised that he was not going to sign it. I asked him to confirm the requirement to provide time for development of an EEO complaint. He responded sharply that I should know the answer to that. I advised him that it was my understanding that he has an obligation to provide the time. He responded that he will advise me as to if he will authorize time as well as for what day, if he decides to authorize time. I asked him to confirm that he was denying me leave to develop an EEO complaint. He responded that he will decide if and when leave is to be granted.

He then advised that I had better get started on the room project. I responded that I would start once we received funding for the project. He loudly advised me that I had two weeks to complete the project and that I had better get started. I responded that there is a process for projects such as this and that I would not circumvent the process. He loudly advised me that I was going to do it and that I had better get started. I left the room and walked past Mr. Kochutin who was near Donna Huber's (Chief Nurse Executive) office as I returned to my office.

Later that same day Mr. Koebrick continued his ██████ demeanor toward me by sending me an E-mail indicating that another project needed to be completed by me and my department immediately (see attachment #3). The project involves the relocation of the electronic messaging board which advises patients when their pharmacy prescription is ready for pickup. It should be noted that this is probably something which should be completed by the IT department, however, maintenance has been identified to perform the work. In the E-mail chain the person indicating the need for moving the sign (Michelle Leach, Director, Resource Mangement) is asked by Mr. Koebrick to coordinate a new location for the sign with CAPT Todd Warren from the pharmacy. This was never done and CAPT Warren even indicates that the sign needs to be located "where patients can actually see it" (something that will be compromised with the proposed location).

I have had separate conversations with both Ms. Leach and Mr. Koebrick during which I had proposed an alternative means of dealing with Ms. Leach's concerns over privacy which would be far less costly and more customer oriented (i.e., patients would still be able to see the electronic board from the hallway as well as the waiting room rather than having to enter the waiting room to see the board as would be required in Ms. Leach's proposed solution). The alternate proposal involves simply taping off an area around the patient registration work areas and putting up a sign asking patients to please stay outside the area designated by the tape in order to ensure privacy for our patients. This is what was done across the hall for the pharmacy where it has been proven to work. Despite the existence of a better and less costly solution Mr. Koebrick would now like to proceed with the more expensive alternative even though it may soon result in having to move the board again (once he authorizes the replacement of vending machines within the waiting room). Despite the fact that it was Ms. Leach's responsibility to coordinate the new electronic board location with CAPT Warren and this was never done, Mr. Koebrick suggests in his E-mail that I am now delinquent since "it should already have been completed…"

On Monday October 26, 2009, Ms. Martin provided me with an alternate leave request form to be used when requesting official time to develop complaints. I presented another leave request to Mr. Koebrick using the new form that afternoon. The request was for 8 hours on October 28, 2009. Mr. Koebrick advised me that he did not think this was the correct form, but accepted it. At approximately 3 pm on October 27, 2009, Mr. Koebrick authorized 4 hours of leave for the following morning. When I picked up the completed form I asked him why he had only authorized 4 hours and he fired back that "4 hours should be plenty of time because [I] should be good at this by now." I asked him again via E-mail to authorize the additional 4 hours that I had requested and he refused. I will note for the record that the development of this complaint took more than 8 hours to complete and that I am fundamentally opposed to having to endure this type of behavior at work and then have to spend my personal time developing the complaint to address it. The related E-mail chain is included with this document as attachment #4. I believe the tone of the messages are attempts to antagonize me. This, combined with his refusal to grant leave for Monday October 26, 2009, and his arbitrary limitation of authorized official time to 4 hours on Wednesday October 28, 2009, would be considered by any reasonable person to be reprisal[51]. Mr. Koebrick's comment that I "should be good at this by now" is disrespectful and implies that he does not take this seriously. It should be noted that Mr. Koebrick's behavior toward me this week occurred after Dr. Roubideaux sent an E-mail on the morning of October 26, 2009, to all IHS staff advising that "we need to treat each other with kindness and respect, and we need to work together in a professional manner" (see attachment #5).

I will also note for the record that Mr. Koebrick continues to involve himself in the management of my department. He apparently discusses various departmental management issues directly with my staff. This has apparently emboldened at least one of my employees to believe that he can behave in a grossly disrespectful manner toward me with impunity. Reference is made to an E-mail dated October 22, 2009, (see attachment #6) wherein I detail the recent behavior of Mr. Ken Prairie Chicken and his demeanor toward me and his repeated responses back to me that he will "just take it higher" or "just take it up the ladder" (implying Mr. Koebrick).

Mr. Koebrick continues to foster and maintain ███████ ███████████████ toward me after his discovery that I do not have Native American lineage. This ████████ is in the form of disrespectful treatment (in tone and message), unfair and unreasonable (and illegal?) demands being made of me, characterizations of me that I am not performing well, and promotion of disrespectful behavior toward me by others. Due to my past experiences with two previous CEOs and one AO it has become clear to me that the Aberdeen Area Indian Health Service (IHS) is apparently unable to provide me with a supervisor who can lead and manage in a racially unbiased manner. I am also noting for the record that during one or more conversations with then *CDR* Ron Keats approximately one year ago he advised me that a senior management official of the Aberdeen Area IHS stated to him that they were "going to change the color of the workforce in the Area." This may very well explain my situations, then and now. Therefore, in addition to the relief requested in the previous grievances and EEO complaint against Mr. Koebrick, I am requesting the following relief:

An anonymous survey be conducted of all non-Tribal employees of the Aberdeen Area IHS to determine the extent of the racial bias and discrimination within the Area. The results of the survey are to be shared with me.

The ██████████████████ end immediately.

Mr. Koebrick be severely reprimanded for his discriminatory actions and █████ demeanor.

Please note that due to the delicate nature of information included within this document I would like to maintain the confidentiality of same.

Sincerely,

Nathan D. Gjovik, PE, RS, MS, MBA, MPH, NREMT-B
CDR US Public Health Service

Cc: The Honorable John Thune, United States Senator, South
     Dakota

Attachments: #1(EEO Complaint Against Fred Koebrick
             Dated October 16, 2009)—26 pages
             #2 (Work Requests #201000226 & 201000227)—2
             pages
             #3 (E-mail Chain Dated October 23, 2009)—7
             pages
             #4 (E-mail Chain Dated October 27, 2009)—2
             pages
             #5 (E-mail Dated October 26, 2009)—2 pages
             #6 (E-mail Dated October 22, 2009)—2 pages

DEPARTMENT OF HEALTH AND HUMAN SERVICES

Public Health Service

Rapid City IHS Service Unit

3200 Canyon Lake Drive
Rapid City, SD 57702

To: Gail Martin, EEO Manager, Aberdeen Area Office
From: Facility Manager, RCSU
Date: November 13, 2009
Subject: EEO Complaint Against Fred Koebrick

This is an addendum to the EEO complaints against Mr. Fred Koebrick, Chief Executive Officer, Rapid City Indian Health Service Hospital dated October 16, 2009, and October 30, 2009.

On Wednesday November 4, 2009, Mr. Koebrick sent me an E-mail (see attachment #1) indicating that he had decided that I was to arrange for completion of construction work for which the Oglala Sioux Tribe had already been provided funding to complete via a contractor. I advised Mr. Koebrick of this and he responded that he had already made the decision and that I was "to proceed as instructed." I believe that Mr. Koebrick did not discuss this with me because of the EEO complaints I have pending against him and that he now has no compunction to ask me to perform work which may be considered inappropriate, improper, or even illegal.

Following the receipt of Mr. Koebrick's directive and subsequent E-mail I hand delivered a station leave request for time to develop another EEO complaint (this one). Upon delivery he stated, "There must be something wrong with you." I responded, "No, there isn't." He replied, "There is definitely something wrong with you." He then advised me that he will decide as to whether or not leave will be granted. I advised him that the request is for this Friday. He responded that if leave is granted it may not be for Friday. Attachment #1 documents this exchange.

Following the directive from Mr. Koebrick discussed above and on the same day there happened to be a special agent from the Office of the Inspector General (OIG) visiting the campus. He was introduced during an Executive Team (ET) meeting which I was attending. I asked to speak to the special agent before he left and he accommodated me. I discussed the directive from Mr. Koebrick with him and he asked me to provide him with copies of the pertinent funding documents. I did same. On November 5, 2009, at approximately 0900 he contacted Mr. Koebrick to arrange for a conference call to discuss the situation. Mr. Koebrick decided to make an example of my whistleblower activity by arranging a conference call and directing the entire hospital ET to attend and invited several ranking members of the Aberdeen Area to also participate. Attachment #2 contains his invitation to the teleconference and my recap of same. At 1210 the same day that Mr. Koebrick had been contacted by the OIG special agent I received an E-mail that he had completed my commissioned officer effectiveness report (COER-performance evaluation) for 2009 (see attachment #3). The COER is incredibly negative and suggests that I am an officer who is highly problematic and should not be promoted or even considered for work elsewhere.

It should be noted that Mr. Koebrick completed a revision of my 2008 COER on October 5, 2009, due to similar EEO issues with the previous acting CEO (who is now Mr. Koebrick's AO). That COER is radically different from the 2009 COER he completed just 30 days later (see attachment #4). Since he has only supervised me for less than 8 months to date the basis for his evaluation was essentially the same. He even included within the 2008 COER a reference to the development of the values statement which occurred in April 2009. However, it is obvious to anybody reviewing the two COERs that something changed between the two reviews. That change is a function of the EEO complaint I filed against Mr. Koebrick on October 16, 2009, and addendum dated October 30, 2009. The first complaint was routed through Mr. Koebrick and he approved leave for the addendum so he is well aware of at least that one.

Following the review of my 2009 COER I felt physically ill as I knew that, if allowed to stand, it would ensure that I would not be considered for ███████████ and I thought of how this would impact my family. I worked up a sick leave request for the remainder of the afternoon and hand delivered it to Mr. Koebrick. He seemed to relish in the fact that I was suddenly not feeling well as evidenced by the smirk he had on his face as he signed the leave slip and chided me about the need to leave if I wasn't feeling well. I asked him about my leave request for the following day. He expressed in a loud and arrogant voice that he "will decide if and when [I] will be allowed leave and, if so, how much." I reminded him that I was leaving for the day and the request was for the following day. He responded, "Nate, you will be the first to know if I approve your leave request!" I inquired as to how this would be done if I was leaving and he implied that he would send me an E-mail. Be that as it may I have heard nothing further on my leave request and there was no reason given as to why it was not approved.

The following day at 0951 I sent another E-mail request to Mr. Koebrick and copied Gail Martin, Aberdeen Area EEO Manager (see attachment #5). I explained that I believed he was attempting to suppress my ability to participate in the complaint process which is, by definition, reprisal. I also explained that I would now be in need of seeking legal counsel and addressing a host of other issues which were outlined on the leave request (see attachment #6). The leave request was for the week of November 9-13, 2009 (exclusive of Veteran's Day). The only response I received to this leave request was Mr. Koebrick sternly advising me of the need to report to duty as required until he authorizes leave. However, he again did not authorize leave and, again, no reason was given as to why he did not.

On the morning of November 12, 2009, I received an odd E-mail from Mr. Koebrick suggesting that I was to meet with him at 1130 in the Lakota Lodge conference room (see attachment #7). I responded with a query as to what the meeting was about. He would not tell me, responding only that he would advise me at that time. I reported to the Lakota Lodge conference room at 1130 as requested. Gerry Birk and Rusty Hale, the two security guards on duty that day, were also present. Mr. Koebrick entered and immediately handed me a document advising me that I had been detailed to the Aberdeen Area Office of Environmental Health and Engineering effective November 15, 2009 (see attachment #8). Nothing like this had been discussed or even suggested to me previously. There was no reason provided for the sudden detail. I noted for the record that this was a reprisal action for the EEO complaint I had filed against Mr. Koebrick. Mr. Koebrick asked the two security guards to escort me to my office to retrieve my personal effects and we all proceeded to do same.

On the way out of the Lakota Lodge Gerry Birk placed a comforting hand on my shoulder in support of me in the situation and then stated that they would hang back a little way "so it didn't look so bad." Mr. Koebrick admonished him that they were to proceed since there is a "safety and security risk." I couldn't believe what I thought I heard him say so I asked him to confirm same and he repeated it. I stated that I objected to his statement and we proceeded to my office. I will note for the record that there has never been even the slightest suggestion of a threat to Mr. Koebrick by me at any time. As a matter of fact, earlier that same morning I was personally helping housekeeping staff move and arrange furniture within his refurbished office (the one that I had ensured was refurbished to suit his needs). I was walking by them in the hallway in the basement of the Lakota Lodge and saw that they were struggling with some large pieces and were not adequately protecting the furniture for the move to the "new" office. I intervened with my assistance physically moving the pieces and providing guidance on protecting the furniture. I then visited twice with Mr. Koebrick to discuss how he wanted the furniture arranged and how to repair a glass desktop surface that had been damaged. The interactions were constructive and professional and I assigned a maintenance worker to repair the glass desktop. This was a typical interaction with Mr. Koebrick when I would initiate same—constructive and professional.

When Gerry Birk, Rusty Hale, Fred Koebrick, and I arrived at my office Mr. Koebrick confiscated my keys and then advised that I was only to take what I absolutely must have from my office. I began collecting my personal effects which included various folders containing personal information I have accumulated over the course of my career. Mr. Koebrick promptly snatched them up and stated that I would not be allowed to bring any documents with me. He then sharply advised me that I had two more minutes to finish. Gerry and Rusty assisted me with loading my boxes (that Rusty had provided to me) and various Native American art and other personal effects. Mr. Koebrick then advised them to escort me off the grounds. I shook hands with Gerry and Rusty and thanked them for being descent. I then left the campus with Gerry Birk following me in the security vehicle.

In the above incident I was made to feel by Mr. Koebrick as if I had done something terrible when, in fact, all I had done was what the regulation demands of me—reported discriminatory activities and brought forward a funding irregularity. This was very embarrassing for me and has resulted in subsequent sleep disturbances for both my wife and I from the stress created by the actions of Mr. Koebrick. I will note for the record that Mr. Koebrick is aware of the delicate nature of my wife's current health status and that she suffered an acute exacerbation of a stress-induced chronic disease from a similar ███████████████ created by his current Administrative Officer, when she was the acting CEO (prior to Mr. Koebrick's arrival).

Based on my recent experiences and the above documentation it is clear that Mr. Koebrick's intent is to try to harm me, my career, and my family. The Federal government should not allow someone with this demeanor to be employed within its ranks and I should not be punished for simply doing what regulations demand. Therefore, in addition to the relief sought in the previous submittals, I am hereby asking for the following relief:

1. Mr. Koebrick's Federal employment be immediately terminated.

2. I be detailed to my home until such time as this EEO action is resolved. This will reduce the stress that my wife is currently experiencing with the thought of my absence from our home in Rapid City while being detailed to Aberdeen.

Please note that due to the delicate nature of information included within this document I would like to maintain the confidentiality of same.

Sincerely,

Nathan D. Gjovik, PE, RS, MS, MBA, MPH, NREMT-B
CDR US Public Health Service

Cc: The Honorable John Thune, United States Senator, South
     Dakota
     Bonita J. White, Esq., Director, DHHS, Division of EEO

Attachments: #1 (E-mail Chain Dated November 4, 2009)—2 pages
#2 (Invitation from Fred Koebrick for Whistleblower Telecon & Recap)—2 pages
#3 (2009 COER from Fred Koebrick)—3 pages
#4 (2008 COER-Revised from Fred Koebrick)—4 pages
#5 (E-mail Dated November 6, 2009)—1 page
#6 (Leave Request Dated November 6, 2009)—1 page
#7 (E-mail Dated November 12, 2009)—1 page
#8 (Memo from Fred Koebrick Dated November 12, 2009)—1 page

APPENDIX 18.
LOG OF INTERACTIONS W/
ABERDEEN AREA IHS

The following is a log of various interactions I had with various Aberdeen Area IHS staff members over the course of the nearly one year I was detailed to the Aberdeen Area Office:

Date   *Start*   *End*   *Discussion Notes*

11/17/2009 0805   0815   I asked to meet with CDR Jon Fogarty and Fogarty accompanied him to his office. I asked for permission to record the conversation. Fogarty replied, "Nate, you know you can't do that, it is illegal." I responded, "Why would it be illegal?" Fogarty responded that I would not be allowed to record the conversation. I then grabbed a notebook to have a written record of the conversation and asked Fogarty, "Why am I here." Fogarty replied, "You have been detailed, temporarily reassigned here." I asked, "Why?" Fogarty replied, "You are here to work, period." I then asked, "What about my request for time to follow-up on my EEO complaints?" Fogarty replied, "You are not getting time to follow-up on your EEO complaints. I have been told that you are ineligible." I asked, "Why would I be ineligible?" Fogarty replied, "At some point in time you will be allowed up to two hours, following my research." I asked, "What about time to follow-up with my whistle-blower complaint?" Fogarty replied, "You are not getting any time for this until I have researched." I asked, "When will I be advised?" Fogarty replied, "When I have time to do it." I indicated that I believed Fogarty's actions to be reprisal and that I wanted them to stop. Fogarty replied, "This meeting is over, get back to work."

11/17/2009 ~0900 ~0930   I asked to speak with CAPT Ron Keats about the nature of my current detail. I asked why I am here in Aberdeen and Keats began to explain that I cannot seem to get along with anyone including the new CEO and that the new CEO has the authority to transfer staff out of the facility. I asked about the statement made by a senior management official within the agency to then *CDR* Keats that "[they] are going to change the color of the workforce." He acknowledged that the statement had been made and asked why I keep having issues. I responded that I was simply doing what was required of me by regulation and the various training we receive every year that demands all employees to report instances of discrimination and waste, fraud, and abuse, and that was all I had done. Keats suggested that I had not treated the CEO with due respect. I responded that I had on every occasion treated the CEO respectfully and then provided an example of how, even on the day I was relieved of my duties I had provided assistance to the CEO on getting his office organized with new furniture—the office that I had ensured was renovated to alleviate the allergic response the CEO had been experiencing prior to the renovation. I then reiterated that I had never treated the CEO disrespectfully—ever. I then invited Keats to call CDR Dayton Newbrough to discuss an exchange that Newbrough had been party/witness to between me and the CEO wherein the CEO was markedly disrespectful to me. I then indicated to Keats that I had worked in an Area office at one time in the past and did not experience discrimination in that environment and that I did not even have a door that I could close on my office (eluding to Keats' office door which is normally kept closed). I then noted to Keats that during our discussion he had been shaking his head "no" whenever I spoke and asked him to please try to keep an open mind and try to understand that there is another side to the story. Keats did not have anything further to say as I then thanked him for his time and left.

11/18/2009   1430   1440   I was asked by CDR Jon Fogarty to meet with him in his office and I accompanied him to same. Fogarty proceeded to advise me that I was no longer to meet with Gail Martin, Aberdeen Area IHS EEO Manager, since she had reported that I had recently visited her office and had a red face. I indicated that I had just found out my wife was having another flare of a stress-induced disease and that I had used the stairs when going to her office to discuss this with Ms. Martin and that may have been the reason for the red face. Fogarty admonished me again that I was not to go to her office and that Pauline Bruce, IHS EEO Director, was now handling my complaints. I responded that nothing was happening through Ms. Bruce's office. Fogarty responded that that is the way it is. I then reminded Fogarty that I had once been Fogarty's supervisor and that I had treated Fogarty respectfully and that I did not feel as if this was being reciprocated and asked if we could speak to each other as people. Fogarty responded that I had come to him as a problem and that he was so busy at time that he felt that his head would explode and didn't need the difficulties that I represented. Fogarty continued by stating that this isn't about you (Gjovik) it is about me (Fogarty). I thanked him for his time left the room.

11/20/2009 0915 0915 CDR Chris Allen advised me that I was free to go home for the weekend.

11/24/2009 ~0820 ~0825 CDR Jon Fogarty asked me to come into his office as I was walking by. I did same. Fogarty indicated that he was going to approve my leave requests for 12/2/2009 for sick leave in the morning and administrative leave in the afternoon. I thanked him and then asked Fogarty if he had made the decision to allow me to leave early the previous Friday. Fogarty responded that he was simply trying to survive this and was responding to new information as it became available.

11/24/2009 ~0845 ~0900 I was having a discussion with CDR Chris Allen concerning a project with which Allen was requesting assistance from me. During the discussion Allen asked me how long I would be detailed to the Area office. During the response I advised Allen of the events leading to my detail to the Area office. Allen responded, "Suffice it to say that I worked for Fred [Koebrick] in White Earth and I transferred to Sioux City."

12/18/2009 ~1130 ~1145 I had been trying to contact CAPT Ron Keats for some time. I sent him an E-mail, tried to reach him by phone but could not even reach an answering service, checked his office several times and knocked on his office door, and left a written note on the dry erase message board on the outside of his office door. He did not respond. On Friday 18 December 2009 at ~1130 I saw Keats talking to another officer within the office where I am now working and approached him and asked if I could speak to him. He said he would be over in a couple of minutes. He arrived at my work station 30 minutes later. Keats and I went into a conference room and I asked him why my billet had been recently downgraded. Keats responded that my supervisor (Fred Koebrick) requested the action and his responsibility was to simply process it. I was surprised by this response as I thought perhaps there should be some "value added" by this O-6 officer. I suggested to Keats that perhaps there should have been some form of communication with me other than simply sending me the completed downgraded billet and that I thought that was the primary function of a liaison. I added that I had worked as a liaison officer on deployment and understood the function to involve communication in both or every direction. Keats then indicated that he did not appreciate being made to feel defensive when he speaks to me and that he is simply of "tool for management—management tells [him] to do something and [he] do[es] it." Again, I was surprised by this response as it implies no advocacy for commissioned officers. I further asked Keats as to what else was being planned or developed as far as actions related to me and he responded that he did not know. Keats was obviously perturbed by our conversation and asked if there was anything else. I thanked him for his time and he left immediately.

12/29/2009 ~0745 ~0750 I spoke with Curt Bossert, Facility Engineer, about Sisseton. Bossert noted that Abe Vinikoor was leaving IHS to work for Children's Hospital in Seattle. I asked Bossert how Vinikoor did with Sisseton and Bossert described Vinikoor's management of the project as weak and that he did not address major issues affecting work quality and schedule. Bossert noted that only about 50% of the planned homes to be constructed by the Tribe had been completed and accepted by the IHS (which was years beyond the approved project performance period).

2/3/2010 ~0830 ~0835 I spoke with Rick Sorensen, Deputy Area Director, in his office after having various E-mail communication with CAPT Ron Keats about the need to get the reviewing official statement (ROS) completed soon. Keats had indicated that he had provided the draft ROS to Mr. Sorensen on 22 January. However, Sorensen indicated that he was unaware of having received anything from Keats and suggested that he would review the document as soon as possible. I emphasized the importance of getting the document completed and forwarded to Keats as soon as possible.

2/3/2010 ~1230 ~1231 I spoke with Rick Sorensen in the restroom while we both happened to be in there at the same time. I asked Sorensen about the status of my ROS and Sorensen indicated that he had been in a meeting all day.

2/8/2010 ~0830 ~0835 I sent an E-mail reminder to Rick Sorensen about the importance of getting the ROS completed and forwarded to CAPT Ron Keats for processing.

2/8/2010 ~1240 ~1242 I called CDR Jon Fogarty while traveling by privately owned vehicle to Aberdeen. I explained that I was traveling through a ground blizzard and was unsure if I could continue to Aberdeen. Fogarty suggested that I should layover in Pierre. I did same and then discovered upon arrival at the Area office in Aberdeen the following day that the office had closed due to inclement weather at 10 am (9 am Mountain) which is around the time that I departed Rapid City for Aberdeen. I had not been notified of this closure.

2/10/2010   ~1305 ~1306   I noticed a person who I believed to be Rick Sorensen enter the restroom while I was in same and quickly leave once they apparently discovered that I was also in there.

2/17/2010   ~1430 ~1435   I was to meet with several members of the OEHE management team, including CDR Jon Fogarty regarding a commitment register project I was working on. I was the first in attendance at the conference table within Fogarty's office and asked if Fogarty had a problem with my attendance via Webex of an APLS (advance pediatric life support) lecture over his lunch. Fogarty indicated that it had better be on my own time because he is not paying me to be attending such courses. I indicated that this was a deployment readiness issue and Fogarty indicated that he was not concerned about my deployment readiness, only that things had to get done. It should be noted that the subsequent meeting lasted well past my scheduled departure time resulting in my spending an additional ~2 hours at the duty station for the day (note that I have provided additional time beyond that scheduled on many/most days without complaint).

3/2/2010   ~1645 ~1645   After receiving a call from Denise Wingo, EEO Counselor, concerning the complaint against Fred Koebrick, I called to speak with CDR Jon Fogarty. His secretary, Connie, answered and informed me that Fogarty was on another line and then asked who I was. I advised of her of same and she apparently went to check with Fogarty who advised her to take a message. I asked her to ask Fogarty to call me as soon as possible. Fogarty never called me back. As a consequence the EEO settlement negotiations collapsed and I advised Ms. Wingo that evening to proceed with a formal complaint. I will note for the record that the sticking point was a simple request made by

Ms. Wingo to Fred Koebrick, Sioux San CEO, on my behalf for the agreement to include a preapproval for a one year extension (two years beyond my planned retirement) for declaration of my home of selection since I would be beginning a training program after retirement. Ms. Wingo explained that this is something specifically allowed within the regulations. However, Koebrick turned it down immediately without consideration stating that they simply want to be done with me and do not want to drag it out any further than necessary. I will note for the record that in a previous discussion on the same day with Mr. Thomas Berry, IHS retirement coordinator, he explained to me that the approval of this extension is routine.

3/22/2010   ~1315 ~1320 During   the   Aberdeen   Area OEHE annual meeting during his opening comments at the annual Office of Environmental Health and Engineering meeting in Aberdeen, SD, CDR Jon Fogarty made mention of a recent difficult meeting he had with various members of congressional staff who visited with him in his office (I believe it was in regard to the American Recovery and Reinvestment Act "stimulus" projects). He commented with a snicker that he "told them [the congressional staff] something that worked." The obvious implication was that he understood the information he provided was not necessarily true or accurate. However, judging by his presentation he seemed to think himself clever to be able to provide such information in order to pacify the congressional staff.

3/23/2010   ~0715 ~0730 During   the   Aberdeen   Area OEHE annual meeting I was having breakfast with CDR Dayton Newbrough at the AmericInn in Aberdeen, SD. Over breakfast there were several discussion topics. One of them was the separation of rooms 230 and 231 (numbers?) within the Sioux San Hospital in Rapid City. Newbrough stated that the project was not completed (over 5 months after I was directed by Fred Koebrick to have it completed within 2 weeks) and that there had been several problematic issues associated with the wall construction and that he was not sure how the project was being funded. LT Craig Grunenfelder, acting Facility Manager, Sioux San Hospital, later confirmed that the work was not yet complete but that he was expecting it to be completed by Friday (3/25). Grunenfelder also responded when I inquired that the Oglala Sioux Tribe had not reimbursed his/my program for the improvement work that was done to the Hope Lodge building (a project for which they had received funding from the IHS and then, after receiving the funds, asked Fred Koebrick, CEO, for the IHS service unit to perform the work, which he then agreed to do, without any discussion with me).

3/24/2010   ~0800 ~0800   The Aberdeen Area Office of Environmental Health and Engineering (OEHE) conducted their annual meeting this week in Aberdeen. My acting supervisor, CDR Jon Fogarty, Director, OEHE, had originally agreed that I could attend various sessions at the meeting since I am cross registered with one of the divisions (Division of Environmental Health Services-DEHS) and have experience in another division outside the one that I am affiliated with (Division of Facilities Management-DFM). Fogarty agreed that I could attend the DEHS session today and tomorrow since I need the associated CEUs to maintain professional registration in that field. However, on the morning of the training as I arrived in the training room I was advised by CDR Chris Allen that I was to report immediately to Fogarty back at the Area office. I did same. Fogarty asked me to step into his office and proceeded to advise me that he did not appreciate my not following orders yesterday. I inquired as to what orders I did not follow and Fogarty advised me that I was to attend the DSFC session yesterday. I responded that it was my understanding that I could attend any of the sessions and that I had attended the DSFC session during the morning. Fogarty responded that he had agreed to allow me to attend the DSFC session. I responded that I am a facilities engineer and thought it appropriate that I attend the facilities engineer session in the afternoon since I had attended the DSFC session in the morning and that I was not aware of a prohibition against me doing same. Fogarty responded that there was no prohibition and he did not say in so many words that I was not to attend but only authorized me to attend the DSFC session. I responded that I was not aware of that and asked what the issue was. Fogarty stated that it was nothing that I said at the session, only that I was in attendance against his wishes. I responded that had I known that I would not have attended and then stated that I only thought it to be appropriate and was trying to help Fogarty and LT Craig Grunenfelder, acting Sioux San Facility Manager, be successful. Fogarty indicated during the discussion that he was upset because he had been provided information from a person that I had confided in about my private thoughts about Fogarty. Fogarty then stated that I thought this person to be my friend when in fact they were feeding information to Fogarty. Fogarty then named that person to be CAPT Kathy Mercure. I said nothing in response. It was clear that the discussion was unproductive and I got up to leave. Fogarty directed me to continue with the work on the spreadsheet (data entry) that I had been performing since my detail to Aberdeen in November 2009. It should be noted that my original billet (position description) was Facility Manager prior to the reprisal actions. My new billet is Facilities Management Engineer. The previous afternoon I had participated in the facilities engineer session. Apparently Fogarty did not want me to attend this session and this was the reason he punished me by denying me of needed no cost training (other than time).

4/8/2010   ~1315 ~1315   I met Rick Sorensen at the door to the men's restroom (I was going in and Sorensen was leaving). I asked Sorensen if he had a response to the various inquiry E-mails pertaining to my reviewing official statement (ROS). Sorensen claimed that he was unaware of such E-mails and referenced his 3/23 E-mail wherein he referenced the settlement agreement and that he was still awaiting a response to same. I advised Sorensen that Fred (Koebrick) "had put the kibosh" on the agreement. Sorensen responded that "Fred works for me, I don't work for him" implying that he authorized the agreement. I explained that he (Sorensen) had been out so the counselor spoke with Fred about the remaining details and that Fred was very negative which turned off both the counselor and me and, consequently, we walked away from the agreement. Sorensen said that he was not aware of that and said he would do a search for my E-mails. I thanked him and we each went about our business.

5/11/2010   ~1030 ~1030 CDR Jon Fogarty brought in some information on a training opportunity to Mark LeBrun, a civil servant Native American IT technician, to see if he would be interested in attending same.

5/20/2010   ~0900 ~0905 I had a conversation with CDR Jon Fogarty morning at approximately 9:00 am about sick leave. I had provided Fogarty with a sick leave request for Tuesday and Wednesday of this week and a station leave request for the remainder of the day today since I was still not feeling well. He advised me that the latter request would have to be for sick leave and I apologized and changed it to same. I then asked if he would be approving the sick leave request for today and he advised that he will "consider it" but that if I didn't feel well that I should not be here. I responded that I assume that means it will be approved and he advised that I should not make such an assumption and then advised me again that if I am not feeling well that I should not be here but that I would require a doctor's statement. I responded that I do have an appointment to see a doctor tomorrow but that he did not have a right to demand a statement. Fogarty responded that I was not to tell him what he does and does not have a right to. I stated that I am not sure why I am receiving such bad treatment from him and he responded that he feels likewise and that I am getting back what I give.

I stated that I simply came in to ask about getting sick leave approved for today since I am not feeling well and he again stated that I should not be here if I was not feeling well. I stated that I would be leaving then as I do not feel well and he advised that I would be leaving by my own volition. I then asked what kind of game is being played here and he directed me to leave his office. I did same.

6/15/2010 ~0915 ~0920 I had a discussion with CDR Jon Fogarty about my retirement paperwork. He asked me upon review if I was going to need an extension for moving my household goods. I responded that I probably would since I was starting a training program. He then stated that he had signed many of them for past retirees and I responded that if he was willing to do so I would appreciate same. He then responded that he believed the process to require a request to be submitted sometime near the end of the first year after retirement.

6/29/2010 ~1310 ~1312 Rick Sorensen followed me into the men's restroom. We were both near the faucets after completing our "business." I washed my hands and then filled my water bottle and he washed his hands. No words were spoken between us (normally he would exchange a greeting with me). He did not even look at me.

7/6/2010 ~1635 ~1635 I saw Alan Davis, AAIHS Executive Officer, on my way into the office. Our eyes met and he said nothing to me (normally he would exchange a greeting with me). However, he glared at me as if he were angry.

7/6/2010 ~1700 ~1700 I spoke to Lois Armstrong, OEHE Administrative Officer, about the JFTR. She confirmed that employees are not supposed to travel without a travel order. She did acknowledge that they have had some individuals in the past who have to travel without a travel order in an emergency circumstance. The context for my need for the information was in regard to CDR Fogarty's directive of me to travel to Aberdeen the late evening/early morning of November 15-16, 2010, without a travel order.

7/7/2010   ~0900 ~0905 CDR Jon Fogarty indicated during our morning huddle that we are not to speak to anyone concerning the Indian Improvement Act or the current investigation being conducted by Byron Dorgan's office. He also indicated that there is a "great deal of work" being put into responding to the various issues underway and that, so far, OEHE was not part of the investigation. Also worth noting was the update from Amy Bohling, DSFC Assistant, on her activities that she is working on transfer agreements. This is the same work I am currently performing.

8/4/2010   ~0900 ~1000 I initiated a discussion with Rick Sorensen to try to resolve the various complaints I have pending against the agency. He agreed to discuss same with me. I suggested that it was in our mutual interests to resolve the complaints as quickly as possible and he agreed by stating that this has been a significant waste of everybody's time. He asked if I had terms for a settlement and I provided a copy of same (which were the same as those included within my EEO complaint against Fred Koebrick). He reviewed them each and agreed that they could probably provide all of the terms except the time for my paramedic training and the monetary damages of $300,000.00. He asked where I had arrived at that number and I explained that it was my understanding that this was some sort of administrative limit on damages but that actual damages were much higher, approximately $1.7 million. He asked me to provide justification for the damages and E-mail same to him (I did same immediately—at 10:50 am the same day). He said he would then check to see what he could do to reach a settlement. It should be noted that he never responded to my E-mail or subsequent E-mail requesting a status update.

8/25/2010   ~0855   ~0900   I delivered a copy of the response to the MSPB order to Alice LaFontaine, Deputy HR Director, Aberdeen Area IHS. She asked what the document was for and I explained same. She responded that it was her understanding that commissioned officers do not have access to the MSPB. I explained that they do in this circumstance. She responded that she had always been told that commissioned officers complaints are not heard by the MSPB. She then signed for receipt on the original document (which I kept) as well as the copy (which she kept). I thanked her and left.

8/26/2010   ~1000   ~1005   I spoke with Clayton Belgarde, HR Specialist, in the restroom during a break he had in the course he was instructing on management. I asked him if he was aware of my MSPB appeal. He said that he was aware that I had filed an appeal with the MSPB and that it was his understanding that COs are not eligible to file with same.

8/31/2010   ~1330   ~1345   I spoke with Deana Long after attending the farewell luncheon for Bill Axlund. I was surprised to see her as she had transferred to the Phoenix Area following significant mistreatment within the Aberdeen Area. She shared some of her experiences with the Aberdeen Area focusing on her mistreatment by Helen Thompson and Marilyn Bad Wound. Apparently Helen would boast about her tie to Charlene Red Thunder, Area Director, and Marilynn would make threats about asking her children to harm those who crossed her. I explained that I was not surprised by this rhetoric as Helen had openly shared a story of her son visiting the home of a hospital patient who had threatened her. The son had apparently threatened harm upon the patient if he ever did something like that again. We spoke for several minutes and I told her I was glad to see her back in the Area.

9/2/2010   ~1535   ~1600   I presented myself at the personnel office and stopped at the reception desk and asked if Geri Fox

(Aberdeen Area Director of Personnel) was in. I was told she was and then I was asked about another individual as to my identity. I provided my name and was then invited back to Fox's corner office. As I walked to her office I could see that there was a collection of individuals sitting around a table outside Fox's office. They appeared to disperse as I approached. CDR Clayton Belgard and Dawn Wilke were among those seated around the table. I entered Fox's office, presented the discovery documents to her, and then sat next to Alice LaFontaine who was seated in front of Fox's desk. Fox inquired as to what the documents are. I explained that they were the discovery documents that I was required to provide in accordance with the acknowledgement order from the merit systems protection board. I then explained that the agency is supposed to provide me with the same type of discovery documents by today. As I referenced the documents I briefly pointed to them on the table next to Fox. Fox then chastised me that I was not to shake my finger at her and reminded me that I was in her office. I explained that I did not shake my finger at her and that I had simply pointed to the documents that I had referenced. She then reiterated that I shook my finger at her and I reiterated my explanation and added that she was being ███████ toward me and that her demeanor was not helpful. She then refuted that she was being ██████. I asked her to sign the document service I had provided. Fox appeared reluctant to do so and then called Belgarde into the room. Belgarde entered immediately and Fox handed him the document packet I had provided. She then explained to me that I would be working with Belgarde on this issue. Belgarde began reviewing the documents and Fox asked me what I wanted. I asked her for clarification on her question and she responded by clarifying that she wanted to know what I wanted in terms of documents. I responded that I simply wanted what the acknowledgement order requires. She asked what that was and I read her the pertinent section from the acknowledgement order. She responded that they do not have a file on me since I am a commissioned officer. I responded that this wasn't necessarily about her files, that I would be looking for all communication concerning me from Charlene Red Thunder and Rick Sorensen all the way down the chain of command. I then asked again if I could get a signature on the receipt for document service I had provided. She asked if I had provided a copy for them. I responded that I had. She responded that Belgarde would provide the signature. I got up to receive the receipt from Belgarde who was sitting at a conference table behind me. He was still reviewing the receipt for document service. I noted for him since I did not know if he had heard my previous statement that the agency discovery docs were due 10 days after the acknowledgement order date which was today. He seemed to be aware of that. Fox explained that they had just received their copy of the acknowledgement order earlier the same day. I responded that I had provided a copy of the document to CDR Jon Fogarty on Monday and Tuesday … and then was interrupted by Fox. She asked if that was that Monday or Tuesday of this week and I responded that it was last week. LaFontaine then referenced the document service that she had signed for last week (the same day that Fogarty had been provided a copy of the acknowledgement order) and explained that she did not know what that was (even though I had explained it to her at the time). It should be noted that I did not reference the discussion I had with Belgarde last week (see notes above) wherein we discussed my MSPB appeal. Belgarde provided me with a signed original of the receipt for document service. I thanked him for same and then turned to Fox and said that I hope we can work through this in a professional manner without being ▆▆▆ She responded sharply that I would not be working with her, that I would be working with Belgarde. Before I left the room Belgarde approached me and extended a hand which I shook and thanked him again before I left.

9/3/2010   ~0655 ~0700   As I entered the Federal building this morning I spoke with Jeffrey Bergstrasser, Protection Security Guard, about my experience delivering the discovery documents as described above and the hostility of Geri Fox toward me. During the conversation Bergstrasser noted that prior to my detail to the Aberdeen the security guards were approached by CDR Jon Fogarty and instructed that when I arrived I was to be treated as a visitor and they were to make sure that I was processed through the metal detector and be treated as other visitors.

10/6/2010   ~1630 ~1715   I spoke with Brian LeBrun, Sioux San Housekeeping Supervisor, about housekeeping management issues at the Sioux San Hospital. He couldn't believe that I was managing the housekeeping department in addition to being the Facility Manager. He explained that he feels as if he cannot properly manage the department and needs an administrative assistant. He also explained that he is having issues with Theresa Brave Eagle. I described my efforts to address her non-performance. He was very disappointed that Helen Thompson and Michelle Keith stepped in to protect her. He asked about Joe Blacksmith's EEO complaint and I described to the best of my recollection what occurred but advised him that I had everything documented for each employee within employee files which were turned over to Michelle Keith. He said that he had never seen them.

APPENDIX 19.
EXPOSÉS ON CAPT RONALD KEATS

The following two items document the poor performance and illegal activities of CAPT Ronald Keats, Aberdeen Area CO Liaison:

Nathan Gjovik

From:	Gjovik, Nathan D. (IHS/ABR) <Nathan.Gjovik@ihs.gov>
Sent:	Tuesday, December 22, 2009 10:55 AM
To:	Rubendall, Richard A (IHS/HQ)
Cc:	McSherry, Paul V (IHS/HQ)
Subject:	Complaint Against CAPT Ronald Keats

As I have previously made you aware, over the past year or so I have been working in a hostile work environment created by various management officials of the Aberdeen Area. During this time CAPT Ronald Keats has apparently been working as a "tool for management" as he described himself during a discussion we had last week. I had been trying to contact him for over one week concerning the recent change of my billet, an action that occured without any discussion with or warning to me. I sent him an E-mail, tried to reach him by phone but could not reach an answering service, checked his office several times and knocked on his office door, and left a written note on the dry erase message board on the outside of his office door. He did not respond. On Friday 18 December 2009 at ~1130 I saw CAPT Keats talking to another officer within the office where I am now working and approached him and asked if I could speak to him. He said he would be over in a couple of minutes. He arrived at my work station 30 minutes later.

CAPT Keats and I went into a conference room and I asked him why my billet had been recently downgraded. CAPT Keats responded that my supervisor requested the action and his responsibility was to simply process it. I was surprised by this response as I thought perhaps there should be some "value added" by this O-6 officer. I suggested to CAPT Keats that perhaps there should have been some form of communication with me other than simply sending me the completed downgraded billet and that I thought that was the primary function of a liaison. I mentioned that I had worked as a liaison officer on deployment and understood the function to involve communication in both or every direction. CAPT Keats then indicated that he did not appreciate being made to feel defensive when he speaks to me and that he is simply of "tool for management - management tells [him] to do something and [he] do[es] it." Again, I was surprised by this response as it implies no advocacy for commissioned officers. I further asked CAPT Keats as to what else was being planned or developed as far as actions related to me and he responded that he did not know. CAPT Keats was obviously perturbed by our conversation and asked if there was anything else. I thanked him for his time and he left immediately.

The following are notes taken from a discussion that CAPT Keats and I had on 17 November 2009 at ~0900:

I asked to speak with CAPT Ron Keats about the nature of my current detail. I asked why I was here in Aberdeen and Keats began to explain that I cannot seem to get along with anyone including the new CEO and that the new CEO has the authority to transfer staff out of the facility. I asked about the statement made by a senior management official within the agency to then CDR Keats that "[they] are going to change the color of the workforce." He acknowledged that the statement had been made and asked why I keep having issues. I responded that I was simply doing what was required of me by regulation and the various training we receive every year that demands all employees to report instances of discrimination and waste, fraud, and abuse, and that was all I had done. Keats suggested that I had not treated the CEO with due respect. I responded that I had on every occasion treated the CEO respectfully and then provided an example of how, even on the day I was relieved of my duties I had provided assistance to the CEO on getting his office organized with new furniture – the office that I had ensured was renovated to alleviate the allergic response the CEO had been experiencing prior to the renovation. I then reiterated that I had never treated the CEO disrespectfully – ever. I then invited Keats to call CDR Dayton Newbrough to discuss an exchange that Newbrough had been party/witness to between me and the CEO wherein the CEO was markedly disrespectful to me. I then indicated to Keats that I had worked in an Area office at one time in the past and did not experience discrimination in that environment and that I did not even have a door that I could close on my office (eluding to Keats' office door which is normally kept closed). I then noted to Keats that during our discussion he had been shaking his head "no" whenever I spoke and asked him to please try to keep an open mind and try to understand that there is another side to the story. Keats did not have much to say as I then thanked him for his time and left.

To my knowledge CAPT Keats has not discussed the above referenced exchange between the CEO and I with CDR Newbrough. I will note for the record that as I was waiting for CAPT Keats outside his office for the above meeting he received a phone call apparently concerning another commissioned officer. CAPT Keats' response to the caller was "That's outright fraud, write him up" and they exchanged farewell greetings and hung up. I will also note for the record

1

that last January, then CDR Keats, participated in an "administrative review" at the Rapid City service unit which was designed to discover the facts associated with my claims against the two acting management officials. However, it was immediately obvious to me during the interview with me at the end of the day that CAPT Keats had already made up his mind that I was the problem as he and the other review participant were immediately confrontational toward me.

Based on my several experiences with CAPT Keats it appears that he has no reservations about making snap judgements concerning the performance or conduct of officers with whom he has not discussed issues that may adversely affect them. They are guilty until proven otherwise. I believe this is neither appropriate management of such issues nor a good personality trait for someone with so much power to affect the careers of so many.

Along with the above complaint I am hereby requesting the assignment of a different liaison to be involved in any further actions related to my remaining career as I no longer trust CAPT Keats to act in my interests.

Nathan D. Gjovik, PE, RS, MS, MBA, MPH, NREMT-P
CDR, USPHS
Aberdeen Area Indian Health Service
Office of Environmental Health & Engineering
115 4th Avenue SE
Aberdeen, SD 57401
(605) 226-7453 (voice)
(605) 226-7689 (fax)
Nathan.Gjovik@ihs.gov

AmericanNews | ARTICLE COLLECTIONS

YOU ARE HERE: *Aberdeen News Home* →*Collections* → *Paperwork*

Aberdeen man sentenced on child porn charge

PAGE 1A
July 25, 2012|BY SCOTT WALTMAN, swaltman@aberdeen news.com

A former Indian Health Service employee has been sentenced to prison on a federal child pornography charge.

Ronald Dean Keats, 55, of Aberdeen was sentenced this week to 44 months in prison and fined $100,000. He must report to prison by Aug. 20 and, after he gets out, spend eight years on supervised release. He previously pleaded guilty.

Keats worked in the Aberdeen Federal Building for the U.S. Department of Health and Human Services' Indian Health Service, according to paperwork filed in the case. The paperwork said that in April 2010, another employee in the Federal Building found a CD in the building's elevator. The disc contained images of child pornography as well as a document authored by the Keats, according to court paperwork.

On May 18, 2010, law enforcers took an external computer hard drive and Keats' government-issued laptop computer from his office at the Federal Building and interviewed him. Keats turned over to them a CD case with four discs that had been in his car. Two of the discs contained images of child pornography, according to court documents. During the interview, Keats admitted to downloading the improper images and saving them to CDs, according to the legal paperwork.

In exchange for his guilty plea, three other charges of possession of child pornography against Keats were dismissed. The crime is a felony punishable in federal court by as much as 10 years in prison and a $250,000 fine.

APPENDIX 20.
SCIA INVESTIGATION OF
ABERDEEN AREA

The following newspaper articles pertain to a Senate Committee on Indian Affairs investigation initiated by Chairman Byron Dorgan on June 23, 2010, and subsequent hearing held on September 28, 2010, entitled "IN CRITICAL CONDITION: THE URGENT NEEED TO REFORM THE INDIAN HEALTH SERVICE'S ABERDEEN AREA":

Senate Committee on Indian Affairs investigates 'potential criminal behavior' in Aberdeen Area of IHS
BY DAVE KOLPACK, Associated Press Writer
Published on Thursday, July 01, 2010

FARGO, N.D.—The chairman of the Senate's Indian Affairs Committee says the group has launched an investigation into Indian Health Service facilities in four states, sparked by revolving door executives at a North Dakota hospital.

Sen. Byron Dorgan, D-N.D., said Wednesday that the committee is looking into alleged "mismanagement, malfeasance, retaliation against whistleblowers as well as potential criminal behavior" in the Aberdeen Area of the IHS, which includes North Dakota, South Dakota, Iowa and Nebraska.

"I believe this type of mismanagement in the region over a long period of time has negatively affected health care provided to the Native Americans," Dorgan said in a release. "These problems must be remedied."

Officials with the Aberdeen Area IHS did not return phone and e-mail messages left Wednesday by The Associated Press.

The investigation centers on the Quentin N. Burdick Memorial Hospital in Belcourt, on North Dakota's Turtle Mountain Indian

Reservation, where there have been five different CEOs in about two years.

"The problems there are such that Sen. Dorgan thinks we need to determine whether it is a problem with mismanagement at that facility or whether it is a problem that is rooted even deeper in the Aberdeen region," said Barry Piatt, Dorgan's spokesman. "He will be looking at the whole region."

Adult patients who need non-emergency care have been sent to other facilities several times in the last three years because of staff shortages, Dorgan said. At one point those patients were diverted for 270 straight days.

A message left Wednesday with Duane Marcellais, acting CEO of the Belcourt hospital, was not returned.

There are 48 IHS facilities in the Aberdeen Area, covering about a dozen Indian reservations and communities. Dorgan said the IHS has had four years to deal with the problem in the region and hasn't made the necessary changes.

IHS Director Yvette Roubideaux is cooperating with the committee and has launched her own investigation, Dorgan said. The committee set a deadline of July 28 for the IHS to provide information and the Senate committee will use subpoenas if necessary, he said.

Aberdeen American News (SD)

Dorgan sees 'gross incompetence' in Aberdeen IHS office
Published on Wednesday, August 25, 2010

BISMARCK, N.D.—The chairman of the Senate's Indian Affairs Committee says it's inexcusable that two Indian Health Service mental health positions remain vacant on the Standing Rock Indian Reservation.

North Dakota Sen. Byron Dorgan says the director of mental health services job has been vacant a full year, while teenage suicides remain a big problem on the reservation that straddles the North Dakota-South Dakota border.

The Senate committee launched an investigation into the IHS area office in Aberdeen, S.D., in June. The office oversees facilities in North Dakota, South Dakota, Iowa and Nebraska. Dorgan says he sees "gross incompetence" and he wants answers from the IHS.

The Aberdeen IHS office referred a request for comment to a national IHS spokesman. Thomas Sweeney said it was premature for the agency to comment before first replying directly to Dorgan.

Aberdeen American News (SD)

REPORT: INDIAN HEALTH SERVICE HIRED CRIMINALS
HUB CITY OFFICE AT CENTER OF FEDERAL FINDINGS
Matthew Daly AP Writer
Published: September 29, 2010

WASHINGTON—The federal Indian Health Service has hired convicted criminals, failed to stop employees from stealing narcotics and allowed workers to take paid leave for more than a year while being investigated for misconduct, a federal investigation has found.

The investigation disclosed years of mismanagement that have led to poor patient care, long-term vacancies and other problems at the Aberdeen Area of the Indian Health Service, which includes North Dakota, South Dakota, Iowa and Nebraska. In one case, an employee at a Rapid City pharmacy stole large quantities of Vicodin and Tramadol, narcotics that are used for pain relief, and resold them for cash. The IHS pharmacy lacked basic security controls, such as security cameras or requiring two people to count inventory, the report said.

Gerald Roy, deputy inspector general at the Health and Human Services Department, told the Senate Indian Affairs Committee that the Aberdeen office was chronically mismanaged, with employee misconduct and even theft of drugs routine. In at least two cases, employees who had been convicted of crimes were rehired by the health service in the same region where the crimes were committed, he said Tuesday.

The Indian Affairs committee is investigating the Aberdeen IHS office, which has been plagued for years by complaints of mismanagement. A final report is expected by the end of the year.

Sen. Byron Dorgan, D-N.D., the panel's chairman, said Tuesday that the Aberdeen office "appears to me to be completely dysfunctional."

Sitting at home

Dorgan said he was stunned to learn that the region's deputy director had been placed on paid leave for undisclosed reasons for more than a year. The official, Shelly R. Harris, has stayed home, at taxpayer expense, while allegations against her are investigated, said Charlene Red Thunder, director of the Aberdeen region.

An IHS spokesman said Harris is paid $125,109 per year. He declined to comment on the allegations against her or say when they may be resolved, citing privacy laws.

Dorgan called the lengthy leave unacceptable and said it was impossible to believe that a private-sector employer would allow such an action. "Not on your life!" he said.

"It all comes back to effective management," Dorgan told IHS officials. "You say, 'Here are our expectations. Meet it or leave.'"

Correcting problems

Red Thunder and Yvette Roubideaux, director of the IHS, said they were working to correct problems at the agency.

"We are starting to hold more people accountable," Roubideaux said, noting that five service unit directors have resigned or been fired in the past two years.

"We have a serious problem at Aberdeen," Roubideaux told Dorgan. "The Aberdeen area must do a better job."

The Aberdeen office serves more than 100,000 Indians on reservations in North Dakota, South Dakota, Nebraska, and Iowa. The region includes nine hospitals, eight health centers, two school health stations, and several smaller health stations and satellite clinics.

APPENDIX 21.
ARTICLE ON CDR MICHAEL TILUS

Article dated 7/28/2012 on Aberdeen Area IHS actions associated with CDR Michael Tilus:

Fort Totten psychologist reprimanded for letter of concern involving Spirit Lake

A clinical psychologist who wrote a letter expressing "grave concern"about endangered children on the Spirit Lake reservation has been reprimanded and reassigned.

By: Patrick Springer and Chuck Haga, (Fargo) Forum Communications

Published July 28, 2012

FARGO—A clinical psychologist who wrote a letter expressing "grave concern" about endangered children on the Spirit Lake reservation has been reprimanded and reassigned.

Michael Tilus, who served as behavioral health director of the Indian Health Service clinic in Fort Totten, wrote a letter dated April 3 bluntly criticizing the Spirit Lake Tribe for what he said were serious failures in protecting children from abuse or neglect.

An aide for Sen. John Hoeven, R-N.D., said Tilus has informed his office that he received a letter of reprimand from the IHS for his letter, and said as of last week he was reassigned to the agency's regional headquarters in Aberdeen, S.D.

Tilus did not return an email from Forum Communications seeking comment.

A former colleague said Tilus said he was a conscientious mental health professional who acted properly by reporting child abuse and neglect.

"My question is, is this retaliation for being a whistle blower?" said Joanne Streifel, a clinical social worker who worked with Tilus at the IHS clinic in Fort Totten. "Are they trying to blackball him at IHS?"

She added: "He is acting in good faith. He is mandated to report. He's not going outside his professional responsibilities here. He's doing what he's supposed to do."

Tilus served as Streifel's supervisor for several years after he joined the IHS clinic in Fort Totten around 2007, Streifel said.

"He has been the best supervisor I have had in all my 40 years of social work experience," she added, "and I can say that without reservation."

A spokeswoman for the IHS declined to discuss the Tilus reprimand and reassignment.

"Consistent with policy, the Aberdeen Area Indian Health Service does not comment on personnel issues relating to current or former employees," said Courtney Mallon, acting public affairs liaison for the IHS.

Tilus was criticized by his superiors for going outside "proper channels" by leveling his criticisms against the tribe in a letter sent to numerous state and federal officials and made public by news reports, said Ryan Bernstein, Hoeven's deputy chief of staff.

"It talks about going outside the direct chain of command," Bernstein said of Tilus' letter of reprimand.

Hoeven's office has been in touch with the IHS to express the senator's concerns and asking for assurances that the reprimand and reassignment were not in retaliation for his "whistle-blowing," he said.

The IHS gave assurances that another mental health professional had stepped in to fill Tilus' caseload at the Fort Totten clinic, Bernstein said.

Sen. Kent Conrad, D-N.D., also is concerned about Tilus' letter of reprimand and reassignment.

"I am aware of the concerns that have been raised regarding Dr. Tilus," Conrad said in a statement to Forum Communications. "I will continue to monitor the situation as all facts become available.

"But through all this, we cannot lose sight of the most important issue here—the wellbeing of the children at Spirit Lake and reservations throughout Indian Country," Conrad added. "Preventable tragedies have occurred that must never be permitted to happen again."

Both Hoeven and Conrad have pressed officials of the IHS and Bureau of Indian Affairs to address gaps in child protection services identified by Tilus and later by Thomas Sullivan, a regional administrator for the U.S. Department of Human Services.

In his letter, Tilus described the plight of endangered children on the Spirit Lake reservation as a growing public health hazard and said social services officials for the tribe were responsible for numerous legal and regulatory violations.

In a letter dated July 18, Conrad wrote Interior Secretary Ken Salazar, whose agency includes the BIA, to urge corrective action for the "epidemic" problems at Spirit Lake described by Tilus.

"Specifically, I request that you take immediate action to supplement existing resources to address the program's serious deficiencies, including, but not limited to, detailing all available social workers within the BIA system to the Spirit Lake Nation."

Conrad also urged a "thorough investigation into the circumstances that resulted in the situation deteriorating to such an alarming level under the oversight of the BIA."

As of Friday, Conrad's office had not received a written response to the letter.

Similarly, Hoeven wrote Michael S. Black, director of the BIA, a letter on July 11 to urge actions to correct "what is by several credible reports a very serious problem."

Hoeven said Spirit Lake Tribal Social Services must be held accountable and must make "immediate improvements." To accomplish that, the BIA must ensure that resources are being used properly.

Hoeven asked for any audits of programs administered by the tribe under agreements with the BIA, as well as any corrective action reports, program reviews or financial reviews.

"If these reports have not been completed, the BIA should undertake such reports immediately," Hoeven wrote in his letter to Black.

As of Friday, Hoeven's office had not received a written response to his letter.

A BIA spokeswoman did not address specific questions by Forum Communications reporters asking about its steps to address the problems at Spirit Lake.

"BIA Regional and Headquarters staff continue to provide support to the Spirit Lake Tribe to increase the capacity to address the circumstances with direct assistance on the ground and engaging partners on the Tribal, State and Federal level to mobilize resources," BIA spokeswoman Nedra Darling said in a statement.

James Yankton, chairman of Spirit Lake Tribe, could not be reached for comment Thursday or Friday, but has said the tribe is working with state and federal officials to address deficiencies.

Earlier this year, Tilus was recognized with the Caraveo National Service Award for his "exemplary dedication to serving the underserved in frontier America, including within Indian country."

A commander in the U.S. Public Health Service, Tilus is a decorated U.S. Army veteran in the Chaplain Corp, according to a summary of his service connected to the award bestowed by a division of the American Psychological Association.

Readers can reach Forum reporter Patrick Springer at (701) 241-5522

APPENDIX 22.
LOG OF APPLICATION
PROCESS WITH VA HR

The following is a log of various interactions I had with various VA human resources staff over the course of a several month application process:

Date	Event
02/25/2011	Application submitted electronically via the USAJOBS.gov web site for a GS-12 General Engineer position with the Fargo, ND VA HCS.
03/02/2011	Notified that application was not considered because of failure to include resume or application form.
03/07/2011	I sent an E-mail to a general mailbox with the VA asking for reconsideration since I am a veteran, was a current Federal employee, and was reasonable certain that I had provided the required documentation.
	I received a response via E-mail from Traci Cole with the VA human resources office in Topeka, KS who explained that they had not received a resume or application form.
	I responded via E-mail with an assertion that I had forwarded my curriculum vitae and asked if an application was necessary if I was already a Federal employee.
03/08/2011	Ms. Cole responded via E-mail that they require a resume or application from all applicants.

I forwarded a copy via E-mail of the curriculum vitae to Ms. Cole that they should have received from my application submittal from the USAJOBS.gov web site.

Ms. Cole responded via E-mail that they are unable to accept late paperwork from applicants, except 10-point veterans (i.e., those with a service connected disability).

I responded via E-mail with an explanation of how the USAJOBS.gov web site forces the user to select a resume before continuing the next part of the application process.

Ms. Cole responded via E-mail by asking for clarification, since she was apparently unfamiliar with the process, and asked if I believed there was an error in the processing of the application.

I responded via E-mail in the affirmative on the error in the application and explained that I am a sophisticated computer user and was familiar with the USAJOBS.gov process. I also again requested reconsideration of my application and, if that wasn't possible, a contact for which I could initiate a protest.

Ms. Cole advised via E-mail that she had setup a case with their system personnel to investigate whether or not an error occurred.

Ms. Cole advised via E-mail less than two hours after setting up the case that she had already heard back from the system administrators and they were unable to find any errors with the system.

I responded via E-mail with another request for a contact person with whom to file a protest.

03/09/2011   I asked via E-mail for a response to my request for a contact person with whom to file a protest.

Ms. Cole responded via E-mail that, barring a screen shot proving that I had attached my resume there was nothing they could do for me.

I responded via E-mail that the reasonable assumption of any person submitting an application via the USAJOBS.gov web site would be that, when prompted to select a resume before continuing to the next step, it would be included with the application packet sent to the agency. I also advised her that I was not aware of anybody who took screen shots of each step of an electronic application process and again asked for a contact person, the Director of her division, to which a protest could be filed.

03/10/2011   I asked via E-mail for a response to my request for a contact person with whom to file a protest.

Ms. Cole responded via a phone message indicating that they had received 10 documents and that there was no resume included within them.

I responded via E-mail requesting a listing of the 10 documents.

Ms. Cole responded via E-mail with a listing of the 10 documents.

I responded via E-mail that the documents she listed were those that I had attached separately and that there must have been a problem with the USAJOBS.gov web site in regard to the forwarding of my resume with the application process. I again requested reconsideration for the position.

Ms. Cole responded via E-mail that I would have had to have attached the resume the same way as the other documents, that the USAJOBS. gov web site does not automatically forward a resume, and that there was nothing further with which they could help me.

I responded via E-mail that her statement concerning the resume was not true and provided a screen shot from my account of a potential application which clearly showed the system prompting me to "Select one of your stored resumes to send:" and then listed the three resumes which I had built within the system. I then advised her that if they did not provide any assistance that I would be forwarding the E-mail chain to my Congressional representatives for their follow-up on my behalf.

Ms. Cole responded via E-mail that the screen shot did not prove that I had submitted the resume and that without any proof there was nothing they could do.

03/11/2011   I forwarded via E-mail the E-mail chain to one of Senator Thune's constituent advocates in Rapid City with a request for their assistance in overcoming the VA's inflexibility in reconsidering my application for the position given an apparent problem with the USAJOBS.gov web site.

03/19/2011   I received via regular mail my disability rating from the VA which qualified me for a 10-point veteran preference when applying for Federal positions.

03/20/2011   I forwarded via E-mail an application for 10-point veteran's preference along with another copy of my resume to Ms. Cole.

03/22/2011   Ms. Cole responded via E-mail that there was not enough detail on my resume to prove that I was qualified for the position to which I had applied and that I would receive an official notification to that effect.

I responded via E-mail that, as shown on my resume, all of the positions I had held while on active duty were engineering positions, the last three being O-5 billets (GS-13 equivalent which was higher than the advertised GS-12 position for which I had applied), and the last two being health care related facility positions, one being project management and the other being facility manager (which was probably the position of the supervisor of the position for which I had applied). I copied my message to Ms. Cole's supervisor, my elected officials, and all of the VA appointed staff for which I could E-mails, including Secretary Eric Shinseki.

03/23/2011   Ms. Cole responded that, since I was a 10-point veteran, I could rework my resume and resubmit same to show my qualifications for the position for which I had applied.

I responded via E-mail with a revised resume and copies of my billets and orders from my last three assignments while on active duty.

03/25/2011   Ms. Cole responded that, with the additional detail provided[52], she had found me qualified for the position for which I had applied, but admonished me that I should have incorporated the detail within my resume because it is not their standard practice to accept position descriptions in lieu of a resume.

04/05/2011   I interviewed in person at the Fargo, ND VA HCS.

04/06/2011   The position was offered by Quincy Lofgren with the VA human resource office in Fargo, ND.

APPENDIX 23.
LOG OF 3ND (CS DUBOIS)
SAFETY CONCERNS

The following is a log of various safety concerns associated with a contractor performing a major contract at the Fargo VA (note that the contractor was performing the contract under the name of 3ND, however, most of their equipment and company identification were badged with CS Dubois):

Date   *Event*

06/07/2011 1. There were several safety issues noted by annual workplace evaluation (AWE) staff associated with the fourth floor scaffold platform being used as a loading and offloading dock via lifting equipment from outside the main building including:

      a. long unsupported spans of railing on the working side of the platform,

      b. lack of toe board protection along the working side of the platform to prevent items from falling off the scaffold platform and the presence of several loose items on same,

      c. leading edge protection for the western approach to the scaffold platform was being provided by a wooden pallet,

      d. lack of an anchoring system of the upper reaches of the scaffold to prevent toppling of the scaffold system (e.g., in the event an element of a lifting device inadvertently attaches to the scaffold system and pulls on it), and

e. it was unclear as to whether or not the required daily inspections were being performed by a competent person for the scaffold system.

06/08/2011   2.   An electrical cable was noted with compromised outer sheath (contractor superintendent informed verbally and via E-mail).

06/09/2011   3.   An electrical cable was noted with compromised outer sheath (the same as noted above).

06/13/2011   4.   There were several safety issues associated with the removal of unneeded materials from the fourth floor by a forklift outside the main building including:

a. failure to secure the site before performing the lifting activity,

b. failure to carefully place the load onto the forklift forks,

c. failure to secure the load to the forks, and the

d. presentation of a callous demeanor by the forklift operator following the incident in which somebody or something could have been hurt (or worse) or damaged.

5. A large temporary light fixture fell from the ceiling in the mechanical room. The fixture shattered onto the floor near an individual who was not wearing his hard hat.

       6. A large electrical cable was noted with compromised outer sheath.

06/16/2011 7. Several scaffolds noted without toe board protection to prevent items from falling off scaffold platforms.

06/20/2011 8. Presence noted of at least one individual on job site without hard hat.

06/22/2011 9. Failure to adequately secure the site before performing a lifting activity by a roofing subcontractor.

      10. Exhibition of a callous demeanor by the subcontractor regarding safety concerns.

      11. Presence noted of at least two individuals on job site without hard hats.

06/29/2011 12. Failure to adequately secure the site before performing a lifting activity by a material supplier.

      13. Lack of fall protection was noted along a leading edge nearby bricklaying operations.

      14. Several scaffolds noted without toe board protection to prevent items from falling off scaffold platforms.

      15. Several scaffolds noted with large gaps in scaffold platform planking which can allow items to fall through.

      16. Presence noted of at least three individuals on job site without hard hats.

07/01/2011 17. Failure to adequately secure the site before performing more than one lifting activity by a masonry subcontractor.

      18. Exhibition of a callous demeanor by the subcontractor regarding safety concerns.

07/08/2011   19. Several axes were noted as being stored on the floor with unprotected sharp edges oriented upward.

20. Steel cabling serving as leading edge protection along the previous north roof perimeter were noted as having only single cable clamps (at least two are typically used to meet OSHA requirements) with approximately 50% installed incorrectly.

21. Several loose items were found unprotected on scaffold platforms.

22. An electrical cable was noted with compromised outer sheath (with the frayed area near a pool of water).

23. Lack of fall protection was noted along a leading edge nearby bricklaying operations (where materials/supplies lifted to and from different roof surfaces).

07/13/2011   24. Lack of fall protection was noted for an individual working over leading edge (noted in the morning—contractor assured this would be corrected immediately, however, the same circumstance was re-noted later in the day).

25. There were several safety issues noted associated with the scaffolds being utilized by the masonry subcontractor including the following:

     a. more than one scaffold structural element which was either not connected or was not connected in accordance with the manufacturer's requirements (e.g., a cross-brace being held onto a connection post by wrapped wire),

b. more than one scaffold structural element which was either not connected or was not connected in accordance with the manufacturer's requirements (e.g., a cross-brace being held onto a connection post by wrapped wire),

c. more than one instance of inadequate railing systems along leading edges for fall protection,

d. more than one instance of inadequate or nonexistent toe board protection to prevent items from falling from scaffold platforms,

e. more than one instance of loose items (e.g., bottled drinks, hardened grout remnants, hardware items, etc.) hanging precariously onto unprotected scaffold platforms,

f. more than one instance of significant gaps in scaffold platform planking,

g. more than one instance of planking having inadequate end extension and/or cleating,

h. at least one instance of planking being used as an access walkway from one scaffold to another scaffold being supported on the unsupported cantilevered end of the platform planking of the receiving scaffold, and

i. nearly all of the planking being utilized exhibiting significant signs of deterioration due to age and weather.

07/14/2011 26. There were several continued safety issues noted associated with the scaffolds being utilized by the masonry subcontractor including the following:

a. more than one instance of loose items (e.g., bottled drinks, hardened grout remnants, hardware items, etc.) hanging precariously onto unprotected scaffold platforms,

b. more than one instance of significant gaps in scaffold platform planking,

c. more than one instance of planking having inadequate end extension and/or cleating,

d. at least one instance of planking being used as an access walkway from one scaffold to another scaffold being supported on the unsupported cantilevered end of the platform planking of the receiving scaffold, and

e. planking being utilized exhibiting significant signs of deterioration due to age and weather.

27. More than one fuel can containing gasoline was noted as being stored outside a protective enclosure.
28. A welder was noted with a comprised electrical cord.
29. A drill was noted with a compromised electrical cord and a missing ground plug.
07/18/2011 30. A temporary electrical panel was identified with a compromised main feed cord.
31. Lack of fall protection was noted along a leading edge in a roof area where materials/ supplies are stored.

32. There were relatively small headed screws with no washers noted as having been utilized to connect a fall-arresting safety connection point to the main building in the new north roof area (looked like more than one had no attachment to the anchor flanges as they had been driven through the anchor flange holes).

08/04/2011 33. Several findings were noted by North Dakota Workforce Safety Insurance inspectors including:

    a. missing scaffold midrails,

    b. planking requiring replacement,

    c. improperly supported outriggers, and

    d. improperly supported bases for several scaffolds.

08/08/2011 34. Several findings were noted by North Dakota Workforce Safety Insurance inspectors including:

    a. missing scaffold midrails,

    b. planking requiring replacement,

    c. improperly supported outriggers,

    d. improperly supported bases for several scaffolds, and

    e. missing plank cleating (to keep plank from slipping off scaffolding).

08/23/2011 33. While performing construction inspection rounds Nathan Gjovik, Project Engineer, asked David Dumonceaux, 3ND Superintendent and On-site Safety Supervisor, about having a spotter (the purpose of the spotter is to maintain site security and safety since it was in close proximity to the main hospital entrance, a smoking shed, and two man doors and one overhead door with direct ingress/egress to/from the hospital interior) for the masonry work being performed by man-basket from the ground. Mr. Dumonceaux responded that this was not required since there was no lifting occurring. Mr. Gjovik also asked if the scaffold system had been inspected that day. Mr. Dumonceaux responded that it had been. Mr. Gjovik asked when it had been inspected and Mr. Dumonceaux responded that "Jared was supposed to do it." This is not in compliance with what Mr. Gjovik had been previously told by Mr. Dumonceaux (circa August 8, 2011) that he was the "competent person" for the scaffold system.

08/24/2011 34. While performing construction inspection rounds Mr. Gjovik noticed what appeared to be the same scaffolding being used which had been used in the past on the northern roof for the thin-brick veneer installation. This scaffold had been identified previously as having safety issues so Mr. Gjovik investigated the setup and discovered two cross-brace posts which were not engaged and at least one old, weathered plank being used as a platform for masons working on grouting the veneer. There were also a number of sharp objects noted on the EPDM surface (waste grout, screws, etc.) so Mr. Gjovik called Mr. Dumonceaux to take a look. Both Mr. Dumonceaux and David Lean,

3ND Sr. Project Superintendent, appeared on the roof shortly thereafter. Mr. Gjovik asked Mr. Dumonceaux if he noticed any issues with the scaffolding. He said he did not. Mr. Gjovik pointed out the two posts which were not engaged as well as the condition of one of the planks being used as a standing platform. Mr. Dumonceaux shouted, "I am sick of this sh@t!", and then he and Mr. Lean proceeded to correct the posts. It is noted that all wooden planks were later replaced with engineered steel frame scaffold platform inserts for use by the masons (this is good).

08/25/2011   35. The contractor was noted driving a piece of rented equipment past the main entrance of the VA hospital. The equipment (Terex man-basket) is apparently driven by the operator within the man-basket mounted on the boom. This was being driven with the boom forward which required the operator to drive facing backwards without any mirrors. The contractor was cautious in his operation. However, there was an ambulance and another vehicle parked in front of the hospital at the time along with a significant amount of foot traffic. The contractor performed the equipment maneuvering without incident. Mr. Gjovik mentioned at the construction coordination meeting that afternoon that he would have liked to have seen a spotter accompany and assist the operator in maneuvering the equipment through the congested area in front of the hospital. The nonverbal communication from the contractor indicated that this was not well received.

08/26/2011 36. Based on continued concerns over the apparent lack of a competent person for the scaffold systems an inspection of the systems was performed by Messrs. Gjovik and John Englund, Emergency Management Coordinator (who has a strong background in safety inspections). There were several findings/questions as follows:

North roof scaffolding:

The contractor was working near a leading edge with a fall protection harness which was tethered to an appropriate fall protection device. He was not wearing a hard hat.

North face scaffolding:

a. No mid-rails along the interior side of scaffolding on the main working level. This was allowed during the previous Workforce Safety Insurance loss protection inspection since the masonry subcontractor described the interior area to be an ongoing work area. However, the work in this area by the masonry subcontractor has been completed.

b. At least three old, weathered scaffold planks on the east end of the scaffold system which appear to require replacement.

c. A variety of small debris noted on the walking surfaces of the scaffold system including screws and waste grout.

d. A questionable top rail on the northeast corner of the scaffold system.

e. At least one old, weathered scaffold plank on the fourth scaffold tower from the east end (north side) which appears to require replacement.

f. Several questionable planks (at least two with questionable cleating) on the highest level of decking.

g. Some planking with greater than 1-inch gaps between them.

h. Unknown access to the easternmost scaffold system, even for removal.

i. Unknown as to whether or not the anchoring system used for the easternmost scaffold system requires design by a registered professional engineer.

j. Two scaffold system towers which appear not to be connected to the building or adjacent towers (east and west ends of the north face). In the case of the west end tower this could represent a danger from tipping since the upper platform has been traditionally used for moving materials to and from the 4th floor work area (e.g., a forklift retraction dragging the platform and causing the tower to tip).

k. Cable clamps tying the eastern side of the western scaffold system tower to the building are incorrectly clamped (this was a past issue with the clamps used for the fall protection cabling along the leading edge of the 4th floor prior to partial enclosure).

l. Questionable support for the western scaffold system platform when viewed from below (appears that plywood edges closest to building have inadequate support for traditional loads placed upon them).

m. Unknown as to whether or not planking used on outriggers is required to be fastened to the outriggers on which they lie.

08/31/2011 37. While performing construction inspection rounds Mr. Gjovik called Mr. Dumonceaux to the north roof area to discuss safety concerns associated with roofers performing work on leading edges on the eastern roof peninsula. Also in attendance were Jared Holland and Darryl Moon, Contracting Specialist. Mr. Gjovik explained that when he arrived on the roof he noticed the roofers working on the peninsula. They had a fall arrest machine in the area. However, it appeared that only one of the workers was actually tethered to the machine. As he continued to watch the activity the only person to appear to be tethered at the time moved approximately 20 feet from the machine while working over another roof which was approximately 12 feet below him (i.e., the tether would not have provided any fall protection). Following Mr. Gjovik's explanation Mr. Dumonceaux became argumentative, expressed his frustration with Mr. Gjovik, and brought up unrelated issues he had with Mr. Gjovik. When Mr. Dumonceaux completed his rant Mr. Gjovik noted that he had pointed out the safety issues to Mr. Dumonceaux and excused himself to return to training and he left the site with Mr. Moon. It should be noted that based on training received this week the contractor is also required to have a competent person for fall protection.

APPENDIX 24.
SCAFFOLD COMPETENT
PERSON REQUIREMENTS

The following are OSHA regulatory requirements for a scaffolding competent person provided by North Dakota Workforce Safety and Insurance on 8/9/2011:

Scaffolding Competent Person

Section 1926.451(f)(3) states: "… scaffolds and scaffold components shall be inspected for visible defects by a competent person before each work shift, and after any occurrence which could affect a scaffold's structural integrity." You ask two questions regarding the competent person requirement.

1. **Does the competent person have to be qualified in safety issues relating to the use of the scaffold, such as guardrails and fall arrest equipment, or just in safety issues relating to scaffold erection and structural integrity?**

    The standard does not specify particular training requirements for competent persons. Instead, it defines a competent person in terms of capability. Section 1926.450(b) defines a competent person as "one who is capable of identifying existing and predictable hazards in the surroundings or working conditions which are unsanitary, hazardous, or dangerous to employees, and who has authorization to take prompt corrective measures to eliminate them." The preamble to the standard further defines the training of the competent person (bottom of the right paragraph on page 46,059 of Volume 61, Number 170 of the Federal Register) by stating:

NETHERWORLD   367

"For example, a 'competent person' for the purposes of this provision must have had specific training in and be knowledgeable about the structural integrity of scaffolds and the degree of maintenance needed to maintain them. The competent person must also be able to evaluate the effects of occurrences such as a dropped load, or a truck backing into a support leg that could damage a scaffold. In addition, the competent person must be knowledgeable about the requirements of this standard. A competent person must have training or knowledge in these areas in order to identify and correct hazards encountered in scaffold work."

The competent person must be able to carry out the tasks specified in the standard. In order to be able to carry out the tasks required in §1926.451(f)(3)—inspecting for visual defects and structural integrity—the competent person needs to have knowledge in the issues relating to the strength and structural integrity of the scaffold. With respect to your question—whether the competent person needs to be knowledgeable about guardrails and fall arrest equipment—the answer is yes to the extent they affect the structural stability of the scaffold. For example, if a personal fall arrest system will be attached to the scaffold, a practice that many manufacturers do not recommend, the competent person must know if the anchor points and scaffold will be able to sustain the loads of an arrested fall.

2. **Does the competent person need both (1) the same training as a scaffold erector, plus (2) additional training on how to inspect scaffolds and recognize hazards?**

Section 1926.454 states that a competent person will train employees involved in erecting, disassembling, moving, operating, repairing, maintaining, or inspecting a scaffold. To meet this requirement, a competent person must be fully knowledgeable about erecting, disassembling, moving, operating, repairing, maintaining and inspecting the scaffold. As a practical matter this will usually mean that the competent person will need the same training as a scaffold erector plus whatever additional training is necessary to carry out these other duties

APPENDIX 25.
VA CONTRACTING OFFICER
MEMO & RESPONSE

The following is my response memo dated 9/12/2011 to an undated memo issued by the contracting officer at the Fargo regarding construction safety associated with 3ND (CS Dubois):

Department of Memorandum
Veterans Affairs

Date: September 12, 2011
From: Project Engineer, Engineering Service
Subj: Response to Undated Memo for Record: Contract #VA263-C-1022, Audiology-ENT-Ophthalmology, Safety Issues by Darryl Moon, Contract Specialist
To: Whom It May Concern

This memo is in response to a memo authored by Darryl W. Moon, Contract Specialist, Fargo VA HCS. The memo from Mr. Moon is not dated but a copy was provided to me on 8 September 2011 (see Attachment #1 below). The memo is signed in concurrence by Stuard Eidenschink, Contracting Officer, and Dennis Langevin, Chief, Engineering Service, both also of the Fargo VA HCS. I will respond to the issues presented by Mr. Moon included within each paragraph generally as they are presented within the memo.

The first paragraph of the memo suggests that Mr. Moon has been party to an effort to address the "underlying root causes for the repeated [safety] deficiencies." I have consistently held that the underlying root cause for the continued deficiencies is very simple: the contractor (3ND, Inc., an offshoot company from C.S. Dubois, Inc.) does not have a competent person, as defined by OSHA, for the various construction activities occurring on the site. I have made Mr. Moon as well as Messrs. Eidenschink and Langevin aware of this on several occasions over the past three months. However, they do not appear to be willing to address this underlying issue. I have also made them each aware of my impression that the scaffolding was looking much better than it did when I started in early June. However, the reason for this was due to the efforts of VA staff (VISN safety professionals and the Fargo VA HCS Project Engineer and Emergency Management Coordinator who has previously worked as a safety consultant), not because of the contractor's inspection efforts. The on-site scaffold safety situation with the contractor evolved from one which resembled something which would be expected in third world countries[53] to something which looks much better. This is due to the iterative process of VA staff finding issues during limited visits to the job sites, primarily by me, who would then inform contractor staff of the deficiencies, who would then correct them. Messrs. Moon, Eidenschink, and Langevin are all aware of this. However, the implication within the text of Mr. Moon's memo is suggestive that the contractor was responsible for the marked improvements in the scaffolding condition. It should be noted that the contract requires the contractor to provide a competent person and to abide by OSHA construction safety requirements (which also require a competent person).

Also included in the memo written by Mr. Moon is a reference to involvement of the Workforce Safety Insurance (WSI -Workman's Comp) safety inspectors. These inspectors became involved due to phone calls which I made to OSHA as a result of the lack of support for construction safety from Messrs. Moon, Eidenschink, and Langevin (phone calls for which Mr. Langevin began a chain of retaliation against me, of which Messrs. Eidenschink and Moon are also aware). If the Fargo VA HCS is truly concerned about construction safety they would have allowed me to schedule a targeted inspection of the contractor's job site. However, I was precluded from doing same. Therefore, the inspectors from the WSI were called in lieu of the true experts from OSHA. I am noting for the record that the WSI inspectors seemed knowledgeable. However, I questioned their level of attention to detail when I pointed out several basic scaffold safety elements which they had overlooked (e.g., compromised planking, missing cleating, etc.). Also, I was in attendance at the debriefing and I did not hear the message quoted in Mr. Moon's memo that the WSI inspectors noted the work site to be "one of the cleanest they had ever seen." It should also be noted that the contractor had ample warning of the pending inspection and, therefore, time to prepare (and several of the old planks had been replaced just prior to the arrival of the WSI staff, again because of my suggestions). Be that as it may, the bottom line for me was the continued absence of a competent person on the job site for scaffold safety (i.e., someone who could actually recognize and correct existing or potential safety issues).

The second paragraph in Mr. Moon's memo states that I began to perform additional worksite inspections. This was done for several reasons including renewed construction activity on the scaffold system, my continued concern over the lack of a competent person for scaffold safety (and then a renewed concern over the lack of a competent person for fall protection), direction by Mr. Langevin to perform same (see Mr. Langevin's hand written review notes second page of Attachment 2 below), and my completion of a VA sponsored construction safety course which indicated that it is the contracting officer's technical representative (COTR) responsibility to review and address safety issues on the job site. These inspection activities were part of an ongoing inspection regimen being completed with the full knowledge and consultation of/with Mr. Langevin who had also just completed the same VA sponsored construction safety course.

The second paragraph in Mr. Moon's memo continues by suggesting that I have been in some way responsible for verbal confrontations with the contractor's "competent person." To the contrary the situation was quite the opposite. During the incident referenced by Mr. Moon in this paragraph I simply advised the contractor's "competent person," in a professional manner, of several construction safety issues that I had just witnessed associated with fall protection (any of which could have resulted in the serious injury or death of one or more of the affected workers). I then simply stood and listened as the "competent person" began what would normally be described as a tirade directed at me which included profanity. When he was done I advised him, in a professional manner, that I had notified him of my concerns and that I needed to return to my (safety) training. I had thought that this sort of response by the contractor would have resulted in sanctions by Mr. Moon or other contracting staff. However, based on the memo it appears that Mr. Moon has seen this as an opportunity to further denigrate me. I am noting for the record that I believe the reason the contractor feels emboldened to speak to me in such fashion is due to one of Mr. Langevin's reprisal actions against me for calling OSHA. He actively solicited comments from contractors regarding my performance which, not surprisingly, resulted in negative feedback from the contractor which was apparently willingly received by Mr. Langevin. This has compromised my authority on the construction sites (I have noticed similar disrespectful behavior by another contractor after they spoke with Mr. Langevin).

The third paragraph in Mr. Moon's memo suggests that I was involved in contentious communication at the face-to-face meeting on 31 August. I am noting for the record that the most "contentious" statement made by me was that the contractor had placed the Fargo VA HCS at risk over the past several months which should be unacceptable to everyone in the room (sensing the lack of support I was receiving by Messrs. Moon, Eidenschink, and Langevin). This was a true statement.

In both the second and third paragraph of Mr. Moon's memo he makes reference to the credentials of those working for the contractor (one a "competent person" employee and the other a "certified safety trainer" hired by the contractor). Mr. Moon seems willing to accept at face value the reports from those supporting the contractor with unsubstantiated credentials who lay claim to being scaffold safety competent persons or experts (to my knowledge nothing has been provided by the contractor proving any of the safety credentials of those working for the benefit of the contractor). However, he is unwilling to recognize the legitimacy of my written reports based on my documented 21+ years of construction experience and registrations as a professional engineer in both civil and environmental engineering. It should be noted that in accordance with OSHA requirements the highest level of scaffold (and trench) safety requirements can only be designed by a registered professional engineer.

The latter part of the third paragraph and the fifth paragraph discuss the findings of the "certified safety trainer" from Acme Rents of Fargo. To no surprise the individual who was hired by the contractor and probably receives significant business from this general contractor (and may be the source of the scaffold equipment for all I know) found no issues with the scaffolding and described it in flattering terms which were readily accepted by Mr. Moon. I am noting for the record that I did not participate in the inspection performed by the "certified safety trainer" because this seemed to me to be completely illegitimate. Be that as it may I performed my own inspection of the scaffold system following that by the "certified safety trainer" and found several additional deficiencies (several of which were recognized and corrected by the contractor via a second individual the contractor has deemed to be a competent person on the job site).

In the fifth paragraph of Mr. Moon's memo he also again references the relatively safe nature of the scaffold conditions during the two inspections. However, he does not acknowledge

NATHAN D. GJOVIK

what I have repeatedly informed him that, again, these conditions are a result of the vigilance of VA staff acting as the competent person for the contractor. Scaffold conditions change constantly and OSHA requires inspections by a person deemed competent (i.e., with the requisite knowledge and ability and authority to recognize and correct existing and potential safety issues with a given construction activity, in this case primarily scaffold safety). The contractor had proven by virtue of a long list of safety deficiencies that they did not have a competent person on the site. The one or two (they have made different claims over time) persons claimed by the contractor to be the competent person have been on the site for the entire time of the development of the deficiencies and, to the best of my knowledge, have not had any scaffold safety training over that time (other than some research to try to avoid having to address items VA staff were bringing forward). It should also be noted that this same contractor had a fatality incident involving some of the same scaffold safety issues VA staff were seeing on this job site approximately four years ago. All of these facts were known by each of the signatories to this memo prior to their signing same.

I am also noting that I had discussed this situation with Mr. Langevin who agreed with me at that time (during and immediately following the VA construction safety course in which we had both participated) that, if the credentials of the "certified safety trainer" could be verified and he found to be legitimate, the contractor would need to hire him or somebody like him to serve as their competent person to perform the OSHA mandated minimum inspections (daily and after each storm and high wind event).

The fourth paragraph of Mr. Moon's memo states that I had "essentially stopped work on the contract." This is only partially true. At the direction of my supervisor, Mr. Langevin (see Mr. Langevin's hand written review notes second page of Attachment #2 below), I did direct the contractor to discontinue operations on the scaffold system until such time as scaffold safety issues were resolved. This should have been supported by all the signatories on this memo. However, it was not and for Mr. Langevin to now concur that activities he directed me to perform (inspect the scaffold and discontinue work on the scaffold) seems quite duplicitous.

This memo developed by Mr. Moon appears to be an effort on the part of the three signatories to thwart VA construction safety directives through dishonest documentation and their perception of strength in numbers (through multiple concurrences of the memo). I am convinced that the work I have been performing on the job site is in accordance with VA construction safety directives. However, I now have no confidence in my supervisor (who now appears to be involved covertly, rather than overtly as in the past, promulgating a hostile work environment for me which started with my phone calls to OSHA) or the contracting staff at the Fargo VA HCS. Since I am not officially designated as the COTR on any of the current construction contracts associated with the Fargo VA HCS which are currently underway, I am hereby requesting to be removed from all construction inspection activities until such time as the Fargo VA HCS chain of command has effectively dealt with construction safety concerns. I am also hereby requesting that Darryl Moon be provided with construction safety training and that Mr. Langevin be formally admonished for his duplicitous behavior in creating a hostile work environment for a new employee who is simply trying to the right things under difficult circumstances.

Nathan D. Gjovik, PE, RS, MS, MBA, MPH, NREMT-P
Project Engineer

Attachments: #1 Undated Memo for Record: Contract #VA263-C-1022, Audiology-ENT-Ophthalmology, Safety Issues by Darryl Moon, Contract Specialist—3 pages

#2 Draft Memo Dated August 29, 2011 with Subject: Construction Safety, Contract #VA263-C-1022, Project #437-306, Audiology-ENT-Ophthalmology 4th Floor Addition—4 pages

Memorandum

From: Darryl W. Moon

Subj: Memo For Record (MFR): Contract # VA263-C-1022, Audiology-ENT-Ophthalmology, Safety Issues

For the past couple months there have been numerous safety issues noted by the project engineer, Nathan Gjorvik, regarding the above contract, especially in the area of scaffolding safety. During that time we, VA Fargo HCS, have communicated these issues to the prime contractor, 3ND in an effort to correct not only the individual issues, but also any underlying root causes for the repeated deficiencies (possible ineffective contractor supervision). In pursuit of these efforts there have been several face to face meetings, as well as telephonic and email correspondence, between different VA organizations (Contracting, Engineering, Safety, EMMS, etc). On/about 8 August a "workforce safety inspection" was arranged via WSI of Fargo to come in and "inspect" the project in question. At the conclusion of the "inspection" an outbrief was held to briefly discuss the results and a recommended path forward. During the outbrief WSI said that the work site was "one of the cleanest they had ever seen" and that any discrepancies noted were relatively minor in nature. It was also determined that WSI would return in a few days to perform a follow-up inspection. It was relayed to the contractor that until this re-inspection was done, and the discrepancies were corrected, work involving the scaffolding would be suspended, and, as a result of the re-inspection, if the discrepancies were corrected, WSI would recommend a resumption of scaffolding work. WSI then provided VA Fargo a written report with recommendations for correction and the follow-up inspection was scheduled. After the re-inspection was accomplished, and the deficiencies had been sufficiently addressed by the contractor, we allowed 3ND to resume work involving the scaffolding.

However, over the course of the past 3 weeks the project engineer has performed several additional worksite inspections and noted quite a few additional safety issues. These, too, were communicated with the both Contracting and 3ND. To add a few opinions, I feel it necessary to say that the environment surrounding the Engineering division and 3ND has become quite contentious and counterproductive. There have been a few instances of verbal "confrontations" occurring between the Project engineer (PE) and the on-site "competent person". I used the term "competent person" parenthetically due to the PE's unwillingness to declare the person as such. I, myself, witnessed one of these verbal confrontations, 1 September 2011, while discussing another safety issue with the competent person--this time regarding workers on the roof and their tethering off procedures.

After a face to face meeting on 31 Aug, between myself, Dennis Langevin, Nathan Gjorvik, Stu Eidenschink, and Jon Dubois (3ND) (which also got quite contentious at times), another "inspection" was scheduled, and performed (which lasted for more than an hour), 1 Sep, by a certified safety trainer from ACME Rents, Fargo, ND. During the outbrief for that inspection we were informed of very similar results to the one performed by WSI. In fact, this inspector said he "felt 100% safe to work on this jobsite", and that "it was one of the best sites he has seen", and that 3ND "has done quite a few things extra that he doubts many other contractors in the Fargo area would do for safety". The inspector is also going to follow-up with a written report to VA Fargo Contracting in the very near future via email, which will then be relayed to VA Fargo Engineering.

Another item that should be mentioned is that in one of the aforementioned communications between the project engineer and 3ND, the project engineer essentially stopped work on the contract, which is NOT within his authority since ONLY a contracting officer can suspend/stop work on a project. This was re-communicated to all parties involved as something that should not and cannot happen again unless imminent personal safety is at risk.

6 September, I received the aforementioned report from CJ Flannery (see attached page with contents of report), who performed the inspection referred to on 1 Sep. In my opinion, one of the most significant parts of the report can be found at the end of "Question 1, which read "Upon asking specific open ended questions of Dave Dumoncueaux I found his judgment sound and awareness to work in a safe applied manner and I would have no problems working on his scaffold set." I can personally testify to hearing numerous of these "open ended questions" being asked of Dave. I also contacted Lindsay Roop, VISN General Counsel, about the situation and inquired about the definition of "competent person" in regard to jobsite safety. Ms Roop told me she was unsure about the definition and referred me to the OSHA website for clarification, to which I proceeded. It is important to note that the definition on the OSHA website and that provided by Mr Flannery were pretty much an exact match. And, after 2 inspections by non-VA safety personnel, the jobsite has been determined to be safe and the contractor was allowed to proceed. Also, while receiving all of the above positive remarks about the contractor's safety performance on this jobsite, there is no guarantee that no accidents will ever occur on this or any other jobsite. It does, however, provide evidence that reasonable efforts are being performed to assure with as much confidence as is reasonably possible that the likelihood of such accidents is greatly reduced.

In summary, numerous discussions have occurred between Contracting, Engineering, Safety, EMMS, and 3ND. Two separate inspections have been conducted, all resulting in overall positive comments regarding contractor and jobsite safety. Based on the preceding sequence of events and inspections, all evidence and opinions from all parties involved, with the exception of Nathan Gjorvik--project engineer, **it is my opinion that 3ND is indeed providing a "competent person", in regard to scaffold safety, and to end the discussion of the topic of "competent person" and not further delay 3ND in performance of this contract at this time.**

DARRYL W. MOON
Contract Specialist

1st Concurrence   STUARD EIDENSCHINK
Contracting Officer

2nd Concurrence   DENNIS LANGEVIN
Chief, Engineering Service

Dear Mr. Darryl Moon;

Thank you for allowing me to address your concerns as it relates to the scaffolding set located on the North side of the VA Facility under control of the General Contractors, questions that were brought to me were concerning the following: who is the competent person and how is that determined, planking used in the scaffold, and guard rails specifications. In addition platform capacities and general construction capacities were noted in an email addressed to Jon Dubois.

As to the who sets the standards for which these tools are used the Scaffold Industry Associations as well as ANSI and adopted by OSHA for enforcement specifically listed in the 29 CFR 1926 OSHA Subpart L 1926.451. As most are aware scaffolding is a temporary elevated platform (support or suspended) and its supporting structure (included points of anchorage) used for supporting employees or materials or both. Subpart L 1926.450(b). As to my understanding that is the accepted standard to which this structure is to be built to and maintained while in use.

Question 1 Competent Person: means one who is capable of identifying existing and predictable hazards in the surroundings of working conditions which are unsanitary, hazardous, or dangerous to employees and who has authorization to take prompt corrective measures to eliminate them. Subpart L 1926.450(b).
Some applications persons are sent to a safety class to attend lecture, administrated test and applied hands on demonstration. The attendee gets a card stated they have attended said class. One can be well versus in the regulations but have no proficient means to put into action what has been learned and thus the employer has final rule over who they deemed competent. Competency is most vital in application and when addressed by enforcement agency they can be questioned on the spot and if that person shows command by use of best practices and has authorization of the scaffold set.
Upon asking specific open ended questions of Dave Dumoncueaux I found his judgment sound and awareness to work in a safe applied manner and I would have no problems working on his scaffold set.

Question 2 Planking used in corners of the set showing sign of weathering however the length of the plank showed viability to support loads required and were fully anchored to the supported platform. The only issue is a slight trip hazard which was noted on the walk around. As for all the working levels the planking are complete and access to platform was a used from the interior building and exterior ladder secured to the set.

Question 3 Guard rails are in the need locations and meet specification with top rail and mid rail and were needed toe board to reduced falling hazards.

In summary I found three end brackets missing toggle pins, overlapping planks , one bent end bracket, one bent frame that would need to be replaced or structural reinforced that was brought to Dave's actions plan to fix. Lastly code of safe practices need to be displayed on each scaffold set to better communicate the requirements associated with supported frame scaffolding enclosed in this email.

All I can says is that due diligence has been done in order to provide a safe and working set and please call me if you may need further information on this set.

Scaffolding
Concerns.msg

Regards,

C.J. Flanery

Acme Tools
Outside Sales
Safety Trainer
cflanery@acme-rents.com
701-219-5671 Cell
701-476-4635 Office
701-232-1196 Fax

Attachment #2

Department of   Memorandum
Veterans Affairs

Date: August 29, 2011

From: Chief, Engineering Service

Subj: Construction Safety, Contract #VA263-C-1022
       Project #437-306, Audiology-ENT-Ophthalmology 4th Floor Addition

To: Chief, Contracting Office

1. On August 23, 2011, while performing construction inspection rounds Nathan Gjovik, Project Engineer, asked David Dumonceaux, 3ND Superintendent and On-site Safety Supervisor, about having a spotter for the masonry work being performed by man-basket from the ground. Mr. Dumonceaux responded that this was not required since there was no lifting occurring. Mr. Gjovik also asked if the scaffold system had been inspected that day. Mr. Dumonceaux responded that it had been. Mr. Gjovik asked when it had been inspected and Mr. Dumonceaux responded that "Jared was supposed to do it." This is not in compliance with what Mr. Gjovik had been previously told by Mr. Dumonceaux (circa August 8, 2011) that he was the "competent person" for the scaffold system.

2. On August 24, 2011, while performing construction inspection rounds Mr. Gjovik noticed what appeared to be the same scaffolding which had been used in the past on the northern roof for the thin-brick veneer installation. This scaffold had been identified previously as having safety issues so Mr. Gjovik investigated the setup and discovered two cross-brace posts which were not engaged and at least one old, weathered plank being used as a platform for masons working on grouting the veneer. There were also a number of sharp objects noted on the EPDM surface (waste grout, screws, etc.) so Mr. Gjovik called Mr. Dumonceaux (only number Mr. Gjovik had in his personal cell phone which was used to make the call) to take a look. Both Mr. Dumonceaux and David Lean, 3ND Sr. Project Superintendent, appeared on the roof shortly after call. I asked Mr. Dumonceaux if he noticed any issues with the scaffolding. He said he did not. I pointed out the two posts which were not engaged as well as the condition of one of the planks being used as a standing platform. Mr. Dumonceaux shouted, "I am sick of this sh@t!", and then he and Mr. Lean proceeded to correct the posts. It is noted that all wooden planks were later replaced with engineered steel frame scaffold platform inserts for use by the masons (this is good).

Construction Safety, Contract #VA263-C-1022   Page 2

3. On August 25, 2011, while performing construction inspection rounds Mr. Gjovik noticed Jared Holland driving a piece of rented equipment past the main entrance of the VA hospital. The equipment (Terex man-basket) apparently requires movement by the operator within the man-basket mounted on the boom. This was being driven with the boom forward by Mr. Holland. He was cautious in his operation. However, there was an ambulance and another vehicle parked in front of the hospital at the time along with a significant amount of foot traffic. Mr. Holland performed the equipment maneuvering without incident. Mr. Gjovik mentioned at the construction coordination meeting that afternoon that he would have like to have seen a spotter accompany and assist Mr. Holland in maneuvering the equipment through the congested area in front of the hospital. The nonverbal communication from the contractor indicated that this was not received well.

[handwritten left margin: which requires the operator to face the opposite direction of travel without mirrors.]

[handwritten right margin: PERSONAL OPINION, OR IS THERE A REQUIREMENT FOR A SPOTTER WE CAN CITE?]

4. On August 26, 2011, based on continued concerns over the apparent lack of a competent person for the scaffold systems, an inspection of the systems was performed by Messrs. Gjovik and John Englund, Emergency Management Coordinator (who has a strong background in safety inspections). There were several findings/questions as follows:

[handwritten left margin: HAVE YOU DISCUSSED THESE ITEMS WITH THE 2ND INC. FOREMAN TO TRY AND GET THEM RESOLVED? IF NOT, PLEASE DO AND INFORM THEM YOU WANT SCAFFOLDING WORK DISCONTINUED UNTIL THESE ITEMS ARE CORRECTED AND YOU HAVE INSPECTED THEM WITH HIM. IF 2ND INC. FAILS TO COMPLY, THIS SERVES TO ENLIST CONTRACTING.]

North roof scaffolding:

This looked good with the above described modifications. The contractor was working near a leading edge with a fall protection harness which was tethered to an appropriate fall protection device. He was not wearing a hard hat. However, there was no other construction occurring in the vicinity of where he was working at the time.

North face scaffolding:

a. No mid-rails along the interior side of scaffolding on the main working level. This was allowed during the previous Workforce Safety Insurance loss protection inspection since the masonry subcontractor described the interior area to be an ongoing work area. However, the work in this area by the masonry subcontractor has been completed.

b. At least three old, weathered scaffold planks on the east end of the scaffold system which appear to require replacement.

c. A variety of small debris noted on the walking surfaces of the scaffold system including screws and waste grout.

d. A questionable top rail on the northeast corner of the scaffold system.

e. At least one old, weathered scaffold planks on the fourth scaffold tower from the east end (north side) which appears to require replacement.

Construction Safety, Contract #VA263-C-1022   Page 3

    f. Several questionable planks (at least two with questionable cleating) on the highest level of decking.

    g. Some planking with greater than 1-inch gaps between them.

    h. Unknown access to the easternmost scaffold system, even for removal.

    i. Unknown as to whether or not the anchoring system used for the easternmost scaffold system requires design by a registered professional engineer.

    j. Two scaffold system towers which appear not to be connected to the building or adjacent towers (east and west ends of the north face). In the case of the west end tower this could represent a danger from tipping since the upper platform has been traditionally used for moving materials to and from the 4th floor work area (e.g., a forklift retraction dragging the platform and causing the tower to tip).

    k. Cable clamps tying the eastern side of the western scaffold system tower to the building are incorrectly clamped (this was a past issue with the clamps used for the fall protection cabling along the leading edge of the 4th floor prior to partial enclosure).

    l. Questionable support for the western scaffold system platform when viewed from below (appears that plywood edges closest to building have inadequate support for traditional loads placed upon them).

    m. Unknown as to whether or not planking used on outriggers is required to be fastened to the outriggers on which they lie.

5. On August 26, 2011, while performing construction inspection rounds Mr. Gjovik greeted Mr. Dumonceaux on the job site within building 51. Hearing no response he followed up by saying "Dave, have we reached the point at which we can't even greet each other?" Mr. Dumonceaux replied, "Pretty much, although I did reply."

[handwritten margin note: WHAT DOES THIS HAVE TO DO WITH MEMO SUBJECT ?]

6. Given the continuing nature of the safety issues and the demeanor exhibited by Mr. Dumonceaux, I am hereby again requesting that construction work on this project be suspended until such time as:

    a. 3ND can find a competent person for the scaffold systems and

[handwritten margin note: WORK Requiring Scaffolding to be suspended.]

[handwritten note at bottom:]

Internal scaffolding:

There is a ~~interest~~ scaffold system tower located inside the roof system which has not been utilized in some time. This has not been inspected by VA staff. It is unknown if it has been inspected by the contractor.

Construction Safety, Contract #VA263-C-1022   Page 4

b. 3ND is able to educate their staff on the importance of safety on the job site and that monitoring safety issues is the job of Mr. Gjovik as the Project Engineer.

DENNIS T. LANGEVIN

WHAT DO YOU EXPECT FOR THIS? HOW WOULD IT BE DOCUMENTED?

APPENDIX 26.
COMMUNICATION WITH ND
CONGRESSIONALS

The following are various communications through the offices of Republican Congressman Rick Berg and Republican Senator John Hoeven regarding construction safety management at the Fargo VA (note that no response was ever received from the office of Democratic Senator Kent Conrad):

January 25, 2012

The Honorable Rick Berg
Member, United States House of Representatives
3170 43rd Street South, Suite 105
Fargo, ND 58104

RE: Construction Safety Management at Fargo VA Health Care
System

Dear Congressman Berg:

This letter is in response to your response letter dated January 13, 2012, to my letter dated December 16, 2011, regarding construction safety management concerns at the Fargo Veterans Affairs Health Care System (VAHCS). Your response letter included an issue brief from the Fargo VAHCS. This issue brief defends the actions/inactions of the Fargo VAHCS and attacks my credibility as the one repeatedly bringing construction safety concerns forward. This is exactly why I feel it is important to continue to follow up on this issue—Fargo VAHCS management does not get it. Rather than viewing this as an opportunity to improve they apparently would rather invest their resources in presenting spin and defamation to defend the actions/inactions of Fargo VAHCS staff which are questionable at best and illegal at worst.

My specific responses to the response you received from the Fargo VAHCS dated January 4, 2012, include the following:

Transmittal letter from Michael J. Murphy, Medical Center Director:

- The reference to "two independent safety consultants reviewed the scaffolding on the worksite" is only partly true. One was independent and the other was hired by the contractor. To the best of my knowledge neither the credentials nor the relationship of the "safety consultant" (employee from a local construction equipment rental company) hired by the contractor were investigated or challenged by Fargo VAHCS staff.

- All deficiencies discovered by the "safety consultants" are classified as "minor." I do not consider compromised planking or absent guard rails (two of the items discovered) to be minor. These represent risks that can easily cause serious injury or death to construction workers or those who happen to be present below the work area (work was being performed above the main entrance to the medical center).

- The statement "we regret that neither of these inspections alleviated Mr. Gjovik's concerns" seems to be designed to marginalize me as some sort of safety zealot.

- The assertion that "no serious worksite injuries have occurred on the construction site" may be true. However, unsafe conditions do not guarantee an immediate negative result. They simply offer the opportunity for bad things to happen.

- The letter does not address my primary concern that the contractor did not have a "competent person" on the job site. OSHA requires this because conditions on a construction site change constantly. The scaffolding system was supposed to be inspected by a "competent person" not just twice by "safety consultants" but every day and after each wind storm and any significant change to the structure. This was not being done. However, the letter suggests that because "safety consultants" inspected the scaffold system on two occasions "the worksite was safe." It should be noted that, as indicated in the letter as well as the associated timeline, deficiencies were noted by inspectors on each occasion, even with the contractor's full knowledge of the dates and times of the inspections and re-inspections.

VHA Issue Brief (attachment to transmittal letter from Mr. Murphy):

- The statement "the project engineer singularly focused on the issue of scaffolding safety soon after his entry on duty…" is not true. There were numerous other safety issues associated with the same contractor. I was also performing the other work expected of me. However, it should be noted that the annual workplace evaluation (AWE) review occurred soon after my entry on duty and VISN 23 safety specialists performing same found several significant safety issues associated with the contractor's worksite including several associated with the scaffold system in existence at the time (which had been in that state of existence for several weeks or months prior to that inspection). This is actually what initially brought my attention to the significant safety issues associated with the contractor.

- See comments noted above regarding statements that "on-site inspections by two independent safety consultants identified minor deficiencies and these issues were corrected" and "facility leadership has verified scaffolding integrity but they have not been successful at alleviating the concerns of the project engineer."

- The actions and findings of the AWE which occurred during the week of June 6, 2011, are not included in this timeline. As noted above VISN 23 safety specialists found several significant issues as follows:

6/7/11   1. There were several safety issues noted by annual workplace evaluation (AWE) staff associated with the fourth floor scaffold platform being used as a loading and offloading dock via lifting equipment from outside the main building including:

    a. long unsupported spans of railing on the working side of the platform,

    b. lack of toe board protection along the working side of the platform to prevent items from falling off the scaffold platform and the presence of several loose items on same,

    c. leading edge protection for the western approach to the scaffold platform was being provided by a wooden pallet,

    d. lack of an anchoring system of the upper reaches of the scaffold to prevent toppling of the scaffold system (e.g., in the event an element of a lifting device inadvertently attaches to the scaffold system and pulls on it), and

    e. it was unclear as to whether or not the required daily inspections were being performed by a competent person for the scaffold system.

- June 29 notes seem to begin a trend to attempt to paint my concerns as being based on some sort of personal issue I had with the contractor. This is not true. The request for replacement of the Construction Superintendent was due to direction from the Chief Engineer (who seemed to have a personal issue with the Construction Superintendent).

- August 2 notes are an example of how information from the contractor was taken at face value by Fargo VAHCS management. During a phone call with an OSHA staff member on August 3 he was unfamiliar with any phone call from the contractor and said he would be very surprised if this actually occurred, especially from this particular contractor due to their past history with OSHA (he was surprised they were even allowed to have a contract with the VA due to this history). I believe this type of carelessness with the truth was one of the reasons the Chief Engineer did not care for the Construction Superintendent and wanted him removed from the project.

- August 2 notes do not include any detail regarding a seminal moment wherein the contractor's "competent person" and his subcontractor's "competent person" both laid claim to certain old, weathered planking being used on the scaffolds to be safe. The contractor's "competent person" then proceeded to demonstrate this empirically by applying a force to the mid span of same after two applications of which a loud crack was heard from the plank. It was clear that any additional loading would have resulted in complete failure of the plank and the "competent person" quickly discontinued the exercise.

- August 3 notes are misleading with respect to my request for a targeted OSHA inspection of the contractor's work sites. My discussions with the OSHA staff member took place over two separate phone calls. During the first phone call the office secretary overheard me speaking to the OSHA staff member and called upper management who then directed me to cease my conversation. During the second conversation I advised the OSHA staff member that Fargo VAHCS management did not desire their presence on the site. Based on this the OSHA staff member suggested Workforce Safety Insurance (WSI) as a possible alternative.

- August 3 notes are also misleading in regard to the WSI inspection. It actually occurred on August 4 and the contractor was notified well in advance of the inspection. The contractor utilized this time to replace nearly all of the remaining bad planking on the scaffolds and to scrutinize the scaffold safety by their "competent persons." However, as the WSI report illuminates, even with the notice and level of effort there were still significant findings, including planking which was recommended to be replaced.

- August 10 notes are misleading. I did indicate to the Human Resources Manager that the scaffolding condition on that day was looking good but explained that this was due primarily to my efforts, not the contractor's (i.e., I was acting as the "competent person" for the contractor by default). This was unnerving to me because I felt as if I was having to assume the responsibility (and liability) for the actions of the contractor (who had a proven record of poor construction safety management).

- August 22 notes do not include detail of the nexus of the memorandum on performance deficiencies and my phone calls to the OSHA. It should be noted that this memorandum was developed following approximately two months of total experience as a VA employee and total exposure to the Fargo VAHCS (my wife and I moved to Fargo for the job). It also came on the heels of the author's (Chief Engineer) 10-day absence followed by a week's absence by me for training (i.e., August 22 was the first real opportunity by the Chief Engineer following my phone calls to the OSHA to serve me with the performance evaluation).

- September 9-13 notes do not indicate that I was not included as part of the organizational assessment. I am unaware of inappropriate workplace behaviors and believe this comment to be baseless and defamatory and another attempt by management to marginalize me in some way. Having said that I will note for the record that I was also very stressed in the office environment and did not trust several of the staff members due to their blind support of the Chief Engineer in situations where it seemed to me to be unwarranted (e.g., the Secretary listening to my phone calls and notifying the Chief Engineer and upper management when she believed I was having an inappropriate conversation with the OSHA—it should be noted that this same secretary was the union steward for the AFGE and probably was the reason for the organizational assessment). It should also be noted that the person I found to be most stable and professionally competent of the individuals working within the Fargo VAHCS Engineering Service recently transferred due, at least in part, to the dysfunction of the office.

It should be noted that I resigned my lucrative position at the Fargo VAHCS and gave up a potential new and rewarding career path with the Department of Veterans Affairs to become unemployed. However, I found this to be a better option than continue to work within the hostile work environment created because I was simply trying to do what is right.

As you read this please ask yourself if too much concern over safety is a common problem found within the Department of Veterans Affairs (or anywhere else)? Also, should safety concerns brought forward by a registered and licensed professional staff member be scrutinized, and the staff member marginalized, while the assertions of a contractor go unchallenged (a contractor who has a past history of a fatality incident and many OSHA violations associated with similar work to that producing the concerns being raised by the licensed professional staff member)? These should be rhetorical questions. However, these are reflective of the demeanor toward construction safety at the Fargo VAHCS. In his letter Mr. Murphy states that "safety is our first priority at Fargo VAHCS…" If this were true then why was the list of safety violations allowed to continue to grow so long and why was I precluded by management from asking the OSHA, the true construction safety experts, to perform a targeted inspection of the suspect work site (and why was I served with a performance evaluation on the heels of my calling the OSHA after only two months of employment)? Actions speak louder than words and the actions show the Fargo VAHCS to be apathetic toward construction safety and several staff willing to compromise their personal integrity to cover up the actions/inactions which demonstrate the apathy.

Following my personal experiences and discussions with National Federation of Federal Employees (NFFE) union representatives I am convinced that safety is, in fact, not the first priority at the Fargo VAHCS. As a matter of fact I am convinced that at least construction safety, although present at some level of the collective consciousness, is not a priority at all at the Fargo VAHCS and after speaking with a national level construction safety specialist within the VA I don't think this problem is unique to the Fargo VAHCS.

As noted in prior correspondence I receive my health care at the Fargo VAHCS. I expect far more in terms of corrective action and integrity from those managing the operations at this facility. I should not have to be concerned about my safety due to staff and/or contractors compromising same knowing that management will be sympathetic toward them and prone to simply overlooking and/or covering up the compromise rather than ensuring my protection.

I am copying this letter to Senators Conrad and Hoeven and Secretary Shinseki so they can be kept appraised of all communications regarding these important issues affecting our collective facility here in Fargo.

Very Respectfully,

Nathan D. Gjovik, PE, RS, MS, MBA, MPH, NREMT-P
CAPT US Public Health Service (Ret.)

Attachment: Letter from Michael J. Murphy Dated January 4, 2012—4 pages

Cc: The Honorable Kent Conrad, United States Senate
     The Honorable John Hoeven, United States Senate
     Secretary Eric K. Shinseki, U.S. Department of Veterans Affairs

DEPARTMENT OF VETERANS AFFAIRS
VA Health Care System
2101 Elm Street North
Fargo ND 58102-2498

January 4, 2012

In Reply Refer To: 437/00

The Honorable Rick Berg
Member, United States House of Representatives
3170 43rd Street South, Suite 105
Fargo, ND 58104

Dear Congressman Berg:

Thank you for your letter dated December 20, 2011, from Mr. Nathan Gjovik, who copied you in a letter dated December 16, he sent to Department of Veterans Affairs Secretary Eric J. Shinseki.

Mr. Gjovik's safety concerns at the Fargo VAHCS were carefully reviewed while responding to allegations that he previously addressed in an email to Secretary Shinseki dated September 25, 2011, prior to his resignation on September 29. A copy of the Veterans Health Administration (VHA) Issue Brief prepared at that time is attached. Safety is our first priority at Fargo VAHCS and we are confident that we are providing a safe environment for the veterans, employees, and contractors at our facility.

The timeline in the attached VHA Issue Brief summarizes both serious concerns raised by Mr. Gjovik and facility responses. Work was discontinued for a total of seven days on two separate occasions, while two independent safety consultants reviewed the scaffolding on the worksite. Minor deficiencies were found and corrected during both inspections, but both consultants confirmed that overall the scaffolding on the worksite was safe.

We regret that neither of these inspections alleviated Mr. Gjovik's concerns. No serious worksite injuries have occurred on the construction site, and the scaffolding, which was the major source of Mr. Gjovik's concern, is no longer required and has been removed.

Thank you for bringing this matter to our attention. Your continued interest in veterans' issues is appreciated.

Respectfully Yours,

MICHAEL J. MURPHY, FACHE
Medical Center Director

Attachment

VA Midwest Health Care Network (VISN 23)
VAHCS FARGO, ND
VHA ISSUE BRIEF

Issue Title: A contracting project engineer from the Fargo VA Health Care System (VAHCS) wrote an email message to the SECVA with concerns about construction safety at Fargo VAHCS.

Date of Report: September 25, 2011

Brief Statement of Issue and Status:
A Project Engineer at the Fargo VAMC wrote to the SECVA about scaffolding safety concerns on a construction project at the Fargo VA Health Care System. Concerns made by the project engineer were brought to the attention of the Network Director on September 25, 2011.

Background, Current Status and Actions:
The Project Engineer is currently an employee of the Fargo VAHCS, but he submitted a letter of resignation to the Chief, Engineer at the Fargo VAHCS on Sept 20 with an effective date of September 29, 2011. As of this date, no construction site injuries related to his concerns have occurred.

Fargo VAHCS leadership is aware of the project manager's concerns and has been actively engaged with the project manager, working with two independent safety consultants to ensure project safety.

The project engineer singularly focused on the issue of scaffolding safety soon after his entry on duty at FVAHCS on June 6, 2011. Local Engineering, Contracting, Safety and VISN Safety staffs have been appropriately involved in monitoring and oversight of the scaffolding safety issue. On-site inspections by two independent safety consultants identified minor deficiencies and these deficiencies were corrected. Facility leadership has verified scaffolding integrity but they have not been successful at alleviating the concerns of the project engineer.

Following is a chronological review on action raised and taken by the Fargo VAHCS. The Network continues to gather information and additional information will be provided as needed on September 26. .

ON/ABOUT ACTION:

June 6   Nathan Gjovik, Project Engineer, entered on duty at Fargo VA Health Care System (FVAHCS).
June 29   Chief, Engineering Service sent memorandum prepared by Project Engineer to Contracting Officer requesting Construction Superintendent be replaced based on safety concerns.
July 14   Chief, Engineering Service sent memorandum prepared by Project Engineer to Contracting Officer regarding safety concerns and alleging that the Contractor had no competent safety person on site and requesting suspension of construction.
July 15   Project Engineer sent email to Contracting Officer questioning competency of the General Contractor Supervisor.

July 18	Project Engineer sent email to Contacting Officer recommending project be suspended until Contractor could provide an appropriately-trained and qualified individual, and requesting superintendent be "changed out."
July 18	Contractor sent email to Project Engineer that provided a copy of the safety inspection policy of 3ND (General Contractor) stating policy was distributed to subcontractors on July 18. This policy identified the General Contractor's new Safety Supervisor.
July 19	Project Engineer sent email to Contracting Officer listing safety violations dating from June 7 to July 18 in response to request from the Contracting Officer.
Aug. 1	Contracting Officer reviewed the General Contractor's progress toward correcting the June 7 to July 18 list of safety violations and emailed General Contractor noting a few safety concerns remaining, but stating that sufficient progress had been observed to not suspend project at that time.
Aug. 2	Project Engineer emailed Contractor noting scaffolding safety concerns previously mentioned and cited several new concerns.
Aug.2	Contractor responded to Project Engineer concurring with several concerns and noting actions taken in response. Contractor stated that discussion had taken place with OSHA regarding expectations for planking.
Aug. 3	Project Engineer emailed Contracting Officer stating he would like to contact OSHA for on-site inspection.
Aug. 3	Project Engineer called OSHA to ask about procedures for focused inspection of scaffolding. OSHA recommended contacting the Workforce Safety and Insurance (WSI) agency – a North Dakota State Workers Safety agency.
Aug. 3	WSI responded the same day and performed an on-site inspection.
Aug. 5	WSI emailed to FVAHCS Safety Officer its suggested solutions to four deficiencies. WSI offered to return for re-inspection August 8, 2011.
Aug. 8	WSI re-inspection completed.
Aug. 10	Project Engineer emails Chief, Human Resources Management Service requesting private meeting and noting that he was considering resigning. Chief, Human Resources Management Service met with him the same day. During the meeting, Project Engineer told Chief, Human Resources Management Service he had noticed 35 construction safety violations and the Contractor "did make adjustments and that it looked good." But he stated that he had subsequently found additional safety concerns. He expressed concerns regarding the management style and direction of the Chief, Engineering Service. He expressed concerns at being associated with an agency that was not concerned about safety.
Aug. 22	Project Engineer emailed Chief, Human Resources Management Service regarding other employment opportunities at the FVAHCS.
Aug. 22	Chief, Engineering Service presented Project Engineer with a memorandum advising Project Engineer of performance deficiencies. (The memorandum was fully coordinated with the HR Employee Relations Officer in advance. This memorandum was IAW NFFE contract requirement for probationary employees.)
Aug. 23	Chief, Human Resources Management Service informed Project Engineer that FVAHCS had no other suitable employment opportunities presently.
Aug. 26	Project Engineer requested and was granted an interview with Medical Center Director during which he summarized his construction safety concerns, engineering working environment, and raised the perception of

	retaliatory behavior toward him by Chief, Engineering Service related to his actions regarding construction safety.
Aug. 26	Medical Center Director discussed Project Engineer's allegations at length with Associate Director for Operations and Resources. Associate Director for Operations and Resources, the former Chief, Engineering Service, was well aware of issues related to safety and the engineering work environment and satisfied the Medical Center Director that actions were underway to appropriately address all issues.
Sept. 1	General Contractor, Contracting and Engineering staff met to discuss scaffolding safety issues. The Contractor agreed to ask for review of scaffolding by an outside safety consultant.
Sept. 2	An outside consultant, ACME Tools Safety Trainer, completed on-site inspection of the scaffolding. The Contractor and Contracting Office participated.
Sept. 6	Contracting Officer received written summary of ACME inspection stating that "due diligence has been done in order to provide a safe and working set..."
Sept. 7	Associate Director for Operations and Resources was notified by VISN Safety Officer that Project Engineer contacted him regarding scaffolding concerns. Associate Director for Operations and Resources briefed VISN Safety Officer on entire issue from his perspective.
Sept. 8	VISN Safety Officer requested more information from the FVAHCS Safety Officer.
Sept. 8	Chief, Human Resources Management Service notified AFGE of intent to conduct an Engineering organizational assessment after AFGE raised concerns regarding the working environment in Engineering. (Non-professional employees in Engineering are AFGE; professional employees are NFFE).
Sept. 9 - 13	HR specialist performed organizational assessment in Engineering Service. Results showed stress in the office related to relationship between Chief, Engineering Service and Project Engineer, inappropriate workplace behaviors by Project Engineer noted by some Engineering employees, and a "singular focus" of Project Engineer on scaffolding safety issues noted by several employees.
Sept. 16	Project Engineer, HR Employee Relations Officer, Chief, Engineering Service and NFFE president met to discuss performance expectations of Project Engineer and priorities of Project Engineer going forward. The information discussed was summarized in a memorandum to the individual dated September 19-20.
Sept. 16	Project Engineer submitted resignation memorandum dated September 16, 2011.
Sept. 20	Chief, Engineering Service discovered Project Engineer's letter of resignation in his in-box.

Contact for Further Information:
Mr. Michael J. Murphy, FACHE, Center Director, 701-239-3701.

Nathan Gjovik

From:	Johnson, Sally (Hoeven) <Sally_Johnson@hoeven.senate.gov>
Sent:	Monday, April 16, 2012 12:31 PM
To:	Nathan Gjovik (ndgjovik@hotmail.com)
Subject:	Senator Hoeven Response
Attachments:	VA Response for Gjovik.pdf

Nathan,

I am attaching responses that I received from the Department of Veterans Affairs. I am sorry that there will be nothing more that our office will do as far as ordering further investigations with OIG or OSHA. You can directly contact either of those agencies. I have attached contact information for the office of OIG and OSHA.

Thank you for contacting our office.

Sally Johnson

Department of State

MAIL
Office of Inspector General
HOTLINE
P.O. Box 9778
Arlington, Virginia 22219

Email: oighotline@state.gov

Phone: 202-647-3320 or 800-409-9926

Department of Labor

MAIL

U.S. Department of Labor
Occupational Safety & Health Administration
200 Constitution Avenue
Washington, D.C. 20210

You can contact OSHA via email.

To submit an information inquiry by **Electronic Mail Form**.

Phone: 1-800-321-OSHA (6742) Toll Free U.S.

Sally Johnson
Constituent Services
U.S. Senator John Hoeven (R-ND)
1802 32nd Avenue S. Suite #B
Fargo, ND 58103
Phone: (701) 239-5389

DEPARTMENT OF VETERANS AFFAIRS
VA Health Care System
2101 Elm Street North
Fargo ND 58102-2498

April 11, 2012   In Reply Refer To: 437/00

The Honorable John Hoeven
United States Senate
1802 32nd Avenue South, Room B
Fargo, ND 58103

Dear Senator Hoeven:

Thank you for your inquiry regarding Mr. Nathan Gjovik and the Fargo VA Health Care System (VAHCS).

Mr. Gjovik's safety concerns at the Fargo VAHCS have been addressed repeatedly; including responses to Congressman Berg, Senator Conrad, and Eric K Shinseki, Secretary, Veterans Affairs. In reply to the various correspondence, it has been noted that our facility has taken all necessary actions to ensure safety for the Veterans, our employees, and the contractors at our facility.

In relation to Mr. Gjovik's concerns, work was discontinued for a total of seven days on two separate occasions, while two independent safety consultants reviewed the scaffolding on the worksite. Minor deficiencies were found and corrected during both inspections, but both consultants confirmed that overall the scaffolding on the worksite was safe. Fargo VAHCS is confident that all safety issues have been analyzed and the facility meets all Occupational Safety and Health Administration (OSHA) guidelines.

We regret that none of the inspections or correspondence has alleviated Mr. Gjovik's concerns, but the facility has taken all appropriate steps to ensure safety. There are no further actions to be taken at this time.

Thank you for bringing this matter to our attention. We appreciate your ongoing support and commitment to our Veterans.

Respectfully Yours,

M J Murphy

MICHAEL J. MURPHY, FACHE
Medical Center Director

Department of Veterans Affairs
VA Midwest Health Care Network
Veterans Integrated Service Network 23

5445 Minnehaha Avenue South
Building 9, Second Floor
Minneapolis, MN 55417
Phone: (612) 725-1968
Fax: (612) 467-5967

April 9, 2012

The Honorable John Hoeven
1802 32nd Avenue South
Suite B
Fargo, ND 58105

Dear Senator Hoeven:

Thank you for your letter on March 29th regarding Mr. Nathan Gjovik's continued concern for safety at the Fargo VA Health Care System (VAHCS). The issues he raised were investigated, implementation of corrective actions verified, and ongoing compliance monitored. Completion of these actions was documented with letters to Secretary Shinseki's staff, Congressman Berg, and Senator Conrad.

The Fargo VAHCS is confident that the safety issues were addressed and that the facility meets all Occupational Safety and Health Administration (OSHA) guidelines. We regret that we have been unable to alleviate Mr. Nathan Gjovik's concerns, but please be assured that the facility took the necessary steps to ensure a safe environment. There are no further actions to be taken at this time.

Should you have any further concerns, please direct all communications to Dale DeKrey, Associate Director for Operations and Resources at the Fargo VAHCS (701-239-3702).

Sincerely,

JANET P. MURPHY, MBA
Network Director

www.visn23.va.gov

ENDNOTES

1   Participation in the review of this document does not imply agreement with any of the content of this book. Reviewers were chosen based on gaining a variety of perspectives.

2   Excerpted from a composition written by the author while attending the University of North Dakota during the fall of 1983.

3   There were a couple of other personal experiences that are only humorous in retrospect. One was during one of my first evenings at the academy. I had to be the minute caller (announce formations, required uniforms, food being served if prior to a meal, and the number of days "before Army beat the HELL out of Navy" at the annual Army-Navy football game at Veterans stadium in Philadelphia) the following day. I was returning to my barracks and had no idea where I was. Unfortunately, the glance I stole of a room number to get a bearing was witnessed by a female upperclassman who was in the hallway brushing her teeth. She ordered me to halt and report to her room where she began dressing me down, figuratively, while finishing brushing her teeth. As the toothpaste was flying into my face she demanded a "4-C" (a 4th class demerit slip, which was used to document various misdeeds by 4th classmen) for my "falling out" in the hallway (we were expected to always have a military bearing which implied always knowing where you are and where you are going). Unfortunately, I was dressed in my gym alpha (uniform consisting of gym shoes, white socks, t-shirt, and gym shorts which had no pockets). I did have some 4-Cs on my person, but they were in my socks and moist from sweat. This moisture prompted another 4-C. The other personal experience involved a white glove inspection of our room one

afternoon. We were not aware of a shelf on the bottom of the back of our closet (apparently for boots). However, the upperclassmen knew it was there and when he swiped it with his perfectly white glove it came back black. He erupted in a shower of expletives and salivary secretions which seemed to last a lifetime.

4   Ironically, I visited the UND campus recently, over 20 years after I graduated, during the summer (i.e., ample parking was available throughout the campus) and got the same type of treatment (parked my jacked-up Jeep in a lot where I apparently was not supposed to and got ticketed within a matter of minutes).

5   I went to Chilkoot Charlie's with my roommate one night. I was in my mid-20's and got carded at the door. I wasn't very happy about getting carded and had to run back to our apartment to get an ID. I grabbed my temporary US Public Health Service active duty ID and presented it at the door. The bouncer, who was the same guy who asked for my ID earlier and knew I was not happy, studied my ID very closely and noticed the USPHS noted on the front and began to apologize for upsetting me. He noted that they did "not want to have any problems." I did not understand at first what was going on and then realized that he thought I was an inspector from the health department. I guess I could have had a lot of fun with the situation but I simply got a beer, joined my roommate, and shared a good laugh with him over the situation.

6   United States Public Health Service. (n.d.). In *Wikipedia*. Retrieved from http://en.wikipedia.org/wiki/US_Public_Health_Service

7   Indian Health Service Introduction. (n.d.). In *Our Mission*. Retrieved from http://www.ihs.gov/index.cfm?module=ihsIntro

8 Indian Health Service. (n.d.). In *Wikipedia*. Retrieved from http://en.wikipedia.org/wiki/Indian_Health_Service

9 The Tribe was split into two primary groups in 1838 when most of the Tribal members were forcibly removed from their homelands in the eastern United States to what was then Indian Territory, which later became Oklahoma. Most of those who were removed became known as the Cherokee Nation of Oklahoma. Many of those who stayed behind became known as the Eastern Band of Cherokee Nation in North Carolina. The Cherokee Nation of Oklahoma has since had a name change to the Cherokee Nation.

10 I was interested to learn while touring the Oklahoma Historical Society Museum in Oklahoma City years later that the Cherokees were generally more literate than the white soldiers who were escorting them on the Trail of Tears.

11 I also worked closely with Harley Buzzard who managed the Tribe's water and sewer construction crews (force accounts). Harley became a friend of mine and we still exchange Christmas greetings. Harley would later go on to serve on the CNO Tribal council.

12 IHS leadership had also significantly changed with the heavy emphasis by the agency on hiring Native American employees. They were now only interested in hiring non-Native persons as a last resort, no matter how talented they are or how minimally qualified the Native American candidate is (i.e., the primary, and sometimes only, criteria was the race of the individual).

13 LCDR Weaver applied for his new assignment at a time when his wife was in the middle of a nursing program in Oklahoma. We were aware that she had issues with substance abuse (alcohol at the time) and believed the nursing program was a very positive direction for her. However, with the new assignment came the end of her training and the beginning of

a downward spiral in her substance abuse which culminated in their divorce.

14 Wikipedia biography of Antonia C. Novello.

15 The PM was Henry Hardnett. Our paths would cross again during a future assignment.

16 Several years later Mr. Bell and I would conduct an E-mail discussion about combining two vacant engineering positions into one in Toppenish. Having worked there previously I felt as if I could perform both functions. However, Mr. Bell made it clear that he did not think I would measure up to the task.

17 It had reached the point in Yakima where "bilingual" meant English and Spanish. During an office get together of my wife's an individual relayed a story of a bilingual person who had been hired in their office. A Mexican appeared for care one day and they called for assistance from the new bilingual person. She replied that she could be of no assistance. When management inquired as to why not since she had been hired because she was bilingual, she explained that she spoke English and *French* (i.e., "bilingual" had become a euphemism for English and Spanish).

18 This would not be the last time CAPT Chadwick would refuse a request of mine. A year later, after receiving a call from a recruiter, I would request the opportunity to apply for an engineering position with the National Park Service (CAPT Chadwick would have to agree to any subsequent transfer). Such positions were highly sought after and would have been a very positive career move (especially since it would be out of the IHS). However, CAPT Chadwick cited an unofficial rule which required officers to stay at a duty station for a minimum of two years. Such rules were routinely waived for others, but not for me.

19 He had even suggested that we should not move our government vehicles as the fire was threatening to destroy everything in the community because "they [were] not our

responsibility." It wasn't like we were short on manpower or time, he was just short on the will do what was right.

20 It is worth noting that, according to Wikipedia, in November 2011 SG Carmona announced he would seek the Democratic Party's nomination for United States Senate in the hopes of succeeding Senator Jon Kyl (R-AZ).

21 That first night I was given a brief tour of a hospital near downtown. We were met in the lobby by several young National Guardsmen carrying M-16s. Apparently the pharmacy (and possibly other areas in the hospital) had been looted so they were there to protect the facility from further loss or damage.

22 In another incident the Tribe modified construction specifications which had been duly reviewed and stamped by engineers and architects and then borrowed the signature page from another set to legitimize the covertly developed specifications. This was brought to the attention of DES management who did nothing.

23 A confined space is any space: 1) that has limited or restricted means of entry or exit; 2) is large enough for a person to enter to perform tasks; 3) and is not designed or configured for continuous occupancy. They are potentially life threatening.

24 It is worth noting that I was told that Lisa Losano was fired from the SWO sometime near the end of the construction of the new health care center.

25 It should be noted that CAPT Weaver had been supportive of my efforts to ensure safety and had even wagered that OSHA would be levying a several thousand dollar fine during their second visit to the site (which he had personally approved). He had led me out on the branch and was now one of the pruners of the branch—makes me wonder how people like him are able to live with themselves.

26 Pezzoni, J., & Eades, M. (2005). *Aberdeen Area Indian Health Service Historic Resources Survey Project Report*. Lexington, VA: Landmark Preservation Associates.

27 Ms. Jewett also felt it important one day to correct me during one of our Executive Team meetings when I referred to the care received by our customers as "free" (after all, it was free to them). She said that the care they receive is "pre-paid" (implying that they are entitled to the care by virtue of some sort of right to same—this is actually not true, but it is a common myth which many tribal leaders try hard to propagate).

28 During the EEO counseling phase of one of the grievances she reportedly told the lead security guard that I should not expect her to have to look at me because she does not like having to look at bald-headed white men (this must be what she meant when she told me that she didn't like the way I look). I logged the comment for inclusion in my EEO complaint and the security guard (whom I respected and had shared with me a story of how Ms. Thompson had possibly been involved in the removal and destruction of official documents from his office) told me that he would tell the truth if he was "put on the stand." However, saying and doing are different things and when his affidavit was developed he suggested that he may have not have understood Ms. Thompson correctly—so much for integrity.

29 Actually the entire state of Oklahoma was a reservation known as the Indian Territory prior to 1907 when Oklahoma became a state. As a point of interest when I was detailed to the Cherokee Nation of Oklahoma we lived in the community of Tahlequah where my wife worked at a local bank. On the old bank safe door was the original name of the bank followed by the bank location—"Tahlequah, IT."

30 I had a subsequent encounter with this individual regarding his brother, George Ghost Dog. George is an outstanding artist and I had purchased many pieces of art from him. However, he is/was an alcoholic and his life was in complete shambles as a result of his addiction. I spoke with his brother

Thomas, a substance abuse counselor and he told me that he had given up on his brother. It seemed odd that the only person who seemed to care about his brother was me, the person presented to be a racist (simply because I'm Caucasian and I call things straight up).

31 The fable of the frog and scorpion begins with a scorpion asking a frog for a ride across a body of water. The frog is reluctant because he doesn't want to get stung by the scorpion. The scorpion explains that if he stung the frog they would both die and the frog agrees to provide the ride. However, when they are in the water the scorpion stings the frog. As they both prepare to drown the frog asks the scorpion why he stung him. The scorpion replies because he is a scorpion and that is what he does.

32 The following is excerpted from the introduction of a US Senate Committee on Indian Affairs report entitled "IN CRITICAL CONDITION: THE URGENT NEEED TO REFORM THE INDIAN HEALTH SERVICE'S ABERDEEN AREA":

On June 23, 2010, Chairman Byron Dorgan initiated a formal investigation of the Indian Health Service's (IHS) Aberdeen Area (hereafter "the Area") in response to years of hearing from individual American Indians/Alaska Natives, Indian tribes and IHS employees about substandard health care services and mismanagement. Chairman Dorgan received complaints about Aberdeen Area IHS-run facilities plagued by frequent reduced or diverted services, mismanagement, poor performing employees, lack of employee accountability, and malfeasance. These conditions negatively impact the care provided to individuals and produce a work environment riddled with waste, fraud and abuse.

33 This performance evaluation would later be described by his supervisor Rick Sorensen as "the worst he had ever seen" and

he had been in the business for decades. However, he still signed in concurrence with it.

34 Agency supervisors are obligated to provide adequate duty time to an employee so they may adequately prepare a grievance or EEO complaint.

35 I had contacted every possible Federal entity charged with the responsibility of protecting employees from the abuses I was being subjected to only to discover that nearly all of them were staffed by minorities who seemed to either sympathize with or have relationships with the IHS EEO office staff.

36 Included with this documentation was a reference to a statement made by a senior management official within the Aberdeen Area to then *CDR* Keats that "[they] are going to change the color of the workforce in the Area." This appears to be a blatantly racist comment which should have been reported by CDR Keats as an EEO violation.

37 This also occurred when I applied for another position with the TSA. Again, I was not considered for the position, probably for this reason.

38 The billets showed that I had held positions at the level of the selecting official of the position for which I was applying.

39 According to the union representative I spoke with about my experiences at the Fargo VA, Mr. DeKrey had been involved in an incident where a technician was ordered to enter an air handler which was not locked out or tagged out (OSHA required safety practice in a situation like this, especially one as dangerous as this since it was inside a confined space). The technician was electrocuted and ended up having to undergo months of rehabilitation. According the story, because he was unable to perform his work as he once had management attempted to remove him until the union became involved and he was reinstated.

40 From information provided by North Dakota Workforce Safety Insurance (workmen's comp) inspectors (see Appendix 24 for full text).

41 It should be noted that this plank was one of the remaining planks after the highly egregious planks had already been replaced. Also, before any of the planks had been replaced (i.e., the highly egregious planks were still in place) the scaffold planking had been supporting two bricklayers, their tools, grout, and brick pallets. I think it is simply miraculous that a major incident did not occur.

42 Mr. Langevin also instructed this individual not go to the contractor's site any longer because he also kept finding safety violations.

43 Basis for Health Services. (n.d.). In *IHS Fact Sheets*. Retrieved from http://www.ihs.gov/PublicAffairs/IHSBrochure/Basis HlthSvcs.asp

44 Yakama Service Unit. (n.d.). In *Locations-Portland Area Office-Health Services*. Retrieved from http://www.ihs. gov/FacilitiesServices/areaOffices/Portland/portland-hs-yakama-service-unit.asp

45 One of my former IHS supervisors, who is Native American, took great issue when in the course of a discussion I described the services being received by our Native American clientele as "free" (which it was to them). She wanted me to make sure I referred to them as "prepaid" in the future. This is simply propaganda.

46 When I began my USPHS career the service was in search of a nationwide mission to (further) justify its existence. It seems to have found same via the Federal Response Plan (FRP). The FRP is what the Federal government uses as a blueprint on how to respond to national emergencies. The FRP involves the DHHS (and USPHS which is within the DHHS) through Emergency Support Function (ESF) #8 Public Health and Emergency Services Annex. This is

the ESF under which I was deployed. However, one could legitimately ask why this function requires uniformed service members.

47 LT Dayton Newbrough is a fractionally Native American engineer who had been assisting me with various project designs as well as acting on my behalf during extended leave periods. LT Newbrough is a good example of an individual who would have no need of the Indian Preference policy in order to be gainfully employed due to his experience, intelligence, and strong work ethic. Our paths would cross again in future assignments.

48 Wanda Jimenez, Secretary, Don Newquist, Engineering Technician, Kevin Sutton, Engineering Technician, and William Thompson, Engineering Technician, were all Native American employees whom I supervised. Ms. Jimenez eventually left for greener pastures elsewhere which caused Mr. Thompson's conduct issues to come to an abrupt end. Mr. Sutton also moved on to become an IT specialist in the local IHS clinic. The year I left we celebrated Mr. Newquist's 76th birthday. He is a WWII vet and one of the friendliest people I've ever known.

49 Mr. Hardnett is an architect and was also the employee union representative. He was one of the few people who had experience working for a private sector company. However, he was apparently fired after only a brief period of private sector employment. I understood this since I noticed Mr. Hardnett spending significant periods of duty time working on his home remodel designs. However, he has a pleasant demeanor and would not find fault with projects while on inspection trips, so I guess he made for an excellent PM in the eyes of DES management.

50 The issue was associated with a move of social service staff to the second floor of the hospital to be in closer proximity to behavioral health staff for the convenience of their mutual

patients. However, the social service staff do not want to move from their current location and have provided a number of reasons why they should not move one of them being that they each need soundproof walls. I had discussed this with Mr. Koebrick on more than one occasion and he saw the reasons put forth by social services as excuses and had threatened to force the move. During those discussions I had reiterated my recommendation to place all staff within cubicles (these were available free of charge from the Area at the time) in one of the large offices. This would leave two relatively large conference rooms and one private room off the larger conference room available for private consultations.

51 Reprisal: An unlawful act to restrain, interfere, coerce, or discriminate against an individual who is involved or participating in the discrimination complaints process (i.e., a complainant, his/her representative, or witness, or an agency official responsible for processing discrimination complaints) From Commissioned Corps Personnel Manual, Part 2, CC26.1, Instruction 6, Equal Opportunity: Discrimination Complaints Processing, Department of Health and Human Services, 2001.

52 That additional detail comprised approximately 10 pages of information. I guess she thought I should have modified my resume by adding all of that information to my already lengthy resume (about which I was later chastised by private-sector personnel staffing specialists because it was too long at four pages).

53 Use of old, weathered, wooden planks which had significant splits longitudinally, were rotting in the middle, some with cross sections significantly compromised from being partially sawed through, or gouged in some fashion, without proper overlap, cleating, or anchoring to prevent slippage which were placed on multi-story scaffold systems framing which were not anchored to the building in any way, some of which

lacked proper cross-bracing, many of which had no toeboard protection, and most had no guard rails in place. One of the scaffold towers was being used in close proximity to various entrances/exits to/from the hospital for patients and staff to support material transfer between trucks on the ground and construction activities on the new 4th floor, much of which were pallets of brick. There did not appear to ever be any kind of load analysis performed for any of the planking being utilized.